# COLLECTOR'S GUI

## HOMER LAUGHLIN'S
# Virginia Rose

## IDENTIFICATION & VALUES

### Richard G. Racheter

**COLLECTOR BOOKS**

*A Division of Schroeder Publishing Co., Inc.*

The current values in this book should be used only as a guide. They are not intended to set prices, which vary from one section of the country to another. Auction prices as well as dealer prices vary greatly and are affected by condition as well as demand. Neither the Author nor the Publisher assumes responsibility for any losses that might be incurred as a result of consulting this guide.

## Searching For A Publisher?

We are always looking for knowledgeable people considered to be experts within their fields. If you feel that there is a real need for a book on your collectible subject and have a large comprehensive collection, contact Collector Books.

*Cover design by Beth Summers*
*Book design by Beth Ray*
*Photography by Richard G. Racheter*
*(unless otherwise noted)*
*Processing by Photo To Go, South Pasadena, Florida*

Additional copies of this book may be ordered from:

COLLECTOR BOOKS
P.O. Box 3009
Paducah, Kentucky 42002-3009

@$18.95. Add $2.00 for postage and handling.

Printed in the U.S.A. by Image Graphics, Paducah, KY

# Contents

# Acknowledgments

Many individuals, collectors, dealers, acquaintances, and friends gave me advice, sent Virginia Rose sample pieces, and offered encouragement. From Michigan to Texas, from North Dakota to Arizona, they cannot all be acknowledged by name. But some must be mentioned: Shirley Freeman, Alvin Daigle, Kim Hanz, Susan Pescatore, Evelyn Honeycutt (for the Bluebirds find), and Sam Portaro. These six people provided some very important Virginia Rose finds. Jack Hamlin telephoned several times to give some vital Virginia Rose statistics. Ruby Roberts of Largo, Florida, not only supplied the set named after her, Ruby's Fall Cosmos (D.31), but she is continually hunting to satisfy my collecting mania. She is a true friend. Muriel Thompson, Lansing, Michigan, wildly peripatetic by automobile, traveled with her aunt from coast to coast (and Alaska), finding Homer Laughlin beauties in great abundance. Rick Gault sent some magnificent specialty bowls, and Jeanne Smiley, another Virginia Rose collector, produced some excellent finds — especially large platters. Both Gary Geiselman and Allyn Rosa aided in this project, Gary through his vast interest and special knowledge of Virginia Rose, and Allyn with his valuable photographs. Then there is Joanne Jasper, author, publisher, and friendly confabulator, whose urgent telephone calls and sympathetic faxes propelled me forward.

Finally nothing could have been accomplished without William Ohman, a true friend and confidante, a pusher, a nudger, himself an energetic writer, a counselor, and a compatriot, often my only touchstone to reality!

# Dedication

*For*
*H. W. O.*
*Always Remembering The Met. Line*
*and Connecticut*

# Author's Notes

Readers! Come join me and wander the realm of Virginia Rose. A mingling of in-depth research, intimate reflection, and personal commentary, this book should not be considered complete. There are deliberately missed decoration numbers waiting to be assigned, there are unknown facts to be discovered, and, of course, mistakes to be corrected. The approach to this book is slightly different from the usual collector book. While the main intent is always to provide information about Virginia Rose, it was decided to do a slight mind stretch and also include photographs of other shapes bearing VR decorations. Thus the reader who truly loves this shape can view how its various treatments and designs appear on Cavalier, Rhythm, Orleans, Georgian Eggshell, etc.

It is admitted not all the treatments covered were, truly and completely, the original property of Virginia Rose. It is conceded, she wears at times the dress of older shapes, and the value of this book is expanded by including these other Homer Laughlin Company shapes. Also to note which treatments were commercial and could appear on the ware of any manufacturer is fascinating in itself. Some of Virginia Rose's most popular decorations were produced commercially, and could belong to anyone. This information spices our knowledge.

Finally, it is clearly acknowledged some critics and American dinnerware collectors will find my opinions presumptuous, my numbering system egocentric, my name choices too personal, and my involvement with detail much too "fussy." But until now, the serious Virginia Rose collector had no base of reference, and was caught up in a web of verbal descriptions given over the telephone between potential purchaser and honest, yet uninformed, dealer. Hopefully, both buyer and seller will have a copy of this book, and the use of the term "D.105" will have more clear relevance than the stumbling description of "tiny pink roses, and a little purple tulip!" Call me egotistical, but now we have, hopefully, some clarity in our pursuit of Virginia Rose!

A good number of photographs in this book show decoration details. Always a great believer in the "magnifying glass syndrome," it is felt a close study of the leaves, vines, flowers, fruits, and filigrees depicted on any piece of dinnerware heightens enjoyment and widens appreciation. A minutely thorough contemplation of the artwork appearing on china opens a treasure of artistic styles: from handpainted free form, to stylized adaptations, to formalized renderings. The artistic detail hidden in many decals can be breathtaking. I call reader attention to the clover detail in Greengage (D.120); seen close up, we can admire the artistic skill of the unknown designer. It is very strongly recommended every collector purchase the best affordable camera, the finest close-up lens/adapter possible, and become a photographer of reasonable skill. To accomplish this wisely, go to a reputable camera shop, tell the salesperson you need to take close-up photographs of china, and set the price range. Accept the advice and with your new camera and lenses, simply start taking pictures, and learn what approaches work best. An entirely pleasurable new collecting facet awaits.

Reader reactions to this book will help answer questions, solve problems, and augment information. In fact, reader help is vital in expanding the total view of Homer Laughlin's most famous line of decalware, Virginia Rose.

Richard G. Racheter
1270 63rd Terrace South
St. Petersburg, Florida 33705

There is no dinnerware in all America more collectible than the china produced by the Homer Laughlin Company. Homer

1871 – 1890

and Shakespeare Laughlin were born on Little Beaver Creek, a few miles from East Liverpool, Ohio. Homer, the elder, had served the North during the Civil War, and both brothers were eager to start a lucrative business. Around 1869, it is believed, Homer Laughlin formed a brief partnership with Nathaniel Simms, and a pottery was established in East Liverpool.

Simms left the business in 1873. At this time, it cannot be ascertained if Shakespeare was connected with the pottery from 1869, but from 1873, the two brothers, Homer and Shakespeare, worked together in the small business situated on the banks of the Ohio River.

This fledgling community, located near some valuable clay deposits, balances wavering at the top of the long spur jutting like an unfinished dorsal fin from the plump body of West Virginia. It was a comparatively new area filled with energy and optimism. Ohio, the Buckeye State, had been long established — gaining statehood as the 17th member of the Union in 1803. But West Virginia, separated by the meandering river from East Liverpool, had been thrust into existence only in 1863, and was basically as new and as fresh as the fledgling pottery. The land, the independent people, the struggling recently formed factories were flavored with a powerful frontier spirit that contributed to the compulsive dynamics of the area. Opportunity lurked behind every tree, and broke forth in every man's dreams and desires.

Caught up in this spirit, the Laughlin brothers determinedly started what is now the oldest, most productive, and largest privately owned pottery still producing American dinnerware. Throughout its long history, so popular and extensive did Laughlin ware become that the company claims to have made about one–third of all the dinnerware produced in the United States.

In 1872, the Ohio Valley Pottery, the name by which the new company was then known, changed from producing a lesser grade of yellow ware and began to manufacture, with some near disastrous setbacks, the more acceptable white ware. But in 1877, Shakespeare sold his interest to Homer, and left for other industrial pursuits in Philadelphia. He died in 1881, never truly aware of the company's potential.

By 1886, the now Homer Laughlin China Company was producing dinnerware of such a high translucent quality as to win medals, and ultimately to challenge the British imports. A new prophetically American logo was devised: the Eagle dominating the prone British Lion — helpless under the assault! This logo epitomizes American youth, vigor, and the need to conquer an aging European influence!

pre – 1900

Just a few years before the demise of the century, in 1897, Homer sold his company to Louis I. Aaron and William E. Wells, removing himself to Los Angeles, and devoting his last years to developing the newly burgeoning city. Thus the pottery slipped from the hands of its originator into the control of two families who, through four generations, still manage the factories, the kilns, and the showrooms.

1897 – 1900

In 1907, there was a bold move across the Ohio River into Newell, West Virginia, where Plant #4 was built. The Newell plant, touted by the company as the largest ever constructed, extended 500 feet along the river banks, and covered over 100 acres. As of this date, the Homer Laughlin Company possessed 62 kilns, 48 decorating kilns capable of producing 300,000 pieces of finished pottery each day. Newell remains the home base of the company.

Two new lines were first manufactured at Plant #4: the Angelus and Empress. Thus, in 36 productive years, between 1871 and 1907, with the aggressive move into West Virginia, the Homer Laughlin Company had created ten highly individual lines of dinnerware which were widely offered and eagerly purchased by thousands and thousands of American consumers. These lines were: 1884 – Victor; 1886 – Shakespeare; 1896 – Golden Gate; 1899 – American Beauty; 1901 – Colonial, Seneca, Niagara; 1903 – King Charles; 1907 – Angelus, Empress.

The growth continued, the energy fed upon itself to flourish, stretch, and expand. In 1911, Marcus Aaron succeeded his father, Louis, as president, and the next year, perhaps to celebrate the new accession, the Hudson line was initiated, captivating the public, and remaining one of the shapes most avidly collected to this day. Genesee, a genteel rounded, less ornate, quietly modeled shape, was also introduced in this year.

The gusty winds of expansion fever whirled over Newell, and Laughlin plant after Laughlin plant was constructed, until, in 1929, Plant #8 rose to handle the production of two new shapes: Virginia Rose, and the similarly designed, daisy-embossed Marigold. Belching smoke, active kiln upon active kiln, densely piled decorating rooms, workers by the hundreds all teamed and seethed to produce dinnerware by the thousand-dozens to gratify America's pride in American products.

With the nation now wrapped in the Depression, mild but insistent philosophical changes were occurring in board room and art laboratories. With the employment of Albert Bleininger, one of the world's leading ceramic engineers, in 1920, and the English born Frederick Rhead, in 1927, the company began to focus its ceramic styles and designs to no longer mimic European models. The world's depressed economy caused each nation to look to itself, to develop its own industries, and cope with its own national problems.

As a fully-fledged feathered and soaring American eagle, Homer Laughlin, under Rhead's tutelage as art director, spurned imitations, and offered new shapes. Rhead, a master designer, created Newell, then the more popular Liberty in 1929. Century, a magnificent ivory-smooth Rhead design was born in 1931, and then followed a spate of shapes: Wells (1930), Jade (1932), Ravenna (1932), Virginia Rose (1932), Marigold (1933), Georgian (1933), and Nautilus (1935). During his first Inaugural Address, March 4, 1933, President Franklin Roosevelt electrified a saddened nation by crying, "The only thing we have to fear is fear itself!", and to help mitigate this fear, Laughlin introduced a rainbow of beautiful designs, a flood of dinnerware to bring color and delight into the homes of a sadly depressed and deprived society.

All these shapes had no obvious European counterparts. While the shape designs were executed and their production supervised by an European, they were cleanly and dramatically American. With Dr. Bleininger energizing the glazes, and Mr. Rhead blueprinting the shape designs, the Homer Laughlin China Company bestrode the world of American dinnerware.

Even with Virginia Rose and other early '30s shapes making a strong showing at dealer outlets, the pearl of great price was yet to be opened. In January, 1936, just two short months before Hitler's Germany reoccupied the Rhineland, Mr. Rhead introduced a sensational new line of dinnerware: vibrant, as never before seen, with rich, primary colors. It caught the dealers and traders within a web of enthusiasm, and consumers followed. Soon Fiesta covered dining and breakfast tables from Portland, Maine, to Portland, Oregon; from Copper Harbor, Michigan to Eagle Pass, Texas. A joyous celebration of color, Fiesta was the thing to have.

The Homer Laughlin Company accepted the laurels brought by Fiesta, and continued to experiment with a variety of new shapes: Brittany (1936), the Eggshell shapes (1937 – 1938), Kitchen Kraft (1939). The commencement of European hostilities stopped the flow of the better imported chinaware, Limoges, Royal Doulton, and Wedgwood, and Laughlin hoped to attract buyers of the more expensive, refined dinnerware with, particularly, the Eggshell shapes.

The company was experiencing an internal dilemma due to Mr. Rhead's growing illness; steps had to be plotted, and decisions explored. In October, 1940, Louis Friedman, and Mr. Rhead traveled to New York City to approach another brilliant ceramist, Eva Zeisel, fresh from the chaos of Europe, and in need of a position. It is my opinion that, for the first time in fifty years, the Homer Laughlin Company experienced a serious blow. Mrs. Zeisel herself told me she believed she was being offered a position in order to assume the art directorship at Mr. Rhead's retirement. Even though Mr. Friedman offered to establish a new market research department and employ as its head Hans Zeisel, Eva's husband, the couple decided against the move to Newell, and the entrepreneurial energy of America's largest pottery company never fused with the innovative genius of Hungary's Eva Zeisel.

After Rhead's death in 1942, another very able designer joined HLC. Don Schreckengost continued to eliminate from the shapes any hint of embossed ornamentation. In 1948, when Mr. Schreckengost became art director, Virginia Rose, still being produced, was considered rather old-fashioned, and slightly fussy — like a maiden aunt come to tea. The new shapes,

Jubilee (1948), Skytone (1948), Rhythm (1949), and Cavalier (1950), gleamed with a sleek modernism, but I believe the glint of genius had died. These were excellent products, ably designed, and stylishly decorated, but 1948 seemed to be the company's most productive year, and the sails were slackening with the wind blowing ever more strongly from the East.

After its disastrous defeat and surrender on September 2, 1945, Japan and her manufacturing skill, under American tutelage, recovered and expanded until, by the mid-1950s her exports of fine dinnerware to the United States began to threaten the remaining potteries. During 1959, Laughlin became competitive and vitreous restaurant and hotel ware came forth from Newell's tunnel and decorating kilns. Retail ware was under siege.

Victor Broomhall, remembered for his abstractly organic ceramic design, was named art director in 1970, and during his tenure, the turning of the tide began to engulf the Cavaliers, the Jubilees, and the Rhythms, and the company's production of vitreous commercial ware surpassed that of retail china. Homer Laughlin again, and wisely, changed as fate decreed. Yet for many of us, born in the seeming innocence of pre-World War II, the demise of an active production of Homer Laughlin dinnerware for the average American family was a saddening blow. The vitreous ware, practical as it may be, will never replace our old friends: Virginia Rose, Art Deco Harlequin, Nautilus, and graceful Georgian.

Lyrica, Gothic, Seville, Royale, and Carolyn are some of the shapes produced today under the present art director, Jonathan O. Parry. With experience as a designer of jewelry, Mr. Parry oversees all design decisions and has created some stunning service pieces, glittering with enamel-like tones. Truly, Homer Laughlin commercial china has a heavy and sincere beauty, but as we grow older, and more nostalgic, we need the presence of old friends. Even new Fiesta, as charming as it is, cannot replace the glow of the original 1930s colors: uranium reds, cobalts, turquoises, and sunny buttery-soft yellows.

Time has altered American dining habits; now often plastic plates and paper cups serve the purpose for eating. Clocks were not made to turn backwards, and the tread of time sounds the forward march: yet, I, for one, wonder about Shakespeare and Homer dreaming dreams and having hopes in the calm and peacefully serene backwater community of East Liverpool, over 120 years ago.

# *Introduction to Virginia Rose*

Virginia Rose — collectors find it difficult to remain neutral about this Homer Laughlin shape. Introduced early in the Depression years and named for the granddaughter of William E. Wells, an early company leader, it is not at all "modern," and yet has not become "dated." It has a charm and beauty not easily characterized. Virginia Rose is either avidly collected or calmly ignored. While this book, hopefully, will appeal to the present Virginia Rose collectors, it is also trusted, once they read it, that the "ignorers" will learn to appreciate what, for me, is the most fascinating of all the decaled lines.

Many collectors, even some advanced in the art of dinnerware, believe the name "Virginia Rose" refers to the decal alone; this decal is the very prevalent rose design officially designated #JJ59. This decorated line, made exclusively for the J.J. Newberry stores, is unofficially called "Moss Rose" or "Pinks." This single decal is to many the only Virginia Rose. Then, often quickly, the budding VR collector notes a very similar decal VR#128, often known as "Fluffy Rose." Soon other treatments are found, Patrician, Colonial Kitchen, and Mexicali, and by this time, the once neutral collector begins to seek the Virginia Rose shape bestrewn with various decals and decorations.

Just how many varied decals, designs, and decorations appear on the VR shape? There are conflicting estimates. Harvey Duke, who specializes in writing about wide-ranging, general pottery subjects, suggests the somewhat extravagant number of 450 treatments. Joanne Jasper, another equally knowledgeable HLC researcher, states about 200 diverse designs decorate Virginia Rose. Other estimates range from 125 to 150. Unfortunately, the Homer Laughlin Company file records were not established for research, and are not definitive. Often the listings and order sheets simply state "Virginia Rose," and give no hint regarding decorative treatments. Although with careful, rather painstakingly sifted reasoning, the company's official number listing can be helpful to the researcher, but, to date, only those for 1937 and 1952 have been located.

Another debated question involves the years Virginia Rose was available to the consumer. Again, Harvey Duke, in the well-received eighth edition of his book, *Official Price Guide to Pottery and Porcelain*, gives the year of introduction as 1933, and further states VR "was produced for over 20 years." We have to infer from this Mr. Duke believes Virginia Rose was produced for 22 to 24 years. Putting these two figures together, 450 different treatments and 22 production years, we can conclude over 20 new designs were offered each year, and this does not take into account those treatments carried over from year to year. Mrs. Jasper, in her book, *The Collector's Encyclopedia of Homer Laughlin China*, suggests the introductory date of 1929. The former based his decision on the appearance of Virginia Rose advertisements in trade papers; the latter arrived at her opinion through the study of material at the HLC factory, and she also concluded the shape was available for some 30 years, from 1929 to 1959. Bob and Sharon Huxford, in *The Collector's Encyclopedia of Fiesta* (7th rev. ed.), state: "Virginia Rose was the name given a line of standard HLC shapes which from 1929 until the early 1970s was the basis for more than a dozen patterns of decaled or embossed dinnerware ... Virginia Rose was one of the most popular shapes ever produced." Here we read of some 14 to 18 patterns produced for about 42 years. Three important writers in the world of American dinnerware, Duke, Jasper, Huxford, and three divergent opinions arrived at honestly, but how confusing for the reader/collector!

Intrigued by this disparity, I went through my personal collection, inspecting each VR plate, bowl, and saucer — about 2,000 pieces. Over 50 of these pieces bear the date 1932, and while the majority lie within the 1930s and 1940s, they continued into the 1950s, and several have the date 1965. Thus, I can determine the introductory year was 1932, the closing year, 1965 — for an availability total of 33 years. If any reader has pieces of Virginia Rose marked with dates before 1932, and after 1965, please contact me through the publisher. As always, writers depend heavily upon the information and samples supplied by readers.

It is logical to surmise the introduction of new decorations was stronger in the 1930s and 1940s, with popular favorites, such as #JJ59 (Moss Rose), VR#128 (Fluffy Rose), and VR#124 (Patrician), being offered year after year. After 1950, we assume there were fewer new decals, and, perhaps, no new decals in the 1960s. It is interesting to note that all the Virginia Rose pieces bearing a 1960s date are #JJ59. Using the figure of 150 individual treatments, and with a little juggling and a not too precise method of computation, we can say between four and eight different VR treatments offered were made available to the buying public each year, the higher number for the 1930s and 1940s. As interest in Virginia Rose lessened, the new offerings also eased until, so it seems, only #JJ59 was sold in the 1960s. All these summations are open to question, but they seem logical, and reflect the extent of my research to date.

Jo Cunningham — Made from 1935 to 1959, "as many as 150 different decals"

Harvey Duke — Introduced in 1933 and "was produced for over 20 years," "decorated in over 450 treatments"

Bob and Sharon Huxford — "1929 until the early 1970s," "more than a dozen patterns"

Ralph and Terry Kovel — 1935 – 1960, "a variety of decal decorations"

Joanne Jasper — 1929, "into the 1970s," about 200 varieties

Through a careful study of my personal collection, the following dates can be verified, but readers should be willing to add a few years and a few treatments. In fact, I continue to request reader input to correct or alter statistical information.

Richard G. Racheter — 1932–1966, 188+ treatments

A firmly flexible statement can be broached: Virginia Rose was available for approximately 33 years, with a total of treatments consisting of approximately 100. This opinion brings me into direct conflict with Harvey Duke, and exemplifies the differences between vast generalization and narrow specialization. Both approaches are valid, but both have restrictive problems. Mr. Duke, casting his wide knowledge over all American pottery, can sometimes miss finer and intricate points; my overtly careful and narrow approach limits the horizons, and minutely focuses the view. One person cannot have, at the same time, two major approaches toward the same subject, and metaphorically speaking, when a man owns a piece of land stretching for thousands of acres, he cannot be expected to know every square foot of his property. Another man, who is involved only with a suburban backyard, is expected to know exactly what is happening within his boundaries.

These two problems set aside, some of the treatments are easy to find, very popular, and command high prices. Others are very rare and unusual. Here the illogical comes into play: "rare" does not necessarily mean "expensive." Some Virginia Rose designs are so rare the collector must despair over ever gathering a sizable representation, much less a complete set. For these impossibly rare, all but unobtainable, pieces, the cost often remains quite low. Ironically, prices are often determined by availability; the more available treatments can be collected in sets, and this incites competition which pushes prices upward.

Some Virginia Rose treatments/decals do not even have known official names, only official numbers. Some have both official names and official numbers; most have neither. In the first category is #JJ59 whose unofficial name, as mentioned before, is Moss Rose. Another is Moss Rose's sister decal, VR#128 known unofficially, but widely, as Fluffy Rose. Belonging to the second category, Patrician, an official name, has the number VR#124. These three treatments constitute the overwhelming majority of Virginia Rose sales. They are vastly different, and appeal to collectors with different life styles. The first two are quaintly old fashioned, conservative, and are gathered by people who look back into the past, remembering grandmothers and cozy kitchen suppers. These two are gentle, sentimental designs. Patrician, however, appeals to the modern, the sophisticated; it is sleek and attuned to the twenty-first century. But irony abounds in American dinnerware: Patrician was one of the first designs, being offered to the public through the Larkin Soap Company in 1932. Frederick H. Rhead became Homer Laughlin's art director in 1927, and he created the Virginia Rose shape shortly after this date. Due to his position, he either directly designed Patrician, or approved it. Mr. Rhead miraculously gazed some 70 years into the future, bringing us this simple and dramatic Virginia Rose treatment, still so popular today.

Lesser performers on the Virginia Rose dinnerware stage are a trio with official names: Bouquet (W#137), Colonial Kitchen (D.167), and Nosegay (VR#423), and two with official numbers, but popular names: Armand (VR#235) and Tulips in a Basket (VR#396). These five are well-liked and reasonably attainable, but are overshadowed by the big three. Finally, a chorus of bit players remains in the wings, curiously interesting, but not yet widely known. One can hopefully theorize one of these players might suddenly erupt into Virginia Rose stars. Columbines (VR#232) and Waterlily (VR#398) are likely candidates.

Once my collection of Virginia Rose commenced, with curiosity peaked, I decided to gather an example of every treatment. As the numbers grew, 50, 60, 70, so did interest, and a near mania prevailed. When other HLC collectors demonstrated a fascination for Virginia Rose, I felt a need to share my findings. Thus, this book was encouraged, engendered, and born.

Not only can one savor the various decals, but the research on individual VR pieces can be stimulating, rewarding, and productive. There are new pieces to be discovered. The 7" oval vegetable and the 7" round nappy, for examples, were found after the publication of Mrs. Jasper's book, but they appear in the revised edition. Any serious collector begins, with time, to formulate a variety of personal opinions about the subject collected. Below are a few random statements arrived at through my observation:

- the 8" plate is the rarest of the five sizes.
- the coupe soup is much harder to find than the rimmed variety.
- ditto the oatmeal versus the fruit.
- the fast-stand sauceboat ceased being produced in 1952 making it difficult to locate.
- of the two sizes of jugs, the smaller 5" version is rarer.
- no known collector has seen the AD cup/saucer, so do they really exist? Mrs. Jasper has seen drawings at the HLC plant, but perhaps this is as far as they went.

Virginia Rose never regularly offered a coffee or a teapot. These two pieces have never been seen in art department drawings, nor were these items ever pictured in early advertisements. But, why did these two pieces show up, fully designed with correct handles and finials, to complete the Blue Dresden set in the late 1940s? And why were these heavier Virginia Rose sets provided with a newly designed butterdish, and shaker set?

Besides referring to a day in June, what is so rare in Virginia Rose? In this shape, in any shape, the hierarchy of availability of any piece can be listed:

- very rare
- difficult
- rare
- common
- scarce
- very common

Remember, we are discussing Virginia Rose <u>pieces</u>, not Virginia Rose <u>treatments</u>! The 6" plate is very common, and in a good number of my "one piece" treatments, that one piece is the 6" plate. Teacups and saucers are common, as are 7" and 9" plates. Rim soups fit into this category also. Difficult to locate? Perhaps the 10" plate, the coupe soup. The oatmeal bowl could be considered scarce along with the 8" plate. In my personal estimation (and other researchers might well disagree), the borderline between "scarce" and the two rare categories is wide: scarce items can be located if the collector is persistent, has a number of friends and dealers hunting, and is willing to wait a considerable time. The rare and the very rare are never, or hardly ever, located even if the collector has networks, stamina, and time. Rare items are virtually impossible to locate, and the very rare are virtually non-existent.

The only criteria any willful collector can use to categorize a Virginia Rose piece is by his or her personal experience. If this experience is positively reflected by other collectors, then the criteria is probably valid. For example, I am not aware of anyone seeing or knowing of the existence of the Virginia Rose AD cup and saucer. Ergo, these sets are very rare. Another characteristic noted by categorizers is confusion in allotting a piece a correct name. Example: Just what is the tray-with-handles? Joanne Jasper listed in her first edition (JJ., p.188) this piece with no size. In the revised edition of the work, the "tray" was deleted and a "bread plate" and a "cake plate" added, still no size. The reader is asked to review the Huxfords' book (Huxford, p.159). In plate 291, is the "tray-with-handles," but the size is 8". We all know a cake plate must be larger than 8".

In my collection, there is one "tray-with-handles," (D.67), and the size is 11"; this could be a cake plate. Since there are two sizes of the "tray-with-handles," could the smaller (8") be the bread plate, and the larger (11"), the cake plate? I have no hesitation in saying "yes" — and will continue to believe until this theory is proven incorrect. As for terminology, I strongly prefer the "tray-with-handles" designation with the sizes added. The reader will then have to assume these "trays" are for bread and/or cake. In this way, there can be no confusion with the Kitchen Kraft cake plate in a Virginia Rose design. Even if my premise is accepted, I know of only two 11" trays with handles, and have seen just the 8" version in a Huxford photograph and in one sent by Allyn Rosa; these two pieces must be considered very rare. These two pieces, bread and cake plates, were discontinued in 1952.

Let us, for a brief moment, return to the question of AD cups and saucers. In the 1952 list (please see Appendices), we are given (1) a listing of the 27 pieces currently offered in the Virginia Rose line, and (2) a listing of ten pieces previously offered, but now discontinued. Neither listing mentions the AD cups and saucers. We have the choice of only two conclusions: (1) the AD cups and saucers were discontinued before 1952 or (2) they exist only as drawing board designs. The question regarding these two pieces is the most pressing, and the most intriguing of all mysteries surrounding the Virginia Rose shape.

Until my research began, and people were kind enough to send me photographs and information, the cream soups were considered very rare. But now, there are seven in my collection, and this piece is known to exist in five Virginia Rose treatments, so its category has been reduced from "very rare" to merely "rare." Not so the cream soup liners. Their elusiveness keeps them "very rare." Cream soups are now known to exist in Signs of Spring (D.1), Columbines (D.20), Maude (D.101), Moss Rose (D.227) (see Duke, p.431), and Fluffy Rose (D.231). Hopefully other collectors have differently decaled Virginia Rose cream soups. The only underliner has been for Maude. Those cream soups seen have all been dated before World War II. Was the Virginia Rose cream soup in the same general category as the Fiesta covered onion soup, and could not make the transition when dining habits grew simpler? This postulation seemed logical until it was learned the cream soup and its liner (called officially a "saucer") were, like the "trays," officially discontinued in 1952 (see Appendices for this important official 1952 list).

The fast-stand sauceboat should be mentioned here. It too should be considered rare, or perhaps even very rare; it was also discontinued in 1952. The only two examples of this piece I have ever seen belonged to Patrician (see D.75) and Red Ring (see D.10).

There is another category of the rarer VR items: lug soup, double egg cup, the Fiesta style double egg cup, coffee mug, St. Dennis cup, butterdish, and the three sizes of shaker sets. The common factor linking these pieces is they were originally designed to go with other shapes, or to stand alone; they were never meant solely for the use of Virginia Rose, do not have the embossed rose, and only when decorated with VR treatments can they be called by that name. The items and their origin are:

| | |
|---|---|
| lug soup – Century | double egg cup – Cable |
| "Fiesta style" double egg cup – unknown, possibly Yellowstone | coffee mug – Generic |
| | St. Dennis cup – Generic |
| butterdish – Jade | small shakers – Swing |
| large shakers – Kitchen Kraft | tall shakers – Debutante |

Only a very few of the 150+ VR treatments were supplied with the above pieces which when located, will prove expensive. They are in great demand. The lug soup is not hard to find dressed in a Century decal, but has, to date, been discovered only in Patrician, Columbines, and Marigold Springtime (D.4). Since this piece has no embossing, the silver rose has been carefully painted on for Patrician. This rare find (a set of four) was discovered by Leonta Bohnert, and is now owned by Bruce Braun.

*The shakers: All three types difficult to locate. Right: Kitchen Kraft large shaker; Center: Debutante shaker, here dressed in Skytone blue. Left: Swing shape with a Rhythm decal.*

The Cable double egg cup exists in many decals, and attaches itself to a number of HLC shapes. It has been seen with Yellowstone, Marigold, Brittany, and Harlequin, among others. It often appears in various decals that seem to belong to no exact line, so it might have been sold as a specialty item. There is a second HLC double egg cup designed in a more rounded, feminine form, and sold with sets of Swing, a very delicate eggshell shape. This Swing eggcup has been found carefully painted to accompany the "Patrician type" Marigold line (J.J., p.69). If the Swing egg cup was painted for Marigold, why not Patrician? Then, Jo Dee Rice discovered another double egg cup having the bouquet decal. This egg cup has been noted on the Yellowstone shape (Duke, p.437), and because of its shape, could have been used as the model for the Fiesta double egg cup.

*Two Cable double egg cups flank the more delicate Swing example in the center. The Swing egg cup has not yet been discovered in a Virginia Rose decoration. Left: Mex-i-cana. Right: an unknown design possibly sold on its own.*

The Virginia Rose St. Dennis cup is a recent rare discovery. At this time, it is known only in Armand, Fluffy Rose, and Olivia (D.111) and comes with two styles of handle, also appearing in a Homer Laughlin coffee cup/saucer set. It is very similar to Hall's Autumn Leaf cup known by the same name. The coffee mug is rare, and highly sought. In my collection the mug appears in Moss Rose, Fluffy Rose, the pheasant decorated Oriental Garden (D.162),

*Left: The ear-handled St. Dennis mother's cup, decorated with dark violets. Right: The coffee mug, this one wearing a Kwaker decal.*

black-trimmed Medieval Rose (D.113), Bluebirds (D.11), and white. Curiously, the Oriental Garden mug had been owned for several years and was thought to belong to Yellowstone. When this treatment appeared on an 11½" Virginia Rose platter, my mug joined Virginia Rose.

The same situation exists with the Jade butterdish. For years thought to appear only in the three popular treatments (Moss Rose, Fluffy Rose, and Patrician), but at the Sanford Glass Show, January, 1996, it was located in the Bouquet (D.107) decal, and, because the dealer did not know what it was, purchased for $20.00. A bargain indeed! But can the collector hedge, using a syllogism of dubious truth?

- Here is a Jade butterdish with a "certain" design.
- This "certain" design appears on the shape Virginia Rose.
- Thus this Jade butterdish is also Virginia Rose.

*Left: The Jade butterdish, here in Harlequin turquoise. Right: The unadorned Century onion soup. Both pieces are scarce with Virginia Rose decoration.*

Clever, but questionable. See Red Beauty (D.16): this striking, bright red, and shiny black decal appears on a large set of silver trimmed Jade, and this set is provided with a butterdish. While the collector can surely place this silver edged butterdish on the Virginia Rose shelves, and nestle it among the Red Beauty pieces, it can never truly be called a Virginia Rose butterdish. It is each collector who must decide.

Readers are very familiar with the small, rounded Swing shakers which are commonly seen with Rhythm and Cavalier decorations and can be inexpensively bought. They are not too hard to discover in the Moss Rose dress, but always command a high price. The large Kitchen Kraft shakers are rare in all situations, and very expensive. A third type of shaker has just been identified as belonging also to Virginia Rose. These small conical shapes were designed for Debutante, but also are used with Cavalier, Rhythm, Jubilee, Skytone, and Kraft Blue. See Moss Rose

(D.227) for the sole example yet found in a VR decal. Thus, both the shaker set and the egg cup piece have a third, very rare variation, appearing, to date, in only one Virginia Rose treatment: i.e., Debutante shakers wearing the Moss Rose decals, and the Fiesta type double egg cup in Bouquet.

When the 1952 official HLC Virginia Rose presentation list (see Appendix H, p.196) was sent to me by Joanne Jasper, it was suddenly understood, two other shapes contrived to be part of the Virginia Rose family:

- the VR onion soup – Nautilus lug oatmeal, regular weight
- the VR square plate – Marigold

We must believe this official company list, and if true, then perhaps the Nautilus lug soup pictured with Hallow's Eve (D.92) actually belongs to the Virginia Rose set? Hallow's Eve appears on the VR listing for 1937, but not on the listing of 1953. Could the possible use of the Nautilus for the VR onion soup have begun in 1937 and ceased by 1953?

The questions persist: with each new important bit of information, new problems or doubts arise. This is the fascination of collecting. The reader is referred to Columbine (D.20), a very interesting 1934 – 1939 treatment which includes the lug (onion) soups; these soups are in the Century shape. And the reader should note, Patrician has these Century soup bowls hand decorated to match its platinum-outlined treatment. There are two answers to this conundrum: (1) the Nautilus bowls were used for Virginia Rose onion soups throughout its history, and the Century bowls not thought to be Virginia Rose are simply Century pieces wearing identical VR treatments, or (2) somewhere between 1940 and 1952, the Century pieces used for VR soups were replaced by Nautilus. If this is the answer, then the lug (onion) soups wearing the Hallow's Eve treatment remain Nautilus.

And the use of the Marigold shape as square Virginia Rose plates seems too fanciful to contemplate. There are no known Virginia Rose square 8" plates, and of the five treatments Marigold shares with Virginia Rose (Gold Rose, Patrician, Snow, Wings, and Marigold Springtime), only the last named actually shares a set of decals, the first four are a sharing of a technique, not a decal. My VR pieces in Marigold Springtime are all dated 1950 – 1952: just at the time of the 1952 Virginia Rose official availability list. I have eleven 8" square plates in the Marigold shape, Springtime treatment. These too are dated 1950 – 1954. Now were these square plates sold with both Virginia Rose and Marigold? This mystery must quietly wait to be solved until more information is compiled. We must locate more duplicate treatments in Virginia Rose and Marigold, and these treatments must be available on 8" square plates. There are still many hidden, shady crannies in the background of the lady Virginia Rose.

For those collectors who wish to become very familiar with Virginia Rose treatments, hopefully this book will be of assistance. The eight generic pieces belong to Virginia Rose only when wearing a VR decal, and as such are very desirable. Many dealers are not familiar with the VR treatments, and bargains can be snapped up. Remember my Bouquet butterdish for $20.00.

A final category to cover before we leave our Virginia Rose discussion: Kitchen Kraft and OvenServe. Members of the Homer Laughlin art department faced the decision of which Virginia Rose pattern to use on the sturdy, kitchenware lines: Kitchen Kraft, with a rounded, easy to scour silhouette, or OvenServe, embossed with full roses and leaves. Unlike the eight cross-over pieces listed before, these lines never lost their true identity to become absorbed by Virginia Rose — or any other HLC shape, for that matter. They maintained their true names: that is, OvenServe with a Virginia Rose treatment. Obviously, the kitchenware lines, or kitchenware pieces, were not obtainable in all VR decorations. At the present time, only 12 are known to have been used on the HLC kitchenware lines.

Even with disagreement among specialists regarding dates, numbers, and nomenclature, all do agree that Virginia Rose is one of the most important Homer Laughlin shapes. It is preeminent among the decaled lines, and entire collections can be, and are, built around Virginia Rose. Wearing decals and decorations ranging from casually common to devilishly rare, and with prices laddering between medium, high, and low, Virginia Rose has become a collector's dream. Share this dream, as we attempt to identify and name some of the numerous decals, designs, treatments!

Welcome to the world of Virginia Rose!

# How to Use This Book

My major concern when writing this book was the system of classification. The first thought was to list the Virginia Rose treatments by date; or, to be more specific, by the date of the pieces at hand. If the collection consisted of only one piece, a saucer or a 6" plate, it would be listed chronologically by the single date on that single piece. This approach was soon seen to be misleading, albeit very convenient for me.

Seated at my writing table, looking at a Virginia Rose 9" oval vegetable bowl, the question was asked: what is the single most noticeable characteristic of this bowl? The answer came immediately: the decoration! Collectors talk about, remember, and identify by the decal or the treatment of a piece, not by the date stamped underneath.

The decal found on this oval bowl was a large orange cabbage rose accompanied by several buds and surrounded by a number of light green leaves. A general term would have been "flower," but since specificity was my goal, the term I chose was simply "rose."

ROSE

What type of rose? Cabbage? But how many collectors can dutifully define a cabbage rose? The most noticed difference between roses is some are double, others single. Since this term would qualify the rose, it should appear in parenthesis, and since this concluded the major part of the entry, it should be followed by a semicolon.

ROSE (double);

After the semicolon would be listed (always in the same order), the color, the size, the number, i.e.

ROSE (double); orange, large, one

And that completes the brief, and hopefully, clear description of the major feature of this treatment. Thus we close it with a colon. Continuing in this logical vein, we add the word "with," and then, with brevity, list the items supporting the major feature.

ROSE (double); orange, large, one: with several small buds; light green leaves.

After this description, we must turn to another feature distinctive to any piece of dinnerware — the glaze. In reality, there are only two glaze colors on Virginia Rose: light yellow, and the much less common white. Handling a good number of VR pieces, it was soon noticed there were variations in the light yellow coloring. It was hard to describe verbally, but some were a softer, creamier color. So three glaze descriptions were decided upon: cream (the richest), light yellow (a fresher, clearer color), and white. Choosing a glaze color can be very subjective, and often the colors do not translate well in photographs, so if any reader locates a treatment on a glaze I call cream and he or she believes it to be light yellow, we must forgive each other. Glaze color names are not etched in stone; they are in the eyes of the beholder.

With the glaze we now have:

ROSE (double); orange, large, one: several small buds; light green leaves. Glaze: cream.

This ends the opening description, and is easily comprehended.

We not only have different varieties of flowers, rose, violet, clematis, and tulip, but there also appear on Virginia Rose pictorial scenes, Mexican designs, bands, and ornate filigrees.

Detailed description of these is handled in the same manner. When a decal is a group of flowers with no one being predominant, the simple term "flowers" is used.

Once a collector has located a treatment, how is this knowledge communicated to others? Joanne Jasper has attempted to solve this communication problem by assigning temporary numbers to much Homer Laughlin decalware. Using this approach, I go a bit farther, and assign each treatment in this book a D(ecoration) number. Since this number must be linked with Virginia Rose, this number formally becomes: VR#D.200. These numbers will appear at the top of each page bearing treatment description and commentary. Since a number of treatments differ only in trim, or number of decals, those will be linked simply by the addition of an "a" or "b," e.g., VR#D.200a.

Directly below the descriptive material, other details will be given for each VR decoration number in the following form:

Name
Official number
Known date
Trim
Also appears on

COMMENTS:

The section, "Also appears on:" greatly expands the usefulness of the book, as the reader can see how a treatment used on Virginia Rose translates into use on other shapes. There is also a subtle implication regarding how HLC viewed a treatment, and whether a decal was designed by the company, or was a commercially supplied design. All this information can greatly aid in the appreciation of a decal, or even the Virginia Rose shape.

The commentary section is composed of subjective material based on logical observation, and often presents personal experiences with the treatment. This section is meant to expand the reader's appreciation in an informal manner.

A final descriptive note at the end of some entries refers to mold differences, especially evident on the bottom of the oval vegetable. This note is given when such a piece has been acquired for an individual treatment. See Appendix B for an in-depth discussion and illustration of the different oval vegetable molds.

Very simply, only those Virginia Rose treatments personally seen, or appearing in clear photographs, have been accepted for inclusion in this book. No verbal or written descriptions have been accepted without illustration. It is sincerely hoped Virginia Rose enthusiasts who own treatments not appearing in these pages, will bring them to my attention for possible future use. We all grow and learn by sharing!

## VR#D.1

APPLEBLOSSOM; pink, white, small, many; with closed darker pink buds, leaves, twigs. Glaze: near white.

Name ..................."Signs of Spring"
Official number...........Not known
Known date............................1934
Trim .......................................None
Also appears on..........Not known

COMMENTS: Pleasant coincidence the first entry in the book is such a pretty, happy decal. This treatment also has among its pieces the very rare cream soup, one of the five known to have this elusive piece: Columbines, Fluffy Rose, Maude, Moss Rose and Signs of Spring. Surely others will come to the fore, but to date, these five form a firm exclusive club. Possibly, the cream soup was not included in all the VR treatments offered to the consumer, just as I believe not all Virginia Rose sets had matching Kitchen Kraft or OvenServe pieces. How the choices were made can never be known. My set consists of 39 valued pieces purchased from Shirley Freeman of Oklahoma. The glaze is also very unusual, a soft mellow white with no hint of yellow. The hollowware bears the gold stamp Second Selection, but no fault can be found by even detailed observation. One of the Virginia Rose treatments a little difficult to acquire, but easy to admire, appreciate, and love.

*9" plate.*

*The rare cream soup.*

Photo courtesy of Gary Geiselman.

*The sauceboat.*

18

## VR#D.3

ASTERS (group); mauve-pink, tiny to small, many; with tiny flowers, blue, yellow; pale gray leaves. Glaze: light yellow.

| | |
|---|---|
| Name | "Fall's Beauty" |
| Official number | Not known |
| Known date | 1938 |
| Trim | Silver |
| Also appears on | Not known |

COMMENTS: China collectors must always be aware that often the same decal looks quite different on various pieces. This sauceboat, the only one in the collection, bears the same decoration as the large bowl below, but the silver trim replaces the border filigree. Sets were, no doubt, available in Fall's Beauty, but none have yet been discovered. The flowers were originally designated as "cosmos" until a friend pointed out there are too many petals. Note the refined curve of the Virginia Rose handle which appears so graceful in the accompanying photograph.

*The only piece in the collection is this sauceboat. Notice how this decal fills out the piece, as compared with the sauceboat in D.1*

## VR#D.3a

ASTERS (group); mauve-pink, tiny to small, many; with tiny flowers, blue, yellow; pale gray leaves, four irregularly placed gold filigrees at the edges. Glaze: cream.

| | |
|---|---|
| Name | "Fall's Beauty Bowl" |
| Official number | Not known |
| Known date | 1940 |
| Trim | None |
| Also appears on | Not known |

COMMENTS: Even though filigree plays a rather prominent part in the treatment of this large bowl, it is placed here because the center floral decal of asters is the same as Fall's Beauty. The bowl looks larger (9½") than it really is because there is no size-constricting color trim, just a creamy uncluttered expanse. The filigree is not the usual type, but consists of a beautifully detailed, stylized bluebell with tiny leaves. This filigree group is randomly placed, some between, some over the rose embossing. Perhaps it would have been more logical to place them all between the embossing. Nevertheless, this is a very impressive piece.

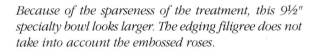

*Because of the sparseness of the treatment, this 9½" specialty bowl looks larger. The edging filigree does not take into account the embossed roses.*

*Detail of bowl's central decal. The shading and detailing work of the flowers is almost oriental in conception.*

Filigree design: Note how this particular one covers up the embossed rose. There is considerable delicacy and detail, and this filigree appears only on this VR bowl.

## VR#D.4

ASTER; white, pink, medium, two to four; with smaller flowers in white, yellow, pale orange; leaves of various kinds, around the edge, four to six floral decals in three separate designs. Glaze: cream.

Name...................."Marigold Springtime"
Official number...........................W#245
Known dates.......................1950 – 1952
Trim ..................................................Gold
Also appears on ......................Marigold

COMMENTS: Virginia Rose and Marigold are shapes closely allied; the latter is much rarer, and adored by a number of adamant admirers. Marigold hollowware is much more sculptural. Strangely, or perhaps, not so strangely, reciprocal use of shapes between the two sister shapes was rare. Wings (D.50) is a good example, and then both shapes had a pure undecorated offering. Here, though, Marigold seems to be supreme. Springtime is a very common, charming design appearing on Marigold, and the dates are at least five years before Virginia Rose. Springtime belongs to Marigold and was borrowed by VR. My collection of the Virginia Rose version consists of a 9" plate, 4" and 6" plates, 1 fruit bowl, a single teacup and an 11½" platter, not an over abundance. I have also seen it on the lug (onion) soup. Marigold Springtime is a devious design. The decals are divided, used separately on various pieces, even reshaped. Unless the collector is aware of this "trickery," mistakes can be taken. Even the large Marigold casserole makes use of only the smaller parts of the overall decal. At least twice, friends have supplied pieces of Marigold Springtime with the assurance it was a new VR decal. The official HLC number was one of those Joanne Jasper discovered in the company's morgue, and we note this treatment was supplied to Woolworth.

*Rear: 11½" platter, and 9" plate. Front: teacup and fruit bowl. Note the use of space: the central rounded decal complemented by the six slightly arching single flowers about the edge.*

*Springtime is quite common on Marigold. Shown is the 11½" platter, dated 1946, but the wide rim of the Marigold example seems to interfere with the spatial beauty seen in the VR platter.*

*The rare Marigold casserole, date 1945. Strange, in such a large and dramatic piece, the decoration is confined to the small edging floral decals. Some collectors find Marigold more "sculptural" than Virginia Rose – it certainly looks more substantial.*

*Detail of floral edging decoration.*

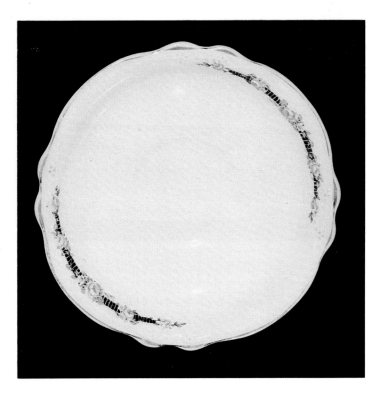

*Only this simple saucer has been discovered in Banded Rose.*

**VR#D.7**

BAND; black, trimmed and striped in pale yellow; with clusters of tiny pink roses, minute yellow flowers; green leaves. Glaze: cream.

Name .......................“Banded Rose”
Official number ............Not known
Known date .............................1942
Trim............................................Silver
Also appears on ............Not known

COMMENTS: One cheer for perseverance. How difficult sometimes when the collector is tired, to rumble through a last pile of worn plates or bowls. Research demands this be done, and this battered item was almost overlooked in a pile of some 20 saucers in a flea market stall. Not in good condition, it nevertheless is the sole representative of an unknown, forgotten Virginia Rose treatment. With a saucer, there must have been teacups, and plates, etc. Where have all these dishes gone?

*A detailed photograph shows considerable detail in the lines, vines, tiny yellow and white flowers gathered around five full blown pink roses.*

**VR#D.8**
**VR#D.8a**

BAND; narrow gold band from which hang floral swags, panels, and medallions; with tiny floral decal; leaves. Glaze: light yellow.

Name: ..............................."Band of Plenty 1"
Official number: .................................VR#136
Known date..............................................1934
Trim: .......................................................Silver
Also appears on: ..........................Not known

COMMENTS: This is a treatment about which nothing is known except it was offered for sale in 1934, a very early date. The collection consists solely of a sugar and lid, but we can assume a creamer also existed. And if a creamer, then also teacups, saucers, plates, perhaps an entire set. Finally, a 9" plate was discovered in the HLC morgue bearing the official number, VR#136. The official listing also includes the number 3893, which informs the researcher that this treatment was available commercially and could appear on non-Homer Laughlin china. With the discovery of this plate, it is now known the band runs along the verge. The golden yellow band is criss-crossed with thread-thin red lines, and a profusion of stylized flowers cluster in a variety of assortments. Art Deco in miniature. Does it appear inside the teacup? Can any collector help with more examples?

Also found in the morgue was a second version of Band of Plenty (Band of Plenty 2). The same without the central floral decal, it has the official number VR#138. The sugarbowl mentioned above could actually belong to either treatment since it has no place for the center decal.

*The flowers floating free on the side of this covered sugarbowl are slightly reminiscent of Bouquet in the use of pink, yellow and blue. The band is opulently ornate.*

*Detail: Note the Art Deco touches. True collectors make good use of the magnifying glass to ferret out the hidden beauties on their dinnerware.*

*These are two Band of Plenty plates discovered in the HLC morgue. Left: Band of Plenty 1 (with central decal), and Band of Plenty 2 (no center decal).*

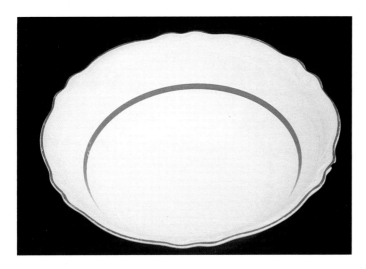

*The large salad nappy dated 1936.*

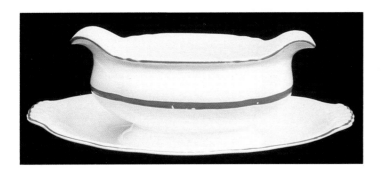

*The fast-stand is rare; this one dated is 1934.*

**VR#D.10**

BAND; red. Glaze: cream.

Name.............................."Red Ring"
Official number...................VR#158
Known dates................1935 – 1938
Trim..........................................Red
Also appears on............Not known

COMMENTS: A simple, pure, understated, very attractive design with a rich, warm glaze. The red ring lies just above the verge, and this placement gives it more emphasis. This treatment appears on the 1937 list, along with three other simple banded lines not yet discovered: litho blue edge with band (VR#156), green edge and band (VR#157), and dark blue edge and band (VR#159). The collection of #158 consists of two 10" plates, three fruits, the rare fast-stand, and the large salad nappy, an interesting mix. What a pleasure to locate the other banded examples someday in a faraway collectibles mall! (Note: does any reader know exactly what is "litho blue?")

*The red trim on this single 9" plate and the three companion fruit bowls is very rare in Virginia Rose. A wider red verge band completes a simple, yet striking, treatment.*

### VR#D.11

BLUEBIRDS; various numbers, small; with orange, yellow, blue small flowers, tiny pink flowers, branches; gray and blue leaves. Glaze: light yellow.

Name...................................."Bluebirds"
Official number.............................Not known
Known date..................................................1936
Trim.............................................................None
Also appears on......Chelsea, Empress, Genesee, Newell, Republic, American Limoges, Buffalo China, French China Company (Martha Washington), Pope-Gosser (Edgemore), Salem China Company, W. S. George

COMMENTS: Suspicions vindicated. All thanks to Evelyn Honeycutt of Georgia. Why, I kept pondering, did bluebirds appear on so many HLC shapes, plus the ware of other companies, but were not used on the highly popular Virginia Rose? My ponderings were just that until Mrs. Honeycutt sent a 6" VR plate in excellent condition with two plump bluebirds twittering their way along flowering quince. This was a spectacular find, and Mrs. Honeycutt is to be greatly thanked. When a St. Petersburg Beach dealer, David Becker, offered me a Homer Laughlin Bluebird mug with no trim, I energetically announced to myself a fourth VR treatment now has the accompanying generic mug.

There are various types of birds of blue on dinnerware — silently skimming blue swallows, thin upright birds with reddish breasts, but most popular, and the ones being discussed here, are those rotund, happy, wide-winged bluebirds that grace so many pieces. Those appearing on Pope-Gosser's Edgemore shape are slightly more red-breasted, but fall into our chosen category (see Jasper II, p.197). In fact, collecting just Bluebirds can be a singularly pleasant hobby. Donna Stenseth's collection is vast, and she is, quite rightly, considered our authority.

This find brings into focus another HLC shape, the early Empress. On this shape, Bluebirds have the official number, E-9303, and are often blue trimmed. These pieces are not too difficult to locate, but they arrive piece by piece. I have never seen an entire set of Empress Bluebirds offered for sale. Prices range from modest to astronomical. Ordinary unmarked fruit bowls have been seen priced at $25.00, yet I purchased an Empress Bluebird sugar/creamer set for $5.00. For years, an Empress large platter remained unbought, in a prestigious St. Petersburg, Florida, mall, with the price of $200.00. So if you relish these delightful songsters, be patient!

*A charming 6" plate. Loaned by Evelyn Honeycutt.*

*The generic mug marked HLC, but not Virginia Rose.*

*Empress: Left to right: sugarbowl; 10" plate dated 1922; 5" oval baker, 1929; and (front) two bone dishes with the early date of 1920. Bluebirds have been delighting collectors for many years.*

*Two relatively rare small platters. Left: 11½" Chelsea (1935). right: 10" unmarked Newell.*

*Liberty 9" plate dated 1930.*

*Two samples of the friendly plump bluebird. Left, the 6" VR plate and right, the Empress sugarbowl.*

*Examples of this treatment on other ware. The platter and sauceboat are French Company. The creamer, American Limoges (1925).*

**VR#D.12**

CHRYSANTHEMUM (double); yellow, pink, medium to large, two to three; with buds; pale gray leaves. Glaze: cream.

Name ...................................."Mums"
Official number............Not known
Known date.............................1939
Trim ........................................None
Also appears on .........Yellowstone

COMMENTS: The rich coloring of the glaze and the muted mauve-pink and soft yellow present a delicate and dreamy aspect. Those treatments without an edge trim also seem less focused. At times, a silver or gold trim can bring a sharp edge to a treatment. Here we have a naturalistic design wherein one section of the decal juts its way into the center of the plate, although this is usually not evident in the smaller items, 6" plates, fruits, etc., but the photograph is of the single Mums piece in the collection, a 6" plate. Thus, this treatment must be considered rare. On Yellowstone, however, the decal is more common, leading us to believe it originated with the earlier shape? The only Yellowstone teapot owned is in the Mums treatment. There is also a mug, probably belonging to Yellowstone, but we use it with Virginia Rose.

*6" plate. Plates of this size seem to the sole representative of a number of VR treatments. To see a 10" plate or large platter with these decals would be welcome. The general tendency is to have larger, more sweeping lines in the larger items.*

*Detail: One can hardly believe the intricate beauty present in American dinnerware decals!*

*A rather rare Yellowstone Mums teapot and the generic mug.*

*Daisies teacup and saucer.*

*A sugarbowl that got separated from its lid — probably many years ago, and a creamer. Rear: fruit bowl.*

*A 9" plate with graceful and larger florals stands between a rim soup (left) and a 7" plate. This treatment is somewhat unusual in that pieces of all sizes only have two decals.*

## VR#D.13

CHRYSANTHEMUM (single); white, pink, lilac, yellow, tiny to small, many; with miniscule blue flowers; tiny yellow-green leaves. Glaze: light yellow.

| | |
|---|---|
| Name | "Daisies" |
| Official number | Not known |
| Known dates | 1935 – 1937 |
| Trim | Silver |
| Also appears on | Kitchen Kraft, OvenServe, OvenServe/Daisy Chain |

COMMENTS: Undistinguished perhaps, but some HLC official must have liked it because it is accompanied by a full line of KK and OvenServe, including the servers. The simplicity of the small floral pattern might have made it quite popular in the mid-1930s. Besides the servers, some KK bowls, and an OvenServe underplate, the only other truly Virginia Rose piece was a saucer until a set of 34 pieces was purchased in an Ormand Beach, Florida, thrift shop. Virginia Rose pieces dressed in this modest decal seem quite hard to find. Could it be Daisies was originally a Kitchen Kraft design, and then was made available in VR? Perhaps this reversal happened more than collectors realize; it would be fascinating to learn exactly which treatments appeared first on what shapes. The careful, interested collector can draw conclusions by deduction, and the official lists help establish a few origins of VR treatments. Of special fascination is the exact relationship between the kitchenware lines and the dinnerware lines, but full knowledge is virtually impossible to obtain.

Research must be careful, systematic, and more importantly, allowed to grow and change with time. The above was written some time ago, but it is left so the reader can understand the "drift" of my mind at the time. Over the years, more and more OvenServe spoons and servers are being located. I already have four sets in my collection, and other sets are known. Once recognized, these Daisies serving sets are easily located. This reinforces the idea that Daisies was independently sold on Kitchen Kraft and OvenServe; indeed, perhaps the spoon and server (lifter) were commonly offered. No forks have yet been discovered, and Daisies remains a rare Virginia Rose treatment.

There is an intriguing point regarding the Daisy Chain pie plate. I own three examples, and know of others; all OvenServe pie plates in this treatment seem to be in the Daisy Chain shape. Maybe there are no regular OvenServe pie plates in Daisies.

*A charming small OvenServe individual casserole/server. Officially known as a baked apple.*

*The handle of the OvenServe server. Servers always seem to have a floral decal on the handle, but not the spoon.*

*The OvenServe spoon.*

*Teacup and saucer.*

*13" platter. The absence of any trim focuses the eye on the two striking decals.*

*7" Chelsea plate. The embossing is similar to Virginia Rose. This plate, like the saucer above, is marked "Chelsea," and could have been made by Taylor, Smith, Taylor.*

**VR#D.16**
**VR#D.16a**
CLEMATIS; red, large, one; with buds, yellow flowers, chartreuse; black leaves. Glaze: light yellow.

Name ................"Red Beauty" or "Clematis"
Official number .........................Not known
Known date ..........................................1934
Trim......................................................None
Also appears on .............................Chelsea, Coronet, Jade, Kitchen Kraft, OvenServe, Tea Rose, Wells, Yellowstone, and Hall's #488 is very similar.

COMMENTS: Red Beauty is the treatment appearing on a total of eight HLC lines, thought to be a record. My first exposure to this semi-stylized decal was through purchasing a set of 34 from Susan Pescatore, Chelmsford, Massachusetts, and, while dramatically startling, it was not thought to be extensively used. As often happens, other lines were discovered flaunting the scarlet "half-flower." The crimson, yellow, chartreuse, and black coloring is disliked by many collectors, and the question arises, why was it so often used? Red Beauty comes in two variations; D.16a has silver trim, and the one piece known, also dated 1934, is a 13" platter. Viewing this combustible treatment, one can understand the use of dainty daisies and pink roses on many VR decals. They are so soothing, and this one lacks any pretense of gentility. Even with all the use, this design's number cannot be identified. The Hall version is very close, but there are differences, so the decal cannot really be called commercial. My opinion: best viewed on the huge Kitchen Kraft bowl with its additional red line. Red Beauty needs space, and the KK bowls allow for the true appreciation of this flaunting treatment.

*Detail of the platter.*

The magnificent Kitchen Kraft large mixing bowl. The addition of the thin red stripe unifies the design.

Hall casserole #298 with the decal known as #488. Note the similarity to Red Beauty.

13" platter with silver trim.

Jade butterdish. Even though the silver trim proclaims this as Jade, it could be used with either the Jade or the Virginia Rose set.

Rear: Jade cream soup (no mark). Lower left: Chelsea teacup and saucer. Lower right: Wells sauceboat, dated 1936, but overprinted with the Wells Peacock, and trimmed in black.

*Two 9" plates. Notice the three columbine decals are of different sizes.*

*The teacup with the decal almost covering the side.*

*Left to right: Covered sugarbowl, casserole, onion (lug) soup (Century shape), and creamer. Columbines is not too difficult to find.*

Photo courtesy of Gary Geiselman.

*The rare cream soup.*

## VR#D.20

COLUMBINE; pink and yellow, lavender, large, two to five; with buds, tiny yellow sprays; leaves and stems.

| | |
|---|---|
| Name | "Columbines" |
| Official number | VR#232 |
| Known dates | 1935 – 1939 |
| Trim | Silver |
| Also appears on | Kitchen Kraft, OvenServe, OvenServe/Daisy Chain |

COMMENTS: Large, naturalistic columbines nod and dance from the verge to the edge on the flatware of this fairly common treatment. The colors are muted and soft; there is nothing harsh about VR#232 though some may find it a little busy, a tiny bit fussy. This decal will appear on the ware of other manufacturers, although none yet has been discovered because VR#232 was obtained from a commercial supply house under the number 707. It did not appear on the inventory of 1953. The main point of interest about this treatment: it is the only one to have been known to include both the rare soups, the lug, and the cream. Allyn Rosa supplied a photograph of the cream soup, and there are four of the lug soups in my personal collection. Please remember, the lug soup is borrowed from Century and there will be no embossing of the VR roses. No doubt as interest in Virginia Rose heightens, there will be other treatments discovered having both these elusive pieces, which make Columbines special.

See discussion of these soups in the Introduction to Virginia Rose.

9" oval vegetable (baker): flat bottom.

*A small OvenServe casserole (missing lid).*

*Detail showing delicate coloring of the woodland flower.*

## VR#D.22
## VR#D.22a

COSMOS; Maroon, white, large, three; with buds, small yellow flowers; yellow-green stems and leaves. Glaze: light yellow.

Name ............................"Sarasota Cosmos"
Official number.............................VR#208
Known date .......................................1933
Trim.....................................................Silver
Also appears on ......................Not known

COMMENTS: The teacup shown below is one of a large set of 57 pieces, including two covered casseroles. The coloring and the presentation of the decals are quite ordinary, in fact, this treatment lacks vibrancy and style; it is a bit "old-maidish." Perhaps it did not prove popular with the public because, while all the pieces available have the single date 1933, VR#208, the number found inside one casserole lid, is not listed on the inventory of 1937. This would hint at a short production period of about four years.

One casserole mentioned above was sold, and not until it was gone was it realized the second casserole was a different version; it had four sprigs. Unfortunately the official number was not under its lid. There is no mention of a four sprig treatment with silver trim on the 1937 list, so we can assume this version also was short-lived.

9" oval vegetable (baker): flat bottom.

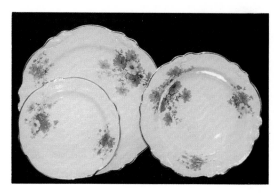

*Left to right: the 6", the 10" and 8" plates. Notice how only the larger plates have the 3 sprigs. This often makes a version difficult to identify when using only the smaller plates*

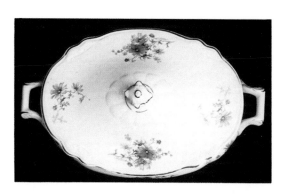

*The covered casserole in the 4 sprig version. I had a 3 sprig version, long sold, that I wish now I had kept. The number of this casserole is D.22a.*

*The teacup and saucer set also with only 2 sprigs.*

*Close-up of the casserole lid. Notice the fine detail of these lovely flowers. Quite remarkable!*

*Two bowls. Left: the more usual 9" oval vegetable. Right: the scarce small 7" nappy. Only Moss Rose and Fluffy Rose to date, have this small verson of the nappy.*

*This teacup and saucer are VR.#135: D.24, two sprigs, no trim.*

Photo courtesy of Gary Geiselman.

*Do not be misled: there is no trim on this 9″ plate; it is D.24b.*

Photo courtesy of Gary Geiselman.

*VR#175: D.24a, two sprigs, silver trim.*

### VR#D.24
### VR#D.24a, 24b, 24c

COSMOS; pink (light and dark), purple, medium to small, four to seven; with green feathery leaves; stalks of goldenrod. Glaze: light yellow.

Name..........................."Meadow Goldenrod"
Official number............................See below
Known dates.............................1937 – 1953
Trim...............................................See below
Also appears on ...............Century, Chelsea, Liberty, Ravenna, Republic, Yellowstone

COMMENTS: This treatment is popular and appears in six versions — sharing this record with the Fluffy Rose series (D.231). The various versions can be interchanged on the table, and only the most discerning collectors will distinguish among them. But the company considered them as separate entities — giving them individual official numbers. The large number of versions makes the treatment quite common, and prices tend to be in the high range.

In her book on Homer Laughlin, Joanne Jasper labels her Meadow Goldenrod example VR#135, (J.J. p.61) but this official number is described as having two sprigs and no trim. Thus the one sprig variation is really VR#404. Of the six known versions, I have seen four, and only these will receive the D(ecoration) number.

| | | |
|---|---|---|
| D.24: | VR#135 | Two sprigs, no trim |
| D.24a: | VR#175 | Two sprigs, silver trim |
| | VR#336 | Two sprigs, no trim (second selection) |
| D24b: | VR#404 | One sprig, no trim |
| D24c: | VR#411 | One sprig, silver trim |
| | VR#437 | Three sprigs, no trim |

9″ oval vegetable (baker): ridge bottom.

*A magnificent casserole and lid, again VR#175: D.24a.*

*Another teacup and saucer set, VR#411: D.24c, one sprig, silver trim.*

*Republic 11" platter and the coupe soup.*

*Rather rare 13" Ravenna platter, dated 1932.*

*Very rare Chelsea 11" platter. The Chelsea shape was also made by Taylor, Smith, Taylor, but this is example is marked "HLC." Except the teacup and saucer, items pictured on this page could be considered examples of VR#135 seen on other HLC shapes.*

*Liberty teacup and saucer.*

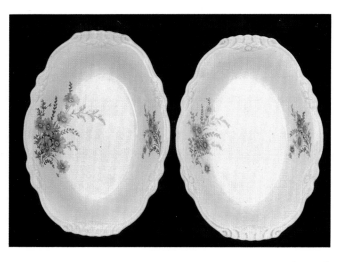

*Two 9" oval vegetables, both VR#135. Notice the difference in the decal size. This also happens occasionally in Fluffy Rose, VR#28.*

*Meadow Goldenrod Bowl. The pale green wash trim is beautiful and uncommon.*

### VR#D.24d

COSMOS: Same as D.24.

Name ......"Meadow Goldenrod Bowl"
Official number .................Not known
Known date ..................................1940
Trim ..................................Green wash
Also appears on ...............Not known

COMMENTS: With the appearance, through the kind offices of Shirley Freeman in Kansas, of a lovely specialty bowl with the Meadow Goldenrod smiling up from the bottom, this decal becomes even more important. It becomes another example of Virginia Rose wearing the very special wash treatment edging. It bears repeating that all these specialty salad or serving bowls were produced in the 1940s, with an occasional overlap into the '50s. Their introduction could have been to stimulate a sluggish dinnerware market due to the commencement of World War II. Housewives were not very concerned with purchasing new dishes in the frantic years of conflict, but they could be induced to add a large bowl to their current set. The bowls must have been popular because they continued to be offered in the late 1940s and early 1950s. One lone example has the date 1959, and this was probably the end of the production.

The green-washed bowl could accompany any of the Meadow Goldenrod variations, and this particular piece must have received considerable use because the decal is faded.

## VR#D.25

COSMOS; pink (light and dark), purple, medium to small, five; with green feathery leaves, stalks of goldenrod. Glaze: light yellow.

Name ................"Upright Meadow Goldenrod"
Official number .....................................VR#133
Known date....................................Not known
Trim .............................................................None
Also appears on..............................Not known

COMMENTS: Quite a conundrum here. I thought initially of placing this treatment under Meadow Goldenrod as its fifth known version! Although it has the same flowers and greenery, it is entirely different, so it was given another designation and number. The Upright Meadow Goldenrod was discovered on one plate in the morgue, with its HLC number written boldly next to the single decal. It looks rather stiff and awkward on the plate. Perhaps it appeared first, and then the cosmos were rearranged into a shape more suitable to dinnerware.

Some months later, Ray Vlach of Chicago sent me a photograph of a striking Century batter set, and it is noted Upright Meadow Goldenrod is a perfect fit for the tall jugs. The same decal is also seen on the accompanying platter. Since examples of Meadow Goldenrod have also been seen on Century, can we assume the upright version was originally used only on those pieces where it fit well? See the morgue section (page 168) for an illustration.

*Note how the decal, tall and elegant, fits the vertical space of this Century batter set. Courtesy Ray Vlach.*

## VR#D.30

COSMOS; pink, blue, medium, one to two; with buds; very few feathery leaves: Glaze: cream.

Name ........................................"Helene"
Official number ....................................VR#431
Known dates.................................1943 – 1947
Trim .............................................................Gold
Also appears on..................Republic, Orleans

COMMENTS: Quite common and widely collected on the Republic shape, these naturalistic cosmos are not seen as often on Virginia Rose and Orleans. My representatives are only three: rim soup, 6" plate, and the oval vegetable. The number was obtained from the oval vegetable. Notice the five year production period represented by only three pieces. It is a relatively late treatment for VR, and perhaps the popularity of the Republic version encouraged HLC to try it in the 1940s. It does not appear on the 1953 listing so presumably it had a limited production life. For all its comparative rarity, about two years ago at a collectibles fair in Sarasota, Florida, a service for ten, plus seven serving pieces was offered for sale at $700.00, a good price. An amusing anecdote: when this same fair was attended in January 1996, this Michigan lady had returned from the depths of her snowy winter with the same set, but this time the price was $850.00! When questioned she replied: "Homer Laughlin sets with decals are becoming very collectible. Don't you know there is a newsletter?"

9" oval vegetable (baker): ridge bottom.

*Photo courtesy of Gary Geiselman.*

*10" plate.*

*9" oval vegetable (baker).*

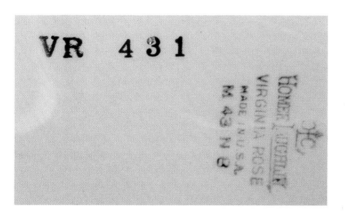

*The reverse of the baker showing the gold VR mark. Collectors are always pleased to see this stamp on the bottom of the baker or inside the casserole lid. Identifies this treatment as VR#431.*

*The small Republic creamer.*

*Left to right: 9" oval vegetable, 6" plate, 9" plate, fruit.*

*Teacup and saucer.*

**VR#D.31**
**VR#D.31a**

COSMOS; Pink, blue, white, large, four; with buds, pale yellow-green leaves, stems. Glaze: light yellow.

Name......................................"Ruby's Fall Cosmos"
Official number............................................VR#221
Known dates.......................................1933 – 1937
Trim...................................................................Silver
Also appears on....................Yellowstone (Y–146)

*Detail of backstamp found on the 9" oval vegetable showing the official VR stamp.*

COMMENTS: A soft mingling of colors and shapes, this presentation is very feminine and pleasing. Its special charm takes it out of the category of "just another Virginia Rose floral decal." Can remember tall spindly, feather-leaved cosmos stalwartly waiting the first September rains, their petals ragged, but they symbolized hope! Even though beaten down into the fall earth, cosmos would rise again in the spring: their regeneration taking form perennially under winter snows. Fragile looking are cosmos, but with tenacious strength. There are 26 pieces of Ruby's Fall Cosmos in my personal collection, all with an early date, 1933, but this official number also appears on the list of 1937, so it was available for at least four years. It is missing from the 1953 list. One of the better VR treatments, supplied by Ruby Roberts, Largo, Florida.

Meanwhile, interest in this treatment is growing. Gary Geiselman discovered a variety with two decals (sprigs) and a silver edge, and from this, the following history of Ruby's Fall Cosmos can be plotted.

| VR#195 | Not seen | | 3 sprigs, silver edge |
|---|---|---|---|
| VR#221 | D.31 | Ruby's Fall Cosmos 1: | 3 sprigs, silver edge |
| VR#324 | D.31a | Ruby's Fall Cosmos 2: | 2 sprigs, silver edge |
| VR#340 | Not seen | | 2 sprigs, no line |

We almost have a family here. The differences between VR#195 and #221 cannot be discerned until the former can be studied, but I feel this will be the same case as with VR#128 and VR#312 in the Fluffy Rose grouping.

9" oval vegetable (baker): flat bottom.

*A 13" platter flanked by two 6" plates. Notice the three large and three small decals almost touching at the rim to form a continuous design.*

**VR#D.33**

COSMOS; pink, blue, white, yellow, small to tiny, many; ringed around edge; with green black leaves. Glaze: light yellow.

Name ......................"Garden Ring"
Official number ................VR#104
Known date...........................1933
Trim .......................................Silver
Also appears on.........Not known

COMMENTS: 1933 seemed to be the year of the cosmos; three separate treatments are known to have appeared. Garden Ring has an open, lacy look, and floats around the edge rim: three larger and three smaller units, tip-touching with a few straggling buds and leaves. The most striking note is the inserted black leaves. These certainly catch the eye. Since the 13" platter and two 6" plates shown are the only examples located in over three years of intensive searching, it can be deduced this is an uncommon decoration. The HLC number was found on a 9" plate in the company's morgue.

*Detail of decal. The black leaves are distinctive.*

## VR#D.35

DAISY; yellow, brown trim, medium large, one to five; with buds; spiky gray-green leaves. Glaze: cream.

Name .........................."Field Ox-Eye 1"
Official number................Not known
Known dates...................1951 – 1952
Trim ...............................Gold
Also appears on ....................Nautilus, Cannonsburg, Paden City

COMMENTS: Both Virginia Rose versions, the Nautilus design, the Cannonsburg and Paden City pieces were offered early in the 1950s. This is a commercial decal. Entire sets of Paden City appear in this treatment, and a healthy number of Cannonsburg pieces can be located, but very few in Virginia Rose, and only the sugar/creamer set in Nautilus. The decal is quite stunning on VR, so its scarcity is a puzzle. The daisies are naturalistically graceful, and do not intrude on the dinnerware. It is, however, one of the decal sets that can confuse, because it appears slightly changed on the various pieces. Version 1 is represented only by the two platters depicted in the photograph; note how the decal seems to be divided and used differently on the smaller piece. Almost as confusing as the Zeisel Hallcraft design, Caprice. It would be useful to be able to obtain some plates or teacups to see if the decal changes even more radically.

*11½" and 13" platters, D.35 (1 sprig, gold trim). Field Ox-Eye is a confusing decal. Note how it changes, as these two pieces show.*

*Regular Nautilus with a rare yellow trim. sugar with lid dated 1951, creamer, 1949. Both unusual pieces.*

*Cannonsburg, pure white, small teapot, no mark.*

*Detail of a forward-looking daisy from the larger platter.*

*Paden City, Shenandoah shape, covered sugar and creamer, no mark.*

*6" plate, D.35a (1 sprig, no trim), with yet another version of the daisy decal.*

**VR#D.35a**

DAISY; this is the same as D.35 except for the trim.

Name..................................."Field Ox-Eye 2"
Official number ..........................Not known
Known dates .............................1951 – 1952
Trim.........................................................None
Also appears on ......Nautilus, Cannonsburg, Paden City

COMMENTS: We discussed some questions regarding this decal under D.35, so here note the decal itself. On this 6" plate, the daisy is depicted in a different mode, and only by looking intensely at the version on the larger D.35 platter can the daisy in D.35a be seen hanging. This treatment seems artistically dissected, but it still cannot be ascertained if the larger plates use the decal as in D.35 or as it appears here. This botanically correct design demands a close-up photograph to allow the reader to appreciate its detail.

*11" platter.*

**VR#D.40**

DAYLILY; orange, medium, one; with yellow bud; chartreuse leaves. Glaze: cream.

Name.........................."General's Daughter"
Official number ..........................Not known
Known date ...........................................1940
Trim .........................................................Red
Also appears on ...............................Century

COMMENTS: Many years ago, when vacationing in the country, I used to pick wild orange daylilies, and present them ceremoniously to my Grandmother as "lilies from the general's daughter!" The origin of this personal game cannot be remembered, but this daylily decal brought back the innocent memories of hot, dusty summer. Daylilies rarely appear on Homer Laughlin ware, and this example is a refreshing addition to the floral decal list. The red trim also pushes this treatment into the category of extraordinary. It was seen at a huge outdoor fleamarket near Orlando, Florida, on four sets of Century AD cups and saucers. On these pieces, the trim was bright green, a really startlingly beautiful combination. The sets were very highly priced, $40.00 each. But patience had its rewards. After nearly two years of no sales in the sets, the dealer sold me one set for $20.00. Collectors can protest outrageously high prices by not buying.

9" oval vegetable (baker): flat bottom.

*9" oval vegetable which unfortunately does not have an official stamped VR number.*

*Century AD cup and saucer, with green trim.*

### VR#D.42

DOGWOOD; pink and white, medium to large, two to four; with buds, brown sturdy twigs, few green leaves. Glaze: light yellow.

Name.............................."Liberty's Dogwood"
Official number...........................Not known
Known date...............................................1936
Trim ........................................................None
Also appears on......................Kitchen Kraft, Liberty, Rhythm

COMMENTS: Rarely seen on Virginia Rose, this is a very popular and common treatment on Liberty, and slightly less available on Rhythm. We can believe the Kitchen Kraft Dogwood was made to go with Virginia Rose, but, no doubt, it officially goes with Liberty. This bold design is very striking on the simple rounded Rhythm shape. Even though called "Dogwood," the blossom in this decal is more likely to depict Magnolia campebelli, the pink tulip tree. See D.43, New England Dogwood, for the true old-fashioned blossom. If one could gather a small set of Liberty's Dogwood on Virginia Rose, would it be wrong to use the Liberty teapot?

*Virginia Rose 9" plate.*

*The massive Liberty casserole and lid.*

*Liberty teapot.*

*Casserole with lid.*

*11" Theme platter.*

*A stately urn-type lamp base. Note the three sizes of the decal. Only identification is a gold "b" inside hollow base.*

### VR#D.43

DOGWOOD; white, pink, medium large, three; with one large orange daisy, other blue, orange smaller flowers; closed bittersweet, green and black leaves. Glaze: light yellow.

Name...."New England Dogwood"
Official number ..........Not known
Known date ...........................1944
Trim.......................................Silver
Also appears on.................Theme
    a series of lamp bases

COMMENTS: Like manna and pennies from heaven, this lovely casserole dropped surprisingly from Clarence Souza of Rhode Island. He included it free of charge when I purchased a set of Spring's Promise (D.183), delightful and thoughtful. This version of the dogwood blossom is truer than Liberty's, which looks suspiciously like a magnolia tree bloom. It reminds the lover of spring woods, the small, pinkish, near white, greenish, uncultivated blooms found deep in sunlight glades. Unadulterated simplicity. One would have wished the accompanying flowers be less color-strident, or, perhaps, simply fresher, paler, more prone to be dewy. Nevertheless, New England Dogwood is a very welcome addition to the Virginia Rose group. The treatment has also been discovered on the delicate Theme shape. But, the most dramatic discovery was seeing this Dogwood decal on three well-designed ceramic lamp bases. This occurence raises a relatively obscure VR treatment to a higher plane! The collector now knows there are three sizes of this decal — probably the smallest appears on the teacup, sugar, and creamer. Of extreme interest, New England Dogwood is a commercially available design, and could appear anywhere.

## VR#D.45

DOOR IN WALL (open); green, large, one; with steps, pathway, country scene beyond door, pots and flowers, border. Glaze: cream.

Name..."Garden Door One" or "Spanish Wall"
Official number ..............................Not known
Known date ................................................1937
Trim ................................................................Red
Also appears on ..........................................Jade

COMMENTS: This beautiful little 11½" platter was once considered quite a rare Virginia Rose piece; in fact it has been exhibited at several shows, labeled a specialty item. Recently another larger example was located. Both pieces continued to be thought of as rare, and were considered specialties. Jade, however, makes use of the decal on a large dinner service. Joanne Jasper made an important discovery from the notebooks of Frederick Rhead, in which the design was named, on Jade, "Spanish Wall." Study the illustration in Mrs. Jasper's book on HLC dinnerware and note the strong emphasis on the wall, missing in the VR examples. The Jade design has been added even though there is no real wall in the Virginia Rose decal. Since many dealers depend on a backstamp, which is absent on my example, it was purchased at a ridiculously low price. It can be considered a rare curiosity rather than a viable collecting possibility.

Then without warning, my "viable collecting" statement was washed away, again by Mrs. Jasper. Her discovery emphasizes the fact that collectors must be flexible and willing to withdraw statements once thought to be nearly self-evident. Garden Door One (and by association, probably Garden Door Two) are not specialty pieces; Mrs. Jasper supplied four 6" plates, three fruits, and three teacup/saucer sets, a total of 13 pieces floating about like the tip of a dinnerware iceberg. There must be more, and since these, except the teacups, were marked, the date became known: 1937. Photographs of the larger pieces would be appreciated. Does any reader own sets of the Garden Doors?

*An unusually small 9" Virginia Rose platter.*

*Detail of filigree border.*

*The existence of these pieces, sent by Joanne Jasper, proves The Garden Door (VR#D.45) is not a specialty design. Note how surprisingly delicate the decal and filigree appear on the smaller pieces.*

*A larger 13" platter (D.45a) with filigree designs between the embossed roses. The Garden Door is slightly askew.*

**VR#D.45a**
DOOR IN WALL: same as D.45.

Name ..."Garden Door Two" or "Spanish Wall"
Official number............................Not known
Known date...............................................1936
Trim.............None on edge, gold on handles
Also appears on.......................................Jade

COMMENTS: How pleasant to receive this 13" platter from Diana Kelly of Arizona because it gives a date that was missing on the smaller version. These gold filigree decorations are unique to this piece, and do not appear on any other Virginia Rose item. They are placed, quite logically, between the embossed roses. However, the absence of trim gives this platter an empty look; the red trim on the smaller version is preferable. The decal seems to have been applied with haste; note it is off center.

Once labeled as a specialty item, this designation is now questioned since a number of Virginia Rose pieces with Garden Door One have been discovered by Joanne Jasper. Is there a set of dinnerware with the door, unique filigree, and no trim?

*Detail of the opened door.*

*Detail of a filigree design.*

**VR#D.50**

EMBOSSED ROSE; green. Glaze: white.

Name ..........................................."Wings"
Official number....................Not known
Known dates.......................1934 – 1940
Trim ......................................................None
Also appears on:................Idea used on Marigold; Edwin Knowles uses same treatment on the Arcadia/Sylvan line.

COMMENTS: Pure white glaze is not usual on American dinnerware, and is used here to emphasize the green, over-painted embossed roses. The effect is very modern, dramatic, and clean, especially for such an early presentation. Collectors either like it, or find its color unappetizing; there seems to be little middle ground. For quite some time the available dates ranged from 1934 – 1936; then pieces dated 1939 and 1940 began to be discovered. No doubt this treatment delved its way into the 1940s. There is one point where the consumer/collector must beware. The embossed rose outline must show through the paint. If there is only a rough, crude chartreuse smear — looking like a 7-year-old daughter roughly smudging her lips — do not purchase it. Except for the rarest pieces, Virginia Rose collectors must not accept second rate. Marigold and Virginia Rose must be considered very close relatives, sister shapes. But like sisters there is rivalry, even though the former has been quite overshadowed by the latter. For a Marigold wearing this uncommon decoration, see J.J. plate 71.

*9" plate showing the pure white glaze. Absolutely correct glaze color is hard to obtain in photographs, especially those done in a studio.*

*Studio photograph of a Marigold 9" oval baker. The official number of Virginia Rose Wings has not yet been discovered, but the Marigold version is HLC#-90.*

Photo courtesy of Gary Geiselman.

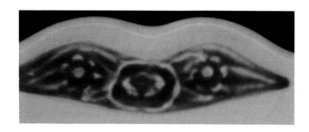

*Detail of over-painted rose embossing. The embossing must show through to be an acceptable example.*

*Sloppy over-painting on the handle of a 13" platter. This piece should be rejected by the discriminating collector.*

# Filigree

The term "filigree" refers to delicate and intricate ornamental design work done in silver or gold, although other colors rarely occur. Early Homer Laughlin abounds in this lovely, lacy outline work. Some early HLC ware appeared with filigree, and several lines of Republic were decorated in filigree, but the shape most closely identified with this treatment scheme is Century. Filigree bows and roses at the edges, snowflakes of varied sizes and degrees in the centers, hoops and swirls of tiny outlined roses, loops of beading and leaves, swags of vines and tendrils all appear at various time on the squarecut corners, deep verges, and marble smooth rims of the stolid, creamy Century.

There is another impression of filigree handiwork and decoration on dinnerware: fussy, old-fashioned, quaint as old dried Parma violets, as passé as cornstarch face powder, paisley parasols, mesh gloves, and wearing pearls to work in the garden. Filigree belongs to a time when Father read aloud after dinner, and Mother assiduously stitched petit point, while the children in starches and knickers, viewed their world curiously, yet safely, from behind tasseled russet velvet portieres.

Today, many collectors smile at and overlook the dainty, fine-lined filigree because it lacks drama and color. Yet there is a refined beauty present for those with a close eye and a gentle view. To the filigree, art directors began to add floral groupings or central flower clusters. This was thought to make it more palatable to a public whose tastes were changing, and as the floral decals grew in size and number, the filigree work diminished. But with careful handling, bold strokes, artistic balance, and a diminished reliance upon feminine intricacy, filigree becomes as sophisticated and contemporary as stainless steel storage frames in the ultra-modern kitchen. No treatment is as cool and progressive as the silver-touched Patrician.

Upon first reflection, it was decided to place all Virginia Rose treatments with any kind or type of filigree in this single category including those pieces with other decals. But this really does work. So here under FILIGREE are those treatments solely using this technique: those using filigree to ornament decals will be categorized according to the individual decal. Hopefully this decision will not lead to confusion.

*11½" platter with some staining. Note how the verge decoration gives the illusion of greater well depth.*

*Detail of "spider" filigree.*

**VR#D.55**

FILIGREE (silver); five-branched, flowers, leaves; with verge decoration of tiny Tudor roses, tulips, leaves. Glaze: light yellow.

| | |
|---|---|
| Name | "Spider Rose" |
| Official number | Not known |
| Known date | 1934 |
| Trim | None |
| Also appears on | Not known |

COMMENTS: The early to middle '30s were awash with dinnerware decorated in silver filigree. Much of the filigree work appearing on Virginia Rose was borrowed from Century, but this piece, sent by Joanne Jasper, seems to be unique. Note how the intricate, delicate verge filigree makes the 11½" platter look deeper. The main design (see close-up) looks much like a threatening desert spider.

### VR#D.57
FILIGREE; silver, medium, six around edge. Glaze: light yellow.

Name ............................................................"Agnes"
Official number......................................Not known
Known date........................................1947
Trim........................................................Red-brown
Also appears on....................................Not known

COMMENTS: What a difference one inch can make in the visual perception of a bowl. Agnes, at 8½", looks very small when compared with the regularly sized specialty bowls, and is the only example yet found in this size. The filigree is also different, slightly crude, but note the filigree designs placed between the embossed roses.

*The Agnes bowl is small, only 7½".*

### VR#D.61
FILIGREE; gold, over rose embossing, edging and line. Glaze: light yellow.

Name ..................................................."Gold Rose"
Official number ...........................................VR#115
Known dates........................................1932 – 1947
Trim........................................................Gold
Also appears on ..................Marigold and Coronet
    use the same technique.

COMMENTS: Another of the Patrician family treatments, this one simply replaces the Patrician silver with gold. Remember, the alternate name for Patrician is Silver Rose. Probably Gold Rose was offered by Larkin Soap Company as a richer alternative to Silver Rose. This treatment is uncommon and hardly ever located, which leads us to believe it was not popular and produced sporadically. Only five pieces appear in my collection as representative of this decoration, dated 1932 to 1944, and Laurie Holmes of San Jose has two pieces dated 1947, a wide span of 15 years for so few examples. Interestingly all seven are in mint condition. A dating of a full set is necessary before determining the relationship between the Silver and the Gold Roses. This is another case where readers could aid in research; more examples must be examined. For now, it must be stated that Gold Rose is hard to locate.

*Gold trim is much more subject to wear than silver trim. Here, however, we have four examples of Gold Rose in perfect condition: 9" plate, 6" plate, teacup, and saucer.*

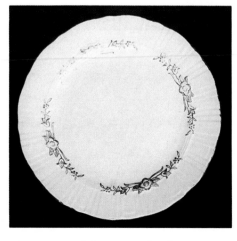

*Coronet used the same idea by trimming the verge embossed rose with gold.*

*Close-up of gold trimmed embossed rose.*

*A stacked assortment of flatware topped by the creamer.*

*Detail of the Woodland Gold decal.*

*Detail of the Golden Rose decal: compare with the Woodland Gold decal.*

## VR#D.62

FILIGREE; gold, rose (or anemone?), small, two; with filigree leaves and stems. Glaze: cream.

Name......................."Woodland Gold"
Official number ...............Not known
Known dates...................1940 – 1946
Trim.............................................Gold
Also appears on ..............The filigree
    appears on other shapes.

COMMENTS: Is this a rose or wood anemone decoration? No matter the true identity of Woodland Gold, it is easily mistaken for Golden Rose. This filigree has a more open look, a clearer, cleaner outline, and certainly has a most modern stance. Also, it never has been seen with any center motif, the hallmark of Golden Rose. The collection consists of some 30 pieces (no teacups or sugarbowl) all in mint condition. How the gold shines! Warm, burnished rich gold of the sun versus the cool, reflective distant silver of the moon, gold trim versus silver trim. Always favor the gold, but it must be realized some treatments would not be advantageously presented with gold trim.

*Closer view of the fruit and 6" plate.*

### VR#D.65
### VR#D.65a

FILIGREE; gold, roses, small, two; with filigree leaves, buds, stems. Glaze: cream.

COMMENTS: Golden Rose is the widely popular filigree pattern best known for its use on the Republic shape; sets are quite commonly available (see Jasper, p.33). It also appears on Century, and, less frequently on Georgian Eggshell and Liberty. Very similar to Woodland Gold, it is less open with more detail, a "fuzzy" appearance. There are two versions:

### VR#D.65

Golden Rose 1. No trim, with a round elaborate, closed medallion in the center of the flatware, bowls, teacups. There is only one piece in the collection, a 6" plate dated 1947.

### VR#D.65a

Golden Rose 2. Gold trim, with the very familiar snowflake medallion appearing as a center decoration. This snowflake is a very old decorative design often seen on Hudson and Colonial shapes (see Jasper II, p.87). Only three pieces in the collection, but Evelyn Honeycutt of Georgia supplied a wide date span from her collection, 1946 – 1961.

*A 6" plate belonging to Golden Rose 2.*

*Detail of the center medallion of Golden Rose 2.*

*Liberty 6" plate duplicating Golden Rose 2.*

*Detail of the center medallion of Golden Rose 1. This version does not have any gold trim.*

*Georgian Eggshell sugar.*

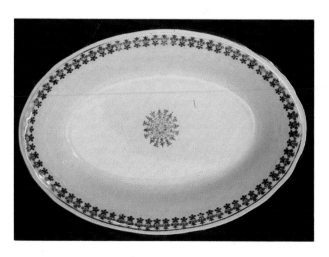

*Notice the center medallion in this Colonial oval bowl, a much older shape.*

*The very rare handled tray. This example measures 12" and must be the cake plate.*

## VR#D.67

FILIGREE; gold, three daisies in groups around verge, narrow gold band. Glaze: light yellow.

Name.................."Golden Temptress"
Official number...............Not known
Known date..............................1935
Trim.............................................Gold
Also appears on..............Not known

COMMENTS: Probably a specialty piece. Its singular, yet not overdone, ornateness and its appearance on such a very rare piece suggests its special nature. The 11" size qualifies it, in my personal opinion, as the cake plate. The smaller size of this tray-with-handles is thought to be the bread plate. But nothing is sure, nor carved in marble (See Introduction). This plate does, however, have a quite unusual additional backstamp, one of four VR treatments bearing a second stamp (others are Ribbons, D.22, Petit Point Rose, D.215, and Signs of Spring, D.1.) This overstamp is in green ink, and depicts an elongated heart. Within is "Pacific China, Fine Quality, Warranted 22 K" (see photograph). What really makes Golden Temptress important is the rarity of the piece.

*Detail of the fanciful bead-hung filigree.*

*This piece has an unusual addition to the backstamp "Pacific China, Fine Quality, Warranted 22K."*

## VR#D.70

FILIGREE; gold, roses with indented leaves, medium, many; with buds, leaves. Glaze: light yellow.

Name......................................"Charlotte's Rose"
Official number.............................Not known
Known date.................................1939
Trim.........................................Gold
Also appears on............................Not known

COMMENTS: Easily mistaken for Golden Rose, this rose filigree differs because the roses and buds have hairy stems, and encircle the entire piece. This lidless casserole is the only example ever seen, and it has a brief story — it is the only Virginia Rose that predates my collecting phase or even my adult years. It belonged to my grandmother, and never seemed to have a cover. She kept it on a table in her sewing room, filled with buttons of all sizes and shapes. I can remember digging through these buttons to locate my favorite set, which she never put to use — probably keeping them for me. Tiny buttons shaped like birds: a bluejay, a cardinal, a canary, a woodpecker with a bright red head, and a green parrot. They were avian friends, and spread out on the floor, they amused me until darkness fell outside the windows, and it was time for supper. These buttons never left my grandmother's room; their home was this Virginia Rose container. After disappearing (I know not when) it reappeared, sans buttons, among my mother's possessions after she died years later. This casserole/bowl will be buried with me.

*The filigree seems similar to Golden Rose, but here buds and hairy stems can be seen.*

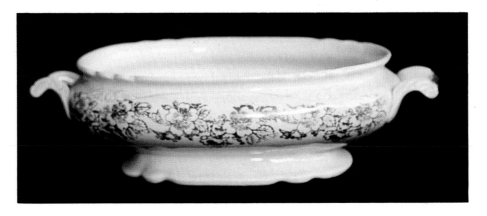

*It can be assumed this casserole bottom once had a lid, but it has been lost for many years.*

*The sauceboat shows the VR indentations on the rim — often overlooked.*

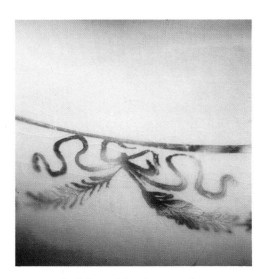

*Detail of the golden bow and swags.*

**VR#D.72**

FILIGREE; gold (lines, bows, swags), around entire center. Glaze: light yellow.

Name....................................."Ribbons"
Official number...............Not known
Known date...............................1936
Trim.............................................Gold
Also appears on...............Not known

COMMENTS: This sauceboat is the sole piece seen, but it can be assumed the treatment existed in sets. An important note: the piece has one of the very few decorator overstamps seen on Virginia Rose: "Imperial 18 Karat Gold" — in a golden diamond. The close-up photograph allows the delicate tracery to be appreciated.

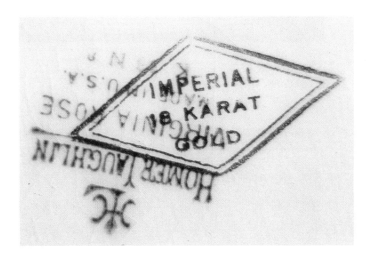

*The overprinted gold diamond backstamp.*

## VR#D.75

FILIGREE; silver, over rose embossing, edging and line. Glaze: light yellow.

Name ..........."Patrician", "Silver Rose"
Official number......................VR#124
Known dates ..................1932 – 1952
Trim.............................................Silver
Also appears on............Same style on
   Marigold, and Taylor, Smith, Taylor

COMMENTS: Patrician is one of the most important Virginia Rose treatments. It is collected and appreciated by modern sophisticates. There is no hint of grandmother's garden here! The approach is sleek and clean, yet it is one of the earliest VR offerings, and was distributed through the Larkin Soap Company. The twenty-some years of production make Patrician quite available, but it is one of the expensive treatments. My own collection of 32 pieces was dated 1933 – 1945, and it was thought adequate to give a good representation of the date span. But I asked Bruce Braun to check his large collection, and you can note, the years were stretched, and Patrician became a very early VR treatment and has one of the lengthiest availabilities. This leads me to repeat, the dates in this book must not be taken too seriously; only when a large number of pieces can be studied will the date span be truly representative. Patrician is one of the three treatments known to have the lug soup (Columbine, D.20 and Marigold Springtime, D.4 are the others). There are persistent rumors that the cable double egg cup is available in Patrician, thus parroting the same piece in Marigold. However, Patrician does not appear on Kitchen Kraft or OvenServe. This is viewed as strange considering the wide popularity of Patrician, although one answer could be the sophistication of the treatment does not transfer well to kitchenware. But I can hardly believe this: the rose embossing on OvenServe, and the wide, dramatic spaces on the Kitchen Kraft bowls are ideal for a clean modern simplistic design. I like to think someday silver Patrician will be found decorating the kitchen lines.

*Series of plates, left to right: 7", 10", 6", and the scarce 8".*

*The teacup and saucer with fruit bowl.*

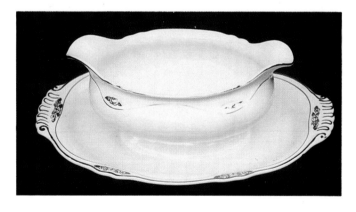

*The fast-stand, dropped from production in 1952, and considered rather rare.*

*Detail of the 9" Coronet plate showing how the verge embossing could be treated in the Patrician manner.*

*Detail of TST silver-covered rose.*

*A Taylor, Smith, Taylor 9" plate, dated 1936, parroting the Patrician treatment, but without the sweeping line.*

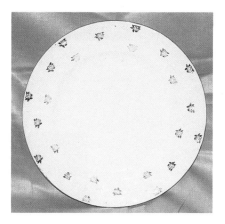

*9" plate, with 18 small silver roses placed in threes between the embossed roses.*

*Rose Sparkle on an OvenServe underplate.*

### VR#D.77

FILIGREE; silver, over rose embossing; with additional small roses around edge in silver outline. Glaze: cream.

Name ....................."Rose Sparkle,"
    "Christmas Sparkle"
Official number..........Not known
Known date.........................1935
Trim ......................................None
Also appears on..........OvenServe

COMMENTS: A real creamy beauty, another of the filigree examples dating from the 1930s. Only one piece, a 9" plate, has ever been seen, but we long to see the teacups and saucers. In my collection are seven pieces of OvenServe covered with these silver roses, but these also have a silver trim, three small underplates, a 9" underplate, and three 3¼" custard cups. On OvenServe, the silver rose decorations are scattered without concern for the embossing, but the result still sparkles. A festive air pervades this design, and it does seem to glitter. What a setting on a bright red tablecloth with green napkins, a table set for Christmas dining. This design speaks more of the holidays than do some of the modern, green and red sets.

*Two details of stamped silver roses.*

## VR#D.79

FILIGREE; silver, over rose embossing; additional scrolling under and between embossed section: Glaze: light yellow.

Name......................................."Silver Scrolls"
Official number....................................VR#172
Known dates ...............................1934 – 1953
Trim.............................................Silver
Also appears on...........:..Same idea as Patrician

COMMENTS: Even though represented by only six pieces in the collection, this treatment was likely as popular as Patrician during the time of its production. Easily confused, these treatments can be intermingled without disastrous results and for years, when I had only one piece, the teacup, it was unknowingly placed with Patrician. When the lovely casserole was obtained, the official number was found stamped in gold on the inside of the lid — and a new treatment was discovered. Silver Scrolls is a more ornate approach than Patrician; it begins with the continual silver line running near the edge, but adds a tracery of delicate scrollwork under the silver trimmed rose, and between the sections. Two closeup photographs show the differences. Remember, please, with extremely close photographs, the colors often change, appearing darker with a gray or blue cast.

*A rarer version of Patrician, this Silver Scrolls teacup and saucer have additional silver scrolling under and between the embossed roses.*

*A very classy covered casserole. The extra scrollwork is delicate, and different, but these pieces certainly could be used with the more common Patrician*

*Detail of Patrician rose overlay.*

*Compare rose overlay of Silver Scrolls to Patrician.*

*On the flatware, the scrolling is close enough to give the impression of a lacy effect.*

*6" plate with center snowflake medallion, D.87.*

*7" plate minus the central motif, D.87a.*

## VR#D.87
## VR#D.87a

FILIGREE; silver, tiny three daisy grouping divided by undulating circles; with miniscule black leaves. Glaze: light yellow.

Name . . . . . . . . . . . . . . . . . . . ."Century's Three Daisies"
Official number . . . . . . . . . . . . . . . . . . . . . .Not known
Known date . . . . . . . . . . . . . . . . . . . . . . . .See below
Trim . . . . . . . . . . . . . . . . . . . . . . . . . . . . . . .None
Also appears on . . . . . . . . . . . . . .Century, Yellowstone

COMMENTS: This filigree design is extremely common on Century, although usually with silver trim, and it appears occasionally on Yellowstone. This older shape dates from the middle to late 1920s, and was the last shape designed by an artist outside the Homer Laughlin Company. Frederick Rhead, hired in 1927, was responsible for the Century shape, and perhaps he was looking around for an existing treatment to try on the new shape. Thus, it is reasonable to say Three Daisies appeared on Yellowstone first, then Century — where it found its best home, and finally a scattering of Virginia Rose was decorated with this edge treatment. It is an elegant, but very conservative, understated decoration, and Virginia Rose sports two versions, with and without the central snowflake, both with no trim lines. We wonder, however, if there are pieces of VR with Three Daisies and a silver trim, especially since both Yellowstone and Century versions had trims.

### D.87

Century's Three Daisies One: with central snowflake medallion, no trim. Date 1934.

### D.87a

Century's Three Daisies Two: with no medallion, no trim. Date 1941.

*Detail of floral and bubble edging.*

*Century batter set. On this shape the decoration is officially known as Garland HLC#C45.*

*Left: 13" platter, D.87.*

*Right: The snowflake version seen on a 6" Yellowstone plate.*

## VR#D.90

FLOWERS (stylized); blue outline; with leaves in a similar manner, smaller blue outlines along edge. Glaze: white.

Name........................................"Blue Dresden"
Official number.....................................Not known
Known dates.......................................1949 – 1950
Trim ..............................................................None
Also appears on..................................Not known

COMMENTS: Here the collector is confronted with several perplexing problems. Blue Dresden is a treatment of the middle period; it is Virginia Rose reworked, heavier, more like restaurant ware with wider, flattened rims, and a pure white glaze. But of central interest is the fact that here, for this rather prosaic treatment, Homer Laughlin makes available a coffee pot, a teapot, reshaped shakers, and butterdish. The handles and finials of the coffee and teapots are pure Virginia Rose.

Blue Dresden offerings include pieces never before appearing in the Virginia Rose shape: ashtray, coffee pot, teapot, 13" chop plate, and AD cup and saucer (again, until proven wrong, I still am assuming "regular" VR's AD set was limited to the drawing board).

Re-worked Blue Dresden offerings: shakers and butterdish.

Virginia Rose items not offered in Blue Dresden: 7½" covered jug, 5" covered jug, 5" open jug, fast-stand sauceboat, coupe soup, cream soup, lug soup, double egg cup, cake plate, bread plate, 10½" platter, and 15½" platter.

All the other hollowware, including the 7½" open jug, was the same except for a slightly heavier weight.

The Blue Dresden flatware, including fruit and cereal bowls, had much wider, flatter rims. It cannot be readily determined why the rim shape was altered, but a good guess is the weightier substance of the line demanded a more rigid rim.

Why the additions and deletions? Since Blue Dresden was a supermarket promotional set, it was felt the pieces should be limited to practical items needed by the average family, and since Blue Dresden was certainly viewed as being for ordinary, everyday use, it could dispense with a variety of soup bowls, platters, and jugs. Practicality was the main thrust with this offering.

The additions tell the collector a great deal about the dining needs of the average household in the late 1940s. The Blue Dresden line, to be acceptable and successful, needed the coffee pot, the teapot, and since so many followed the example of Bette Davis, ashtrays. For the first time we actually can see and handle the AD cup and saucer. These small cups are quite rare in Blue Dresden; the only sets personally known belong to Bruce Braun of Wisconsin.

Artistically, this treatment is clean, fresh, and modern. The dark blue stylized floral bouquets are quaintly, old-worldly charming, like a Dutch tile, and the pieces are ideal for kitchen and other informal dining. The blue color is not obtrusive and would blend nicely with certain Fiesta or Harlequin colors. And it most certainly was quite inexpensive; what else could a housewife of the early 1950s desire?

Blue Dresden flatware is readily available; the 10" plates are seen frequently in malls. The hollowware is not common, and the pieces collectors most desire, the teapot, coffee pot, 7½" plate, and those fascinating AD cup/saucer sets, must be considered rare.

*The only time VR produced a coffee pot; these are quite rare.*

*7½" jug. The Blue Dresden jugs do not seem weightier than the other jugs.*

*The 6" plate, the 10" plate, and the sauceboat. One of the points about this treatment, the decals can appear cobalt, or a softer blue, depending on the light.*

*The covered casserole which, like the Marigold example, uses only the small decals.*

*This teacup, saucer, and fruit bowl have a bluer cast to the decal. Note the wide, flat flange totally different from the other Virginia Rose sets.*

*Detail of central design. The name Blue Dresden is very appropriate; it looks like a Dutch tile.*

### VR#D.92

FLOWERS; orange, red, small, many; with feathery gray leaves. Glaze: light yellow.

Name..........................."Hallow's Eve"
Official number ....................VR#376
Known dates.................1936 – 1937
Trim ........................................Orange
Also appears on .................Nautilus

COMMENTS: Another treatment with personal special significance. Homer Laughlin rarely comes up at Florida auctions, but this set was purchased at my first auction for $12.00. Some of the 42 pieces are worn, but still a fantastic buy. The trim is rare for Virginia Rose, rare even for any Homer Laughlin dinnerware, chosen because it matches perfectly with the stylized floral pattern. Even the gray foliage was artistically chosen. The official number was easily discovered on the 1937 list as only one entry for "two sprigs, orange edge" exists. The orange trim is so perfect, the Nautilus shape also is edged in orange. A lovely set, more exciting due to the unbelievable price. (Note: The Nautilus version was produced first with the number, N-234. There is also a Virginia Rose treatment with exactly the same orange floral decal, but without trim, VR#375.)

*7" plate with the teacup and saucer. The orange trim is unique.*

*Nautilus lug or onion soup, dated 1936. See discussion in the Introduction about how this piece might have originally been meant to go with VR set.*

*Detail of decal. Note the closed bud bottom center. How closely this matches some parts of Hall's Autumn Leaf design.*

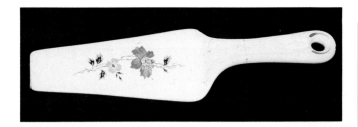

*Server with blue around the opening on handle.*

*Shirley plate with red trim.*

*The floral decal is insignificant on this creamer; it is the apple green wash that is fascinating. It suffuses the piece, but darkens to become a more solid trim at the top and along the handle.*

**VR#D.94**
FLOWERS (stylized); blue, red, yellow, medium to small, three to six; with small black leaves, wheat, thin branches. Glaze: light yellow.

Name ..........................................................."Shirley"
Official number ...Not known (see comments below)
Known date .......................................................1937
Trim .................................................................Red
Also appears on...............Kitchen Kraft, OvenServe

COMMENTS: Shirley Freeman sent this information the day before this manuscript was shipped to the publisher and justified my faith in human goodwill. The Missouri lady who sent Folly (see D.122) was kind enough but Mrs. Freeman charged me only $5.00 for a plate much more interesting than Folly. I decided to name the plate after my benefactor, realizing there will be critics more knowledgeable who will deplore my attempt to impose my will to the naming of Virginia Rose treatments. For me, this fresh treatment of red poppies, soft blue chicories, and yellow nasturtium-like flowers will always be "Shirley."

Also read Folly (D.122) for the problem of the official number (VR#360). This treatment also fits the same conditions and all that was said for Folly applies to Shirley. Also please note, the server has blue trim around the hanging opening. Does anyone have Shirley with blue trim?

**VR#D.96**
FLOWERS; pink, small, one; with tiny blue flowers, green leaves. Glaze: light yellow.

Name........................................"Apple"
Official number.................Not known
Known date...................................1936
Trim.......................Apple-green wash
Also appears on ...............Not known

COMMENTS: A very atypical approach to a Virginia Rose treatment. Take a very ordinary little floral decal, place it on the VR shape, then wash it with a silvery apple-green coating, heavy near the top and handle, delicate at the foot. The entire piece is transformed. The photograph gives a truthful account of the coloring. Where the wash is thin, the yellow glaze shows through. There is no usual trim; the wash takes its place. What a wonder to see the Virginia Rose 10" plate so decorated. Unfortunately, only the single creamer has been found.

## VR#D.97

FLOWERS; pink, marigold, cosmos, tiny, two; with miniscule flowers, blue, yellow; bright green leaves, silver over rose embossing. Glaze: light yellow.

Name...............“Flowers and Filigrees”
Official number .......................VR#231
Known dates.....................1933 – 1935
Trim ...............................................Silver
Also appears on.................Not known

COMMENTS: Randy and Kerry Dunn have an extensive collection of Virginia Rose in this treatment, but it cannot be said this is a common pattern. Without the silver embossing, it would be listed as just another of the many VR floral designs. The use of a silver stamped verge line is unusual, and also sets this treatment apart. The early dates are rather intriguing; pieces found in California, Florida, Illinois, and Michigan all have date marks within the three years stated above. While this is not proof, it is an indication this might be a treatment with a very limited production.

*Teacup and saucer with silver embossed rose and filigree ring inside teacup and on the saucer's verge. In March 1997, Joanne Jasper found a casserole with the official number VR#231.*

## VR#D.98

FLOWERS (group); anemones, tulip, daisy, medium-large, four with small blue flowers, pink buds; dark green leaves. Glaze: cream.

Name ...........................“Hidden Meadow”
Official number........................Not known
Known date.........................................1946
Trim ......................................................Gold
Also appears on ...........................Republic

COMMENTS: This is another contribution from Gary Geiselman, a 6" plate. Once, very long ago, while walking through an overgrown, unused Connecticut pasture, I happened upon the foundations of a small, long abandoned house. Yet the hands of the wife were still evident in the remainders of a once flourishing border garden. There were tulips, some black-eyed susans, a straggle of iris, a spreading pink rose wildly growing over the foundation. This cluster of flowers, once tamed, reminded me of this spring experience in the rocky pasture some 40 years ago.

Lynn Fredregill mailed a photograph of a beautiful Republic set — highly filigreed, but the floral decal in the center was Hidden Meadow. Often a collector can be confused if there are intrusions, e.g., filigrees, color differences. Perhaps Hidden Meadow's appearance on Republic pre-dated Virginia Rose.

*Photo courtesy of Gary Geiselman.*

*6" plate, the only example of D.98 ever seen, dated 1946.*

*Lynn Fredregill submitted this photograph of a set of Republic dishes wearing the floral Hidden Meadow.*

*The creamer shows the pale delicacy of this treatment and the extra heavy silver trim.*

*Wild Hyacinth on Chelsea.*

*Detail of floral decal showing the extreme attention to shading and the use of blue chicories to balance the design.*

### VR#D.100

FLOWERS; pink, small, many; with blue cornflowers; tiny leaves and stems. Glaze: light yellow.

Name............................"Wild Hyacinth"
Official number ..................Not known
Known date ..................................1933
Trim ................................................Gold
Also appears on...Yellowstone, Chelsea

COMMENTS: Study Plate 39 in Joanne Jasper's book; the Yellowstone plate on the right uses the same decal as Wild Hyacinth, yet it takes some study because here we have an example of a treatment using various sized decals. The smaller designs tend to appear on the smaller pieces, and sometimes what is believed to be two treatments is only one. The larger decal has many more cornflowers (chicory) which lend a welcome contrast.

Quite surprisingly, the rare shape Chelsea again appears; the pieces observed have the simple mark "Chelsea" which means it could have been produced either by Homer Laughlin or Taylor, Smith, Taylor. Determining the production source would assign the decal as either commercial or exclusive. On the larger Virginia Rose items, it is assumed the decals are larger. This very early treatment is represented in my collection by only the creamer shown above. Wild hyacinths grow along stream beds, and the smaller, looser flower heads are much more delicately colored than the gaudy, heavily-scented commercial strains.

**VR#D.101**

FLOWERS (group); pink, yellow, blue, tiny, five; with leaves and two extra flowers at the end of bare craggy twigs, ornate scrolled band. Glaze: cream.

Name...................................."Maude"
Official number .............Not known
Known dates .................1933 – 1935
Trim..............................................Silver
Also appears on .............Not known

COMMENTS: Maude is a very exciting treatment. Its verge line and inner teacup line are the most elaborate of any Virginia Rose design. Look carefully at the close-up photograph to understand and appreciate the acute detailing. If you asked me to state the rarest piece of Virginia Rose, the answer would be the AD cup and saucer — these have never been encountered, and perhaps they exist only on the drawing boards. But, the cream soup underplate gets a close nomination as the rarest piece, rarer than the cream soup itself. This treatment possesses the only underplates ever seen. Even if the above two points did not exist, the decal of Maude is unusual enough to make it exciting, a rough and straggly design. Maude came early in VR's life, and should be on the 1937 list, but the only entry mentioning a verge line is VR#136, and the sprigs (decals) number seven. Since there are no larger pieces in the collection (only teacup, saucer, three cream soups, and underplates), the 10" plate cannot be examined. Perhaps there are seven decals! No matter, Maude would be a very worthwhile addition to any Virginia Rose collection!

*Teacup and saucer, note the elaborate ring inside cup; cream soup liner (or saucer), one of the rarest Virginia Rose pieces; and cream soup stacked on two 6" plates.*

Photo courtesy of Gary Geiselman.

*The cream soup with liner; it also has the elaborate ring border.*

*Teacup and saucer showing the verge decoration which duplicates the cup's inner border, a very intricate design.*

*Detail of floral decal and section of the verge band.*

*Left to right: 7" plate, 6" plate, 9" plate, oatmeal bowl.*

*The 6" plate showing the warm gold-brown spatter trim.*

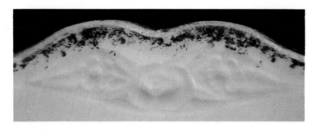

*Detail of the trim above the embossed rose.*

### VR#D.103

FLOWERS (group); pink, blue, yellow, tiny, many; surrounded by undulating cream band with stripes and scattered flowers. Glaze: light yellow.

Name ...................................................."Rose Quilt"
Official number ....................................Not known
Known dates .....................................1932 – 1934
Trim .................................................. Spatter gold
Also appears on.........American Limoges, Sebring

COMMENTS: Unusual and fascinating, this Virginia Rose treatment has a rare style of trim, spatter gold. This edging is exclusively HLC, because it does not appear in the ware of other manufacturers. Rose Quilt was extensively used by American Limoges and Sebring Pottery, sister companies located in Ohio, that often exchanged shapes and decals; this particular design was called Toledo Delight. It was a common, very important line for Sebring, appearing on the heirloom Corinthian shape (see Cunningham, p.263), and yet it was supplied commercially. Why Homer Laughlin chose to place another pottery's popular design on Virginia Rose cannot be determined. Since it is a very early offering, perhaps HLC was just testing customer tolerance before investing much money in original treatments.

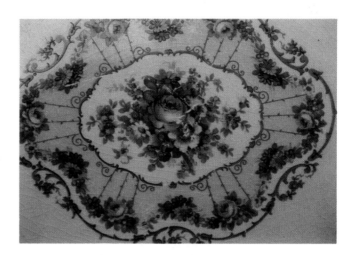

*Detail of the center of 13" platter. To fit the shape of the piece, this treatment also changes shape.*

*Left: The American Limoges 13" platter, marked "Delight IT208."*

*Right: Sebring teacup and saucer. The oval decal is positioned inside the bowl of the cup.*

## VR#D.104

FLOWERS; anemones, cosmos, small, many: with blue forget-me-nots and leaves. Glaze: cream.

| | |
|---|---|
| Name | "June Morn" |
| Official number | Not known |
| Known date | 1934 |
| Trim | Brown wash |
| Also appears on | Not known |

COMMENTS: Another platter entry thanks to the kind courtesy of Jeanne Smiley, which has to be considered a specialty piece until seen on regular dinnerware. This platter is large, just over 15", and while the central floral decal is rather uninspiring, the brown-washed trim is of great interest. Also, the very early date makes Ms. Smiley's find quite important. As has been stated over and over, each new find, large or small, expands the collector's understanding of Virginia Rose. June Morn was located in a mall between Charlottesville and Culpeper, Virginia. It has to be noted, although, the washed trims seem to be appearing more often on larger Virginia Rose pieces. One vital point Ms. Smiley makes is the rising costs of Virginia Rose; she has seen platters tagged as high as $45.00.

*Huge, heavy platter, slightly over 15". The warm creamy glaze color is very evident.*

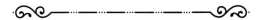

## VR#D.105

FLOWERS (group); pink rose, purple tulip, etc., medium, four; with buds, tiny flowers; green leaves. Glaze: light yellow.

| | |
|---|---|
| Name | "Four" |
| Official number | Not known |
| Known date | 1946 |
| Trim | None |
| Also appears on | Not known |

COMMENTS: Known by only one 6" plate, this treatment is very similar to April (D.142), and, except for an open, innocent quality, rather boring. Strangely what saves Four from being totally without merit is the factor of no trim. Gaze long at the photograph, and perhaps you will see what is meant. I am almost certain this treatment appears on Century, but cannot prove it; it simply looks like a Century decal.

*6" plate. The absence of any trim gives an open, vacant look. Would the teacup treatment be the same, or have only portions of the decal?*

*Magnificent large salad bowl with Harker salad servers.*

*Reverse showing the Stetson gold second mark.*

### VR#D.105a

FLOWERS (group); same as D.105; with elaborate filigree filling sides of bowl. Glaze: light yellow.

Name ........................"Four Flowers Bowl"
Official number......................Not known
Known date.........................................1946
Trim ..................................................None
Also appears on......................Not known

COMMENTS: Sows' ears and handsome princes suddenly emerging from enchanted frog bodies! Look carefully at D.105: small, meek, honest, but certainly not conducive to extensive praise. Now, thanks to Sam Portaro, Chicago, the D.105 Cinderella has blossomed into a most stunning, filigree bordered princess: D.105a. Here is another striking specialty bowl. This time, however, there is no question as to the use. The bowl is accompanied by two salad servers: the spoon, and the very uncommon fork. A very dramatic special salad set. In mint condition — as Sam said, "right out of the box" — we have lucked into a spectacular find and it also has a gold Stetson China Co. mark. Fuzzy caterpillar into flamboyant butterfly D.105a, we salute you.

*Detail of gold filigree.*

*Detail of bowl's center.*

67

## VR#D.106

FLOWERS (group); roses, daisies, pink, medium to small, four; with tiny blue, yellow, orange flowers; green leaves, silver filigree around edge. Glaze: light yellow.

Name.............................."Sunny Morning"
Official number....................Not known
Known dates........................1947 – 1950
Trim .................................................None
Also appears on .........Century (filigree),
   Orleans (flowers), Yellowstone (filigree)

COMMENTS: What a surprise to discover the central floral bouquet on Orleans. This sharing is quite unusual. Of course, the filigree is the most common one to appear on Century, and also can be seen on Yellowstone. Four mint cereal bowls (oatmeals) were purchased in Ocala, Florida. Remember, the Virginia Rose oatmeals are much less common than the smaller fruits. Each one of these bowls had a different date, and when the 7" plate was added about one year later, it had the date 1947. Five pieces and four dates we sometimes have entire sets with a narrower date range.

*Four oatmeal, or cereal, bowls with a 7" plate behind. Note filigree is Century's Three Daisies.*

*Orleans is a rarer shape. Here a 13" platter duplicates the floral design.*

*Close detail of the pink mallow.*

*9", 6", and 7" plates.*

*The scarce 36s bowl with the rim soup.*

### VR#D.107

FLOWERS (group); yellow, blue, shades of pink, small, many; with buds, drooping sprays. Glaze: cream.

Name ..........................................................."Bouquet"
Official number.............................................W#137
Known dates ...........................................1937 – 1949
Trim .................................................................Silver
Also appears on .......................................Not known

COMMENTS: So many unusual pieces have been discovered that Bouquet has as many individual pieces, except the Kitchen Kraft and OvenServe, as Moss Rose (JJ#59) and Fluffy Rose (VR#128). The answer seems to be Bouquet, produced for Woolworth's, was in direct competition with Moss Rose, produced exclusively for J.J. Newberry. Both popular chain stores wanted "their" Virginia Rose offerings to be equal. This is a satisfactory answer. Both the official name and number are available for this sprightly, happy treatment. As reported by Joanne Jasper, the "W" in the number shows it to be a Woolworth exclusive, and this chain would not allow Bouquet to be outdone by the Newberry stores. It is a bright and popular, early middle period design, offered by HLC for some 12 years, and readily available. If a collector is patient, sets for 6 – 8 can be located with some regularity. The serving pieces seem to be scarcer, but I have owned three casseroles, and now ignore them when seen. Someone at HLC liked this treatment and it has some interesting, yet conflicting, characteristics. As mentioned above, Bouquet ranks after Moss Rose and Fluffy Rose in the variety of pieces that can be collected, yet no Kitchen Kraft or OvenServe utilizing Bouquet has been found. Appearance on these two kitchen lines is thought to signify a pattern's importance. Note some statistics: the butterdish (Jade shape), the egg cup (Cable), the Virginia Rose 36s bowl, and the 5" open jug have only been located in Moss Rose, Fluffy Rose, and Bouquet. This alone would make Bouquet important. But then there is also the "Fiesta-type" double egg cup seen only on Bouquet and perhaps produced solely for Woolworth.

Still to be located: the generic mug, and the shakers (these would break the Kitchen Kraft absence), but with the butterdish and jug located, were these not also for sale at the Woolworth counters? But how can the absence of the kitchen lines be explained? One answer is perhaps Newberry had, as a contractual agreement, the right to sell Moss Rose Kitchen Kraft and OvenServe through its stores, and Woolworth could not present Bouquet on the kitchenware lines. Only a surmise, but it will stand until a Bouquet KK mixing bowl is discovered, or an OvenServe cake lifter.

Here, again, readers can help. The connection with the country-wide 5 and 10 cent store certainly can explain the absence of the Bouquet decal on any other HLC shape — just as Moss Rose does not seem to do double duty. It was probably designed solely for the ubiquitous chain of popular stores, and belonged exclusively to them.

All these fascinating points cause Bouquet to weigh in as quite a desirable addition to any collection. Aside from these considerations, this sunny, sprightly treatment can be enjoyed on its own merits. For brunch on the garden patio, or by a bubbling stream for an elegant picnic during a lazy summer afternoon, Bouquet is the Virginia Rose set to use.

*The rare small jug flanked by creamer and sugarbowl.*

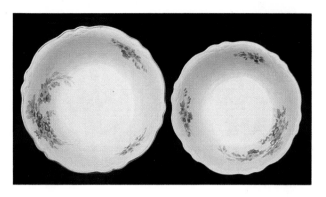

*The regular 8½" nappy (left) shown with the scarcer 7" variety.*

*Left to right: "Fiesta-type" double egg cup, 6" plate, Cable double egg cup, and butterdish (Jade).*

*The Bouquet official number W-137 shows it was produced for the Woolworth Company.*

*Close-up of the Bouquet decal.*

**Confusion among Muriel One (D.108), Muriel Two (D.108a),
Louise (D.192), and Little Louise (D.193).**

There is a strong possibility that readers will be confused about these four treatments, and a brief discussion of the similarities and the differences should help clarify the problem.

Muriel One (D.108) is represented by a single 9" plate dated 1939. The left side of this plate is swept by a large multi-floral decal. There are also gold filigree designs between the six embossed roses; there is no trim.

Muriel Two (D.108a) has been identified using a studio photograph supplied by Gary Geiselman. This plate has the identical floral decal, without the gold filigrees. The trim is silver.

Louise (D.192) was originally known only by a 15" platter, but subsequently a few other pieces were added: 9" plates, a 6" plate, and an oval vegetable. Luckily, the oval bowl had the official number, VR#390. But the 6" plate was the hero of this situation, for it was quite different from Little Louise's 6" plate, proving we have two separate treatments, and not versions of the same.

Little Louise (D.193) is now recognized as a separate decoration, as proven by the 6" plates. The confusion concerns the use of identical smaller decals on both Louises. To more strongly cement our opinion, a 9" plate or a bowl of Little Louise is needed.

Now, where is the further puzzlement concerning these four? Carefully view the large decal placed on the 9" and 7" plates (we have no such plate for Little Louise), and the reader will note the central section of all three is identical: a large, loosely petaled pink rose, a lemon rose, three white translucent daisies below, plus dark leaves, and a sprig of forget-me-nots. But here the similarity ceases. The Muriels' decal arcs into a quarter moon shape, rather rigidly bound, while Louise stretches and dips into the central section of the plate. Once these points are recognized and acknowledged, confusion ceases.

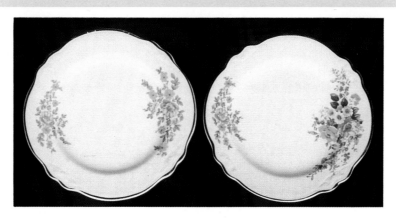

*The very important 6" plate solves a mystery. Little Louise (left) and Louise (right) share the smaller decal, but notice the difference in the larger decal.*

*Detail of the Little Louise decal.*

*Detail of Louise decal.*

### VR#D.108

FLOWERS (group); pink, yellow, white, tiny to large, many; with buds; pale green leaves, four to six filigree designs around edge. Glaze: light yellow.

| | |
|---|---|
| Name | "Muriel" |
| Official number | Not known |
| Known date | 1939 |
| Trim | None |
| Also appears on | Not known |

COMMENTS: This treatment's smaller flatware is not at all distinguished, but on the larger plates and platters the decal becomes sweeping, and arches toward the center of the piece. This is not a common design, but Muriel Thompson of Lansing, Michigan, found a 9" plate which allowed the above observation. The most distinguishing feature of this treatment is the lovely gold filigree that decorates the edges, four details in the smaller, six in the larger pieces. Unlike some others, this delicate filigree is placed between the rose embossing to create a unit of decorative edging. The floral part of Muriel could be, by the careless observer, mistaken for the design on the 6" plate of Little Louise. There can be no final decision yet; we need to see a 6" filigree plate of this treatment in order to determine if Muriel and Little Louise are simply two versions of the same decoration.

*The 9" plate sent by Muriel Thompson.*

### VR#D.108a

FLOWERS (group); same as D.108 without filigree.

| | |
|---|---|
| Name | "Muriel Two" |
| Official number | Not known |
| Known date | 1944 |
| Trim | Silver |
| Also appears on | Not known |

COMMENTS: What a tangled web is woven for us, especially those who try to piece together dinnerware puzzles. Muriel was all settled, new treatments were quite rare, and suddenly, Gary Geiselman mails the photograph at right. Indeed it was new, but still a version of Muriel. And Muriel is a rather rare treatment, and here was a version of it, or so we assume. The four previous Muriel pieces are all dated 1939, and this example is 1944. It may be that Muriel is a version of Muriel Two. Does any collector know? During the war years dinnerware manufacturing slowed. No assumption can be made about which version appeared first. Giving the public a choice between two versions of one treatment was, during times of cut-back, more suitable than presenting two completely different decorations. They could have been used interchangeably; the dinner plates and serving pieces having the filigree, but the presence of the silver trim on Muriel Two makes me believe two sets were the idea. Whatever the answer, here is a later addition to the list of Virginia Rose treatments.

*Detail showing the graceful, artistically executed sweep of the bouquet.*

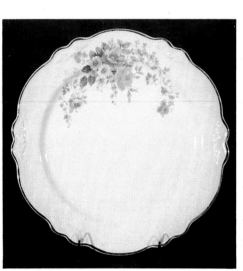

*7" plate. Notice the decal was not assigned to the center of the plate, and the silver trim.*

*This impressive 16" teal-washed platter, courtesy of Gary Geiselman and Allyn Rosa.*

## VR#D.109

FLOWERS; rose, tulip, pink, yellow-orange, medium, two; with tiny blue florets; green leaves. Glaze: light yellow.

Name ............................................"Het Loo"
Official number........................Not known
Known date........................................1938
Trim ............................................Teal wash
Also appears on ..............................Theme

COMMENTS: Het Loo was, and still is, the largest house in the Netherlands. The estate was purchased by William of Orange (William III of England) in 1684, and he and his English wife, Queen Mary II, built a grand symmetrical palace of red brick. The gardens are extensive, and they and the house are open to the public. The Dutch royal family gave the property to the state in 1987 although Queen Beatrix reserved the perpetual use of a moated castle in a far corner of the vast estate. The magnificent gardens are filled with Holland's best tulips, roses, and other flowering bulbs, hence, the name of this treatment.

This is a grand 16" teal-washed VR platter with a center decal, probably a specialty item as no washed edged dinnerware services have been discovered in Virginia Rose. Readers are reminded this particular floral arrangement is known as Nova Rose, a large rose in the center, and a tulip extending out of the mass. The decal appears on Theme, but in a more rounded form.

## VR#D.110

FLOWERS (group); peony, tulip, anemone, aster, medium, four; with a variety of cluster of small flowers; leaves, and tiny branches. Glaze: cream.

Name .................................................."Garden Theme"
Official number...............................................Not known
Known date .................,....................................Not known
Trim ...............................................................Silver
Also appears on.......Republic, Rhythm, Swing, Theme

COMMENTS: Apologies are in order because very little can be told about this Virginia Rose treatment. Gary Geiselman had it on display at a show some years ago, and he believes it was sold. All that remains, at this time, is the photograph. The rim soup bears the same decal as Theme #11, and VR using Theme designs is noticeably unusual. It does appear on Swing and Rhythm, and occasionally on Republic, but no one can really be sure which shape was the first to be decorated in Garden Theme. A careful study of all five shapes and their dates might help solve the problem, but that is in the future. While it is one of Theme's most common decoration, Republic is the older shape. The round, tight compactness of the decal makes it shine to great advantage on the flatware: the abbreviated portions appearing on the sides of teacups, and creamers do not suitably portray the original sense of unity. Meanwhile Garden Theme adds another treatment to the Virginia Rose list.

*Virginia Rose rim soup.*

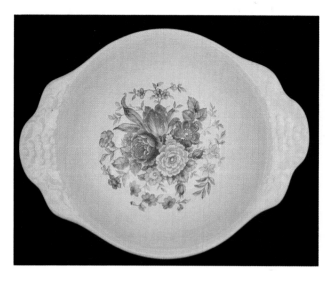

*Theme shape lug or onion soup, dated 1940.*

*Swing teacup and saucer trimmed in a band of pale blue, dated 1943.*

**VR#D.111**

FLOWERS; yellow rose, white narcissus, red poppy, medium, three; with bud; green and black leaves. Glaze: light yellow.

Name ................................................"Olivia"
Official number .......................Not known
Known date ........................................1947
Trim......................................................None
Also appears on.................Brittany, Ivora, Kitchen Kraft, Kwaker, Nautilus, Republic, Yellowstone

COMMENTS: This treatment is very common on Kwaker, can be seen occasionally on Yellowstone, and I own a large set of Olivia on Brittany teacups and saucers. Several pieces of Kitchen Kraft have also been located including the very desirable large shakers. But its appearance on the Ivora shape, made exclusively for Colgate, adds a true "zing" of interest. Joanne Jasper discovered the official description: rose and poppy decoration. Since Ivora flatware is practically indistinguishable from Kwaker, the two can be interchanged. The single piece of Ivora wearing the Olivia treatment is the tall large jug with a Kwaker-like handle, sporting rings at the base, not unlike Harlequin. Also to be noted is the existence of the St. Dennis cup. This piece was probably produced for Kwaker, but it fits in very well with Virginia Rose.

*9" trimless plate flanked by the Kitchen Kraft shakers.*

*Brittany teacup.*

74

*Left to right: Kwaker creamer, 9", 6", and 7" plates with a coupe soup in front. These pieces could be Kwaker or Empress since they share flatware, but we will call them Kwaker.*

*The very impressive and rare Ivora jug. Often mistaken for Kwaker because of the handle, it does have three Harlequin type rings near the base. It is marked with the usual HLC stamp.*

*The unusual, scarce Nautilus AD cup and saucer, one of a set of five. Cups are unmarked, all saucers dated 1952.*

*Another unusual piece, a small mug-like cup; it could be an AD cup. The small saucer is marked HLC. Could this be another example of Ivora?*

*Left: Republic teacup and saucer.*
*Right: St. Dennis cup.*

### VR#D.112
### VR#D.112a

FLOWERS (group); pink rose, blue forget-me-not, tiny, eight, with miniscule blue, orange flowers; green leaves, miniscule gray leaves. Glaze: light yellow.

Name...................................."Spring Song"

COMMENTS: Again and again, new and interesting developments constantly come into the foreground of Virginia Rose collecting! For some three years, I owned a single 6" plate, tentatively named "Pink Rose Swags." Not very exciting, but a sturdy, honest treatment. Then very recently, Gary Geiselman sent me a 10" plate for photographing. This large plate was the only one in his collection, but he knew of more in Savannah, Georgia. The photo was taken, the plate returned, and the name Spring Song affixed. Nothing more.

Months later, when reviewing my photographs, a bolt struck — Pink Rose Swags was Spring Song with a central decal! These two slightly ordinary treatments immediately gained new stature. Both were dated 1933, a very early date. Can we ever discover why this treatment appeared in two versions during the same time? Or, it is possible, although improbable, that some of the individual pieces of the set had a decal in the center of the flatware? Who can honestly know? We will have to wait until more Spring Song pieces are found. A good reason to get in my automobile and sojourn to Savannah.

The final ending involves the morgue collection where Spring Song was discovered bearing the official number VR#106. Now the listing can appear as follows:

D.112  VR#106     7 sprigs, silver trim, 3894
D.112a            6 sprigs, silver trim
       VR#203     7 sprigs, gold verge, stamp, trim

The only date known is the very early 1933, seen on D.112a. The VR number has not yet been discovered for this second version, and the gold trimmed piece has not yet been seen — something else for which Virginia Rose collectors can be looking.

*Gary Geiselman found a small set of Virginia Rose in Savannah, Georgia. A rather unremarkable treatment except for the early date 1933. This is the 10" plate.*

*The 6" plate formerly known as Pink Rose Swags, but now identified as a version of Spring Song, D.112a.*

*Detail of central decal of D.112a. The presence of this centerpiece distinguishes it from D.112.*

*The stately and impressive VR casserole and lid.*

*The treatment on Yellowstone is not difficult to find, especially on the smaller platters.*

## VR#D.113

FLOWERS (stylized); yellow, red, black centers, small to medium, one to three; with red buds; black and gray leaves. Glaze: cream.

| | |
|---|---|
| Name | "Medieval Rose" |
| Official number | Not known |
| Known date | 1946 |
| Trim | Silver |
| Also appears on | Georgian Eggshell, Kwaker, Yellowstone |

COMMENTS: When this casserole, the only example possessed, arrived in the mail, I just knew the official number would be stamped in gold under the lid, but, as often happens, the fates did not allow such. This treatment lacks an official number. But this is one of the joys of collecting American dinnerware; research never ends! The matching Kwaker casserole does have a number, K-8604B. Perhaps some reader can use this and work backwards. The roses are highly stylized, reminiscent of the flowers appearing in medieval painted panels. The Kwaker piece is itself unusual, departing from the usual wide rimbands so prevalent in the shape. In the time sequence: Kwaker, Yellowstone, and then some designer at HLC liked Medieval Rose and placed it on Virginia Rose. It must be considered quite rare and is difficult to locate.

*Close-up of stylized rose and bud.*

*This is the only Kwaker piece discovered wearing a treatment later belonging to Virginia Rose.*

### VR#D.114

FLOWERS; pink, yellow, medium, three; with tiny blue flowers; rose leaves, tulip leaves. Glaze: light yellow.

Name ................................................"Liza"
Official number .......................Not known
Known dates .........................1936 – 1940
Trim.....................................................Silver
Also appears on .....................Not known

COMMENTS: An eye-catching design, especially the large plates where the Nova Rose decal (see Duke, p.950) is beautifully spaced and realistically rendered. For a few years, Liza was known only by a single coupe soup in the possession of Gary Geiselman, but recently other pieces have been seen — and this is welcome because if given a chance, Liza could become very popular. Only the flatware has been discovered but small sets (minus teacups and service pieces) have been reported. Even though Americans are peripatetic and regional dinnerware can be discovered far from where originally introduced, I feel Liza belongs to the southeastern section of the United States. It is unwise to make statements such as these, but the charm, grace, and delicacy of this pattern bespeaks easy warmth and sunny, magnolia-scented patios; it is a summery treatment, more relaxed, with less energy than the spritely cool-weather Bouquet.

*6", 7" , and 9" plates, with fruits and 11½" platter.*

*Coupe soup.*

*A beautiful rendering of the floral detail.*

*The hibiscus-like flower with an unusual black accent seen on 6" plate and teacup.*

*Paden City Bak-Serve 13" platter and coffee server (no lid), and Paden City Papoco underplate (center).*

## VR#D.115

FLOWERS; white, pink, medium, two; with small orange, blue flowers; leaves, buds. Glaze: light yellow.

Name.................................................."Roulette"
Official number...........................Not known
Known date...........................................1956
Trim .......................................................None
Also appears on:........Paden City Bak-Serve
    and Papoco

COMMENTS: Again Joanne Jasper must be thanked for sending two pieces of this unusual treatment: a 6" plate and a teacup. The main flower is a variant hibiscus nearly hiding an orange poppy. A small orange tulip juts from the top, while a bluebell droops lazily. There is a startling black area included, almost as an afterthought. Roulette needs to be viewed on a larger piece because, as often happens, the small pieces show only a portion of the decal. As if answering my request, Roulette was found on a Paden City Bak-Serve covered casserole, priced at $45.00. Too high for purchase, but it was accompanied by an embossed Papoco underplate with a reasonable $8.00 price. Later in other Florida cities, Roulette was noted on Paden City jugs, coffee servers, and platters. As surmised, there a dramatic enlargement of the decal, with more flowers, and played-down black area. Roulette then, is a commercial design commonly used by Paden City. Still it would be interesting to view this treatment on larger Virginia Rose pieces: the platters, 10" plates, or round bowls. Any help?

*Detail of the decal. Note how the top and bottom flowers balance the treatment.*

/The Virginia Rose Treatments _____

## VR#D.116

FLOWERS (stylized); yellow petals, blue center, medium, one; with stylized orange buds; leaves. Glaze: light yellow.

Name............................"Medieval Garden"
Official number..........................Not known
Known dates............................1933 – 1935
Trim ......................................................None
Also appears on..........Kwaker, Yellowstone

COMMENTS: Looking exactly like an ornate flower woven into a medieval herbal tapestry, this photograph of the sugar with lid was sent by Gary Geiselman; the glaze photographs creamier. The very early date is interesting, as each treatment pushing on the date of introduction is of great value. Medieval Garden appears with considerable frequency on the earlier Yellowstone, and the 20+ examples of the Yellowstone owned all have 1927 – 1928 dates. Using decals that have already appeared on known shapes is a good business plan when attempting to interest the public in a new shape. A quick flip from Yellowstone 1928 to Virginia Rose 1929 (the date Mrs. Jasper tends to use for the introduction of VR) makes more sense than to wait for four years. Medieval Garden is the treatment that might push the dates of Virginia Rose back to 1929. If any reader has any Medieval Garden, please check the mark dates.

Photo courtesy of Gary Geiselman.

*Medieval Garden sugarbowl and lid. Please remember under studio lights the glaze looks creamier.*

*On flatware, the ornate stylization of the treatment can be better appreciated. From the collection of Evelyn Honeycutt.*

*Kwaker 12" platter.*

*This treatment is not difficult to locate on Yellowstone. The rim soup (left) is unusual because of its wide lip; the coupe soup is at the right. In front is the sauce boat.*

*Detail of the stylized flower. Vaguely similar to Medieval Rose (D.113).*

80

Photo courtesy of Gary Geiselman and Allyn Rosa.

*Even chipped, this is a charming treatment.*

### VR#D.117

FOUR-O'CLOCKS (stylized); pale blue, pale yellow, medium, two: with pink soapwort; blue-gray leaves, stems. Glaze: light yellow.

Name..........................................."MoonGlo"
Official number.......................Not known
Known date..........................................1946
Trim....................................................None
Also appears on.......................Not known

COMMENTS: Just a month or so before this manuscript was finished, the photograph at left was sent to me by Allyn Rosa of Washington, D.C. This VR treatment exists presently in a single, badly chipped 8½" bowl. MoonGlo has a faded, dusty, silvery appearance that anyone who has seen flowers by moonlight will recognize. While colors cannot be determined by the light of the moon goddess Artemis, it seems that one can see them, as if the retina remembers that a rose is deep red, a buttercup a rich yellow, or four-o'clocks pink and blue. For those collectors and those Virginia Rose detractors who find endless VR roses boring, this treatment is very refreshing and a striking alternative. Hopefully the magical moon will open some long-locked cupboard and a pristine set of MoonGlo will become available for circulation.

### VR#D.118

FRUIT (pear, apple, grapes); yellow, red, pale purple, tiny to small, many: with yellow bowl; tiny leaves. Glaze: light yellow.

Name ..................................."Medley of Fruits"
Official number .............................Not known
Known date ...............................................1934
Trim.......................................................Yellow
Also appears on ........OvenServe/Daisy Chain

COMMENTS: Many of the Virginia Rose treatments have some detail that captures and captivates the collector. This gracefully simple early design does so for three reasons: (1) the yellow trim is very unusual, and perhaps exists only with this treatment; (2) fruit designs are quite rare on Virginia Rose; and (3) the same treatment can be found on the newly identified Daisy Chain shape. The one plate in my collection was among a set of six displayed in a lighted cabinet in a mall booth in north Tampa, Florida, and was the only one in mint condition. Sadly, the other five were purchased by someone else. This was in 1989, and no other examples have since surfaced. Late in 1996, the Daisy Chain 9" pie plate was spotted and snatched at the Webster, Florida, Monday flea market; my eyes are peeled for the Daisy Chain casserole. Any other VR collector have Medley of Fruits pieces?

*10" plate with unusual fruit decals and much-desired yellow trim, the only Virginia Rose to appear trimmed in yellow.*

*Close-up of center basket of fruit. A tiny Art Deco design.*

*Daisy Chain 9" pie plate Medley of Fruits.*

*Close-up of the pear edge decal. The other fruit looks suspiciously like a tomato. Could this be?*

*This is the largest Virginia Rose platter ever encountered, 18".
The teal-washed edging is also unusual.*

**VR#D.119**

FRUIT (pear, apple, plum, cherry, grape); pale tints, red, yellow, black, tiny to small, many; with pale green leaves, in wicker handled basket, on grass and floral swag. Glaze: light yellow.

Name..............................."Bountiful"
Official number...............Not known
Known date..............................1944
Trim ...................................Teal wash
Also appears on ...Georgian Eggshell

COMMENTS: A massive 18" platter with a very unusual washed border trim; this type of edging is very rare, not only on Homer Laughlin dinnerware, but with other American manufacturers. The central decal has the quality of a faded lithograph. A very impressive, dramatic piece. A slightly smaller, 16" Georgian Eggshell platter has the same decal, and uses the same wash technique along the edge, although here the color is pink.

*The same old-fashioned fruit decal appearing on a 15"
Georgian Eggshell platter with rose pink wash.*

*For comparison, another old-fashioned print of fruit seen on the square 8" Nautilus Eggshell plate. Not many fruit decals appear on Homer Laughlin dinnerware.*

*Detail of grapes from the Georgian Eggshell platter.*

83

**VR#D.120**

FRUIT (stylized); yellow/green plum, large, one; with leaves, two red clovers; clover leaves. Glaze: white.

Name .................................."Greengage"
Official number.....................Not known
Known date.....................................1947
Trim ................................................None
Also appears on .............Hall's Hallcraft,
    Tomorrow's Classics

COMMENTS: As always, luck is a determining factor in the collection of any material. With a heavy cold, I did not really want to travel, on a damp and chilly Florida day, to an outdoor flea market — but I did so, and the first piece noticed was the large platter shown here. In perfect condition (except for a few tiny scratch marks on the decal), prominently placed and priced so low, it was hardly possible it was unsold. Treatments that look handpainted appear on other shapes, e.g., Liberty, but this is the first sample noted on Virginia Rose. It is easy to see the large brush stokes on the plum and the spatter technique for the red clover. Does this dramatically executed treatment appear on other flatware, and if so, what form does it take? This particular piece might be a specialty platter but whatever its role, it is a truly fascinating addition to any Virginia Rose collection.

Then, as so often happens, the same decal, drastically reduced but still very recognizable, was found on Eva Zeisel's Tomorrow's Classics gravy bowl: same color, same clovers, same plum. Immediately, the Greengage decal becomes known as a commercial venture and as such may be found anywhere.

*A pure white 15" platter with a striking "hand-painted" decal.*

*Close-up of a single clover showing the quick, watercolor technique.*

*Tomorrow's Classics gravy with Greengage decal.*

*9" plates. The lack of trim emphasizes the tall hollyhock.*

**VR#D.121**

HOLLYHOCK; mauve, medium large, 2 stalks; with buds; leaves, orange florets. Glaze: light yellow.

Name ..................................................."Sentinel"
Official number ................................Not known
Known dates ...................................1934 – 1941
Trim ................................................................None
Also appears on....................Wells, Yellowstone

COMMENTS: How I wish it could be reported that Sentinel appears on Century. Like Iris (D.125) there is a rigidity that is reminiscent of the square, scalloped-corner Century! But it does appear on Wells (see Cunningham, p.179). What is thrilling about Sentinel? Of the three 9" plates supplied by Joanne Jasper, two are dated 1941, and the last, 1934. These plates also have the heavy molding described as Mold #1 (see Appendices).

Hollyhocks are an old-fashioned, self-seeding perennial, found in most English gardens and abounding in New England fields beside crumbling foundations of old dwellings. Strong, persistent, marking other lives, this treatment stands sentinel over the past.

*Virginia Rose cup and saucer.*

*Detail of the flower.*

*Yellowstone pieces.*

## VR#D.122

HONEYSUCKLE; orange, small, four; with gray, green leaves. Glaze: light yellow.

Name ..........................................."Folly"
Official number .................VR#360 (?)
Known dates ...................1937 – 1942
Trim ................................................Red
Also appears on ..............Marigold (?)

COMMENTS: A lady in Missouri kindly sent me the 9" plate shown here. This deed was a pleasant surprise, doubly so because Folly has the rare red trim that is quite desirable to Virginia Rose collectors. Naturally, I wished to add it to my own collection, and the woman seemed fair. Since money does not really replace a plate (or so I thought), she was offered two replacement VR plates and a signed copy of this book; these are standard ways to make parting from a piece of Virginia Rose more palatable. Some sellers have accepted, others have refused. However, this woman refused my offer, but would "seeing I was the 'expert' in the field," sell the plate for $150.00. Was this a serious offer to sell or a gentle way of declining the sale? I returned the plate.

While trying to identify the 1942 plate I consulted the 1937 list, and found one entry VR#360 had 3 sprigs, trimmed in red. Since red is a very rare trim color and since the number of individual decals (3) matched, I laid claim to this official number. Of course, the proof is not yet in this pudding, but it seems very logical. For clarity, I added a question mark whenever necessary. Another interesting aspect is #360 was taken originally from a Marigold treatment, M-167, so we can assume it appeared on that shape. A further bit of very exciting information is M-167 was also used on VR#344 and VR#345, the former with a rather ordinary silver trim, the latter sporting a "celestial blue edge line." The combination of orange honeysuckle with sky-blue trim is very appealing. It is worth the chance of being incorrect, just to anticipate such a mixture.

*The red trimmed 9" plate.*

*Detail of the honeysuckle decal.*

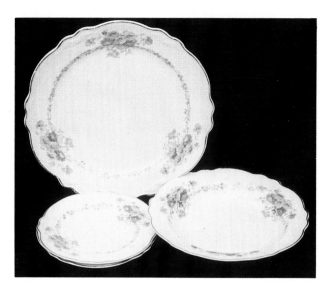

*Two stacked 6" plates, and the rim soup in front of a 10" plate. Without the verge ring of tiny flowers, this would be an undistinguished treatment.*

### VR#D.123

IMPATIENS; yellow, pink, small, many; with buds, tiny blue, yellow flowers on the verge; small green leaves. Glaze: light yellow.

| | |
|---|---|
| Name | "Four O'Clock Delight" |
| Official number | Not known |
| Known date | 1935 |
| Trim | Silver |
| Also appears on | Not known |

COMMENTS: What impresses here is the verge design. This decorative scheme exists infrequently on Virginia Rose. No entry for 3 sprigs and a verge line appears on the 1937 list, so this very early design could not have proved very popular. It might have been slated for distribution in a single store but until more pieces are found, we are left to wonder. The verge decoration sets this treatment apart, and the tiny flowers are in perfect, jewel-like detail. Wonder why Homer Laughlin did not make more use of the verge line decoration?

For a second use (not version) of these impatiens, see the morgue example, Temptation, DM.407.

*Photo courtesy of Joanne Jasper.*

*9" plate decorating a rustic cabin wall. Have no idea of the owner, or where it is — although the back of the photograph says "Seattle Filmworks," this proves the treatment's existence.*

### VR#D.125

IRIS; pink, maroon, medium, three; with green leaves. Glaze: light yellow.

| | |
|---|---|
| Name | "Iris" |
| Official number | Not known |
| Known date | Not known |
| Trim | Gold |
| Also appears on | Not known |

COMMENTS: Cannot offer much information about this treatment because, while it does fit our criteria for inclusion, it is known only by the photograph at left which was supplied by Joanne Jasper. Three stalwart irises march on the left side, three-bears-style, baby, mama, and papa. The style of the decal is reminiscent of Century. Irises are rare flowers on dinnerware, probably because the stately stance does not lend itself to a graceful interpretation. Leigh-Crescent has a decal entitled Iris Bouquet (see Cunningham, p.213) and Universal has a soft swaying version on its Fleur-de-Lis Iris kitchenware (see Cunningham, p.297). But beyond these examples, irises are difficult to locate. HLC does put three realistic, old-fashioned bearded irises on a heavy cream-glazed early 1930s mixing bowl. Again, readers are asked to help. If anyone has some pieces of Virginia Rose, or of Century in Iris pattern, please supply dates and photographs.

*Depictions of iris are very rare on Homer Laughlin. So rare, in fact, that this decal is included: it appears on a heavy cream-glazed 1930s mixing bowl.*

## VR#D.126

JESUS; portrait, halo, blue surround; with orange groups of filigree scrollwork around edge. Glaze: white.

| | |
|---|---|
| Name | "Jesus Plate" |
| Official number | Not known |
| Known date | 1950 |
| Trim | None |
| Also appears on | Not known |

COMMENTS: A beautifully rendered portrait obviously intended as a specialty plate to hang with reverence on a wall. A partially winged, semi-circled swag filigree frames the pieces. It is 9½", and a most unusual piece. Collection of Joanne Jasper.

*The 9" plate that obviously was meant as a devotional wall decoration.*

*An expressive detail.*

*The filigree border decorations have no particular religious significance.*

## VR#D.127

LINE; gold, verge and edge lines. Glaze: light yellow.

| | |
|---|---|
| Name | "Double Gold Band" or "Gold Circle" |
| Official number | VR#116 |
| Known dates | 1937 – 1948 |
| Trim | Gold |
| Also appears on | Not known |

COMMENTS: Only two rather worn examples were in my collection, 10" and 7" plates, both dated 1948. Enough remained, however, of the gold edge and verge line, to label it VR#116. Then a pristine sugarbowl and lid were discovered, and the rich sophistication of this glamorous treatment was clearly apparent. Truly, with its rich, almost cream glaze, it has more class than Patrician. Darlene Nossamen names this very appropriately, Gold Circle, and this is used as an alternate name. Mrs. Nossamen also reports this was a 1950s treatment; will wait for verification in order to expand the known date. These sophisticated understated treatments can be said to belong to the Patrician family, relying as they do only on silver and gold lines and narrow bands for a delicate, conservative decorative effect.

*A sculptural sugarbowl and lid. The simple treatment makes this piece almost as elegant as Snow (D.275). Note the refined touches of gold on handles and finial.*

*Two blue lupines on a 6" plate. A very unusual design.*

### VR#D.132
LUPINE; blue, large, two; with leaves. Glaze: white.

Name............"Amherst" or "Bluebonnet"
Official number..............................VR#420
Known date .......................................1943
Trim.........................................................Gold
Also appears on ......................Not known

COMMENTS: Leota Bohnert of West Virginia sent me one piece in this striking treatment: a 6" plate that she found in Gallipolis, Ohio. What a craving to possess some Amherst teacups and saucers — how would the vertical decal be adapted? Names always have special associations for me. When living in a tiny village in New Brunswick, Canada, we used to go the back pinewoods-skirted way into Nova Scotia to shop in Amherst, gateway to the province. During the early summer, the roadway shoulders, for mile after mile, were shrouded with masses of tall blue lupines. This gorgeous sight will remain in my mind's eye forever! Collecting dinnerware has a special added attraction: through a collection a person can remember past joys and bittersweet sorrows, and it is healthy to do so.

Upon reading Darlene Nossamen's *Homer Laughlin China* (p.20), we learn of a decal she calls Bluebonnet. But her description notes one large spray. Our Amherst has two! So technically, with the difference in spray numbers, Darlene's example is a new treatment, but until I have visual verification, it cannot stand in my listing. Incidentally, the Texas bluebonnet is technically Lupinus subcarnosus or L. texensis, so the vote for exactness belongs to Mrs. Nossamen. But, we still remember those early summer Nova Scotia days, drowsy and freshly pine-scented.

*Detail again proving HLC designers were masters at the subtle touches necessary in good botanical decaling. Note the faint pink flush touching the tips of the florets.*

### VR#D.134

MEDALLION (oval); blue, yellow, red center, large, one to six; framed in two floral swags. Glaze: cream.

Name ......................"Matinee Medallion"
Official number..........................VR#399
Known date ....................................1937
Trim................................................None
Also appears on........Century, Tea Rose

COMMENTS: The two pieces in the collection, an oval vegetable and an 11" platter, were supplied by Dick Pastor of New Hampshire. At first, he did not wish to part with these unusual pieces. Fortunately, the oval vegetable was stamped with the official number. Although both pieces were dated 1937, the number does not appear on the 1937 list: #399 comes directly after Waterlily (#398), so perhaps both were offered late in the listing year. This decal appeared on thousands and thousands of unmarked Century pieces given away at movie houses during the Depression. It also graced Tea Rose, a somewhat unknown shape also used by HLC as premiums. A curious find, locating this decoration on marked Virginia Rose. We need to determine if this medallion can be found on VR teacups and flatware; if none is ever located, perhaps the Virginia Rose were the serving pieces purchased to go along with the give-away Century. Until further research, this VR treatment remains a mystery.

9" oval vegetable (baker): flat bottom.

*Rear: 11½" platter, and front: 9" oval baker. This baker, fortunately, had the official number stamped in gold.*

*Decal of the intricate Art Deco medallion design.*

*Century creamer (see Huxford, pl.269, for additional examples). Since Century with this decal was a movie premium, it was not marked.*

*The teacup and saucer, the only examples found on Virginia Rose.*

*Detail showing the intricate scrolling with attendant tiny flowers.*

**VR#D.135**

MEDALLION; wedgwood blue, medium, one; with ornate scrolls, topped by pink double roses, yellow daisy, and other tiny flowers; leaves. Glaze: cream.

Name.............................................."Wedgwood"
Official number ....................................VR#456
Known date.............................................1956
Trim .......................................................Gold
Also appears on..Georgian Eggshell, Republic

COMMENTS: A very late Virginia Rose offering, it does not appear on the 1952 list. We can postulate Wedgwood was not available for any great length of time. Logical speculation is rampant when dealing with dinnerware dates and information. It does seem rare on VR: the teacup/saucer are the only examples located, but it does appear in the morgue collection (p.168). It is more common on Republic and Georgian Eggshell, so perhaps it can be assumed that Republic is the mother shape. A little fussy and ornate, but the inset of the famous blue does hold attention. Do not confuse Wedgwood with Aristocrat or Rochelle (see Jasper, pls.136, 137), two rather common, similar treatments appearing on Nautilus Eggshell.

*This treatment is never common, but it is seen more often on Republic. Here is the small sugarbowl and lid.*

*Georgian Eggshell sauceboat, dated 1950, looking ever so much like a child's imaginary ship sailing off to fairyland!*

## VR#D.137

MEDALLION; gold, chains, hanging cross from bottom. Glaze: unknown.

Name.................................................................."Charms"
Official number..............................................Not known
Known date ....................................................Not known
Trim .........................................................................None
Also appears on..............................................Not known

COMMENTS: This treatment stretches the parameters of our inclusion rules to the utmost. Known only by a small photograph of a 6" plate in Cunningham, p. 197, it nevertheless is a legitimate Virginia Rose treatment. Qualifying as a mystery decal, it can be hoped some reader has examples of Charms and will provide more information.

## VR#D.140

MEXICAN SCENE; man sleeping amid pots by the wall of a Mexican house; with tall palm tree. Glaze: cream.

Name.................................."Mexicali"
Official number............................Not known
Known date................................................1943
Trim............................................................Red
Also appears on..................Harlequin, Swing

COMMENTS: Glazes are always problematic in photographs, but I can vouch that the photograph at right is the true color of the 9" plate lent by John Moses. If the reader looks in Huxford (pl.171), the color is very yellow, and since Mexicali is extremely rare on Virginia Rose, it does not seem possible it was available in two glazes, but this might be an incorrect assumption. The dozing Mexican design is unbelievably rare on Harlequin and rare on Swing. I have seen only the Moses plate, and anyone owning pieces of VR with Mexicali is lucky indeed.

*9" plate from the collection of John Moses. Note the red trim; color trims on Virginia Rose are quite uncommon.*

*Part of a set of Century wearing this treatment. Platter, fruit bowl, teacup and saucer.*

**VR#D.143**

MEXICAN SCENE; with various pots in orange, red, blue, small red pig. Glaze: cream.

Name..............................."The Red Pig"
Official number..................Not known
Known date....................................1944
Trim ................................................None
Also appears on.......................Century

COMMENTS: Four or so years ago a set of Century was purchased in Sarasota, Florida. Very unusual because it was a "new" Mexican/Indian design, with a funny little squat red ceramic pig standing boldly in the front. When shown to other HLC colectors, it caused a flurry of interested delight which quickly died. Imagine my delight when in the summer of 1995, Muriel Thompson of Lansing, Michigan, offered me a "strange," small Virginia Rose platter with a red Mexican decal. When it arrived, there was my delightful tiny friend, the red pig! A little worn, but very welcome, addition to the Virginia Rose collection. This should be considered a rare find and now we crave more.

*11½" platter obtained through Muriel Thompson. Slightly worn, it is still highly valued.*

*Close-up of my friend, The Red Pig.*

### VR#D.144

MEXICAN SCENE: various pots in deep oranges and yellow with stalks of cactus. Glaze: light yellow.

Name .............................................."Mexicana"
Official number ..........................Not known
Known date ...........................................1947
Trim........................................................None
Also appears on.......Century, Kitchen Kraft, Nautilus Eggshell, W.S. George, Mexi-Gren

COMMENTS: The reader must remember these pots appear in varying arrangements in these designs. Various arrangements of the same decaled pots should not be viewed as separate treatments. This decoration is very rare on Virginia Rose (see Huxford, pl.177), and I appreciate John Moses, Manhattan, New York, sending me this particular saucer to photograph. It is one of the very few in his collection and it had no date. The other HLC shapes to carry this design often have different trim colors: Century, red; Nautilus Eggshell, blue. It should be mentioned that while the Virginia Rose in the Huxford book looks white, Mr. Moses' piece was definitely yellowish. Were there two glaze treatments? Does any reader have VR Mexicana with a white glaze? A fascinating bit of information was found during research; the decal was used by W. S. George (see Cunningham, p.83), an example of a decal so closely identified with Homer Laughlin having been supplied by a commercial distributor.

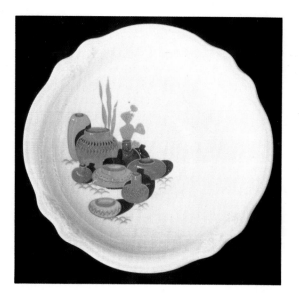

*John Moses sent me one of his few Virginia Rose pieces of Mexicana to photograph (see Huxford, pl. 177, for other examples).*

*The medium 8" Kitchen Kraft mixing bowl. Purchased, covered in grime, at a flea market for 50¢.*

*Two sets of Mexicana Kitchen Kraft shakers. Remember, often the pots and plants in HLC's Mexican designs were rearranged. From the collection of Gary Geiselman.*

*Known only through this 6" silver trimmed plate, April is very similar to the treatment called Four (D.105).*

### VR#D.146

NARCISSUS: pinkish-white, pink center, medium, two; with pink double rose, blue, mauve asters, yellow daisy-like flowers, tiny florets; pale green leaves. Glaze: cream.

Name ........................................"April"
Official number..............Not known
Known date...............................1947
Trim..............................................Gold
Also appears on............Not known

COMMENTS: Perhaps this treatment should have been listed under the category "Flowers," but the two narcissi seemed dominant and rarely rate a position in a decal, yet here they are with their own category. There is little to recommend this treatment beyond the narcissi. Probably not a very important Virginia Rose offering. The collection has only one 6" plate.

*9" plate with very unusual green trim. This color trim appears only here and on Madame Gautier (D.196).*

### VR#D.147

NASTURTIUM (stylized); red, light blue, orange, large, three; with buds; yellow-green leaves. Glaze: light yellow.

Name ...................................................."Bugles"
Official number...............................Not known
Known date.................................................1940
Trim.........................................................Green
Also appears on.................Georgian Eggshell, Universal

COMMENTS: An example of how a collector must persevere in hunting. In The Feed Store, Dunedin, Florida, one hot summer day, I noticed a large set of Georgian Eggshell with this decal and very special green trim. For some reason, the 9" plates were sorted through, and suddenly, near the bottom was this single, lonely piece of Virginia Rose. Whether it was part of the original set can never be determined, but it would have been easy to miss. So pleased was I to find the VR, none of the Georgian Eggshell was bought, and this I regret. Neither did I purchase the Universal water jug. Happily, several months later, a platter was discovered locally, and this time, was purchased for only $4.00. As more time passed, it was confirmed that Bugles was a regular treatment appearing on Universal. A very attractive refrigerator stack set was photographed in the Antique Mall of Tampa, proving that Bugles is a commercial decoration. Still, wish at least one piece of the Georgian Eggshell were mine.

The large Universal oval platter, here with red trim.

The small Universal teapot wearing the bright Bugles decal.

Universal refrigerator set. Courtesy of Frankie Moscatello.

Close-up of the very colorful flowers.

*9" plate and 6" plate. Notice the decal comes in different variations.*

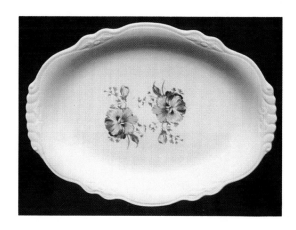

*The 13" platter with two of the smaller decals arranged to present a different aspect.*

## VR#D.149

PANSY; purple, yellow, medium, one to three; with buds; pale green leaves. Glaze: light yellow.

Name........................................"Funny Face"
Official number........................Not known
Known dates...........................1954 – 1956
Trim....................................................None
Also appears on........................Not known

COMMENTS: Pansies, which I consider an unusual decal on dinnerware, are charmingly portrayed on Funny Face, purple and yellow, the common pansy colors, with lacy green leaves more like maiden hair fern than pansy leaves. The saucers have a characteristic often seen in Jade; the decal is in the center of the well and obscured when the teacup is in place. Gloria DePasquale of New York supplied 24 examples in a mint set. It is amazing how many striking, unusual decals appear on the VR shape. As a child, I purchased baskets of pansy plants with allowance money in an attempt to enliven my parents' Depression era front yard. Pansies, or violas, are personally special to many people over the age of 50 — their smiling, delicate human-like expressions in rich or pale colors decorated yards and window boxes of countless small homes in the 1930s. Funny Face brings back memories!

*Detail of the decal on the larger plate.*

*Teacup and saucer and cereal bowl. When the teacup is in place, the wonderful tiny "Funny Face" disappears!*

### VR#D.150

PATIO SCENE: table with umbrella, chairs, red, yellow, blue, trailing flowers and vines, pots. Glaze: cream.

Name ................................................"Sunporch"
Official number...........................Not known
Known dates.............................1950 – 1954
Trim.........................................................None
Also appears on .......Century, Kitchen Kraft,
   W.S. George (Bolero), Harker

COMMENTS: Sunporch, the most desirable treatment to grace the dinnerware of Homer Laughlin. Sunporch, the treatment that can often bring out the negative characteristics in any collector. Sunporch, rare, very rare, stimulates greed, and the powerful urge to acquire. Could Sunporch compel me to sell an aged maiden aunt, or trade a babe-in-arms for a teacup? To define the magnetic power of Sunporch is difficult. It is rare, but so are many other Virginia Rose decals. The only other treatment coming close to the mighty strength inherent in Sunporch is Bluebirds (D.11), and this softly gentle bird treatment is still a distant second. All collectors want to add the Bluebirds treatment to a collection but the overpowering covetousness that overtakes anyone involved in Sunporch is absent. No holds barred when dealing with Sunporch.

Some collectors acquire this treatment on any shape; it can be relatively easy to find on W. S. George's Bolero and Ranchero, rather less common on Harker kitchenware. Among collectors, this fascinating treatment on HLC ware is not for sale! Those very few people who have a Century teapot, some Virginia Rose pieces, or other bits and pieces of Sunporch, wish to remain anonymous. To locate the whereabouts of HLC Sunporch requires diligent ferreting, a bit of surreptitious poking about, and considerable sniffing around. When Kim Hanz some years ago told me she had just sold some Virginia Rose Sunporch, she refused to name the new owner. Anonymity is absolute unless the Sunporch owner wishes to raise the veil.

John Moses lent me a Sunporch plate, as did Jeanie Milburn. These two collectors implied the above information. In my collection there are the Kitchen Kraft platter, a round casserole, and a Virginia Rose teacup. Rare indeed!

*9" plate and teacup.*

*Kitchen Kraft casserole with Sunporch decal.*

*Kitchen Kraft platter.*

*Right: Detail of the KK platter decal.*

*Left: Detail of the 9" plate decal. Note the Fiesta dishes on the umbrella table.*

## VR#D.151

PARROT; green, small, one: with small red, yellow, orange flowers; green leaves. Glaze: cream(?).

Name .................................................."Parrot"
Official number .........................Not known
Known date ............................................1937
Trim.............................................Green wash
Also appears on .........................Not known

COMMENTS: The inclusion of this treatment was the result of much soul searching. Parrot is the only inclusion based solely on another's viewing. There is no photographic record, but I trust to a tooth Jeanne Smiley, who has supplied me with a series of large platters, and whose veracity is unquestioned. When she called me about her find, she mentioned the embossing was large and crude, and this was the reason she did not automatically purchase it. When I requested she get it, she returned to the mall, and it had disappeared! Disappointing indeed! Can we believe some HLC collector in the area now owns this fantastic platter?

In Ms. Smiley's own words: "The parrot platter was seen Labor Day weekend, 1996, at Mechanicsville Antique Mall, Richmond, Virginia, and was the same size as the rose platter, 15" (see p.141), dated 1937, and had the same chartreuse (green wash) trim. The decal was centered on the platter with the parrot and foliage reminding you of the Art Deco style. The parrot's color was very close to the green (wash) trim with red, yellow, orange flowers and foliage. This all reminded me of the Oriental theme noted in Joanne Jasper's Homer Laughlin book (Jasper, p.132). It was also backstamped Virginia Rose."

Where is it? It would be deeply appreciated if the new owner of this Virginia Rose parrot platter would contact me, and perhaps provide a few photographs for my research records.

*13" platter with beautifully modeled peony blossoms. Peonies are quite uncommon on American dinnerware, especially naturalistic ones such as these. This platter is the only example of Summer's Garden found at this time. The beauty of the execution makes me want to find more!*

## VR#D.155

PEONY; pink shades, large, one to two; with buds; green, gray leaves, stems. Glaze: pale cream.

Name...................."Summer's Garden"
Official number.................Not known
Known dates...................1936 – 1938
Trim ...............................................None
Also appears on................Not known

COMMENTS: Soft and naturalistically shaded ruffled single peonies. My grandmother grew peonies, and, as a child, I marveled at the sweet juice oozing from the tightly furled buds. These flowers were never picked and brought into the house because they were attractive to numerous tiny ants. The peonies of this 13" platter, so realistically and sweetly portrayed, caused remembrances of my grandmother to flood my mind. This is a design with a very special personal meaning.

*Detail of peonies, a near masterpiece of delicate shading. Note the color nuances in both flowers and leaves.*

### VR#D.160

PEONY (stylized); pink, large, one; with yellow lily, rosebuds, blue, yellow smaller flowers; various green leaves. Glaze: cream.

Name ................................................"Spring Wreath"
Official number.........................................CAC 186
Known dates .....................................1947 – 1949
Trim ................................................................Gold
Also appears on .....Kitchen Kraft, Liberty, Republic

COMMENTS: It would be improper to state uncategorically Virginia Rose borrowed this decal from Republic because the latter shape was produced from the early 1900s until about 1940, although this theory is probably correct. The Republic version entitled Spring Wreath did appear in the 1930 Sears catalog. We have used this example in naming the Virginia Rose treatment. Gadroon-edged Liberty was brought into production in 1928; both it and Virginia Rose were closely tied to Frederick Rhead, and, as head art designer, he had persuasive control over a shape's treatments. Yet all this discussion leads us to no clear and positive conclusion as to which shape first used Spring Wreath. What does matter is that the design is reasonably available and its strong hand-painted quality makes it very popular, although artistically the decorative approach seems over-abundant, excessive, and slightly domineering as the three rich swags touch at the tips. On the sides of the Kitchen Kraft jar and the Republic sauceboat, the decal is smaller and more restrained. Ironically, on the KK server, it is too small. The official number shows it was a distributor exclusive. Besides being easy to locate, Spring Wreath appears on the rare KK shakers.

There is a French Provincial or country kitchen flavor that suggests wooden trestle tables, bright linen napkins, bouquets of field flowers, and a Dutch door open to a lazy summer garden: this is the setting for Spring Wreath.

9" oval vegetable (baker): ridge bottom.

*9" plate. Notice how the three decals almost touch, forming a continual edge decoration.*

*Kitchenware pieces: Rear: KK cake plate and cake server. Front: Small KK mixing bowl, and a pair of very rare KK shakers. Spring Wreath is quite commonly seem on KK bowls.*

*Small KK covered jar.*

*Liberty teacup, but no saucer was found.*

*Republic sauceboat. Spring Wreath modifies its decal to fit on the smaller pieces.*

*11½" platter, the only known piece to date.*

*Ravenna 6" plate. Ravenna is a very scarce HLC line, and to find one with a Virginia Rose decal is even more exciting.*

### VR#D.162

PHEASANT: purple, green, yellow, small, one; perched on a twisting branch, stylized flowers in several groups, pale maroon, purples; with leaves and branches. Glaze: cream.

| | |
|---|---|
| Name | "Oriental Garden" |
| Official number | Not known |
| Known date | 1934 |
| Trim | None |
| Also appears on | Georgian Eggshell, Ravenna, Yellowstone |

COMMENTS: Thanks to Rick Gault of Laurel, Mississippi, for this very attractive and unusual very early 11" platter. For many years I have owned several pieces of Yellowstone with the pheasant with a gracefully curving tail, and was quite fond of it. Then a single 6" plate in the Georgian Eggshell shape was given to me, and on my own, I located one piece of Ravenna (a rare shape). Then, finally, all wrapped up, the knowledge the decoration also was used on Virginia Rose. Was the mug actually made to be sold with Virginia Rose? Let us beg the question and assume it was, for then we can announce the discovery of a VR mug outside of JJ#59 and VR#128. This, in itself, is worth an assumption. As mentioned before, birds are unusual on American dinnerware, except perhaps for the many bluebirds that flutter expensively on plates, platters, and bowls. Pheasants are more aristocratic and elegant, lacking winsomeness, but, in a stylized form, grace a series of early heavy mixing bowls. To be perfect, this platter should have some edge trim, and the central decal could be a tad larger, but this is still a major find.

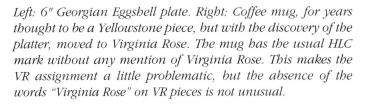

*Left: 6" Georgian Eggshell plate. Right: Coffee mug, for years thought to be a Yellowstone piece, but with the discovery of the platter, moved to Virginia Rose. The mug has the usual HLC mark without any mention of Virginia Rose. This makes the VR assignment a little problematic, but the absence of the words "Virginia Rose" on VR pieces is not unusual.*

## VR#D.163

PICTORIAL; black outline, small boy presenting an unusual Christmas greeting; rose embossing covered in chartreuse. Glaze: cream.

Name..............................."Christmas Plate"
Official number .....................Not known
Known date ......................................1941
Trim......................................................None
Also appears on.......................Not known

COMMENTS: Like the Jesus Plate, this delicately irreverent plate must have been intended as a wall decoration. Where it would be hung is an intriguing thought! Size is 9½", and the rose embossing is covered with chartreuse in the same manner as Wings.

*Detail: For some reason, this simple portrayal reminds me of the 1930s comic strip, "Little Nemo in Slumberland."*

*Was this 9½" plate originally an example of Wings (D.50), and then the decal was added, or vice versa?*

## VR#D.165

PICTORIAL; Los Angeles scenes with broken filigree sections about the border. Glaze: cream.

Name ......................................"Los Angeles"
Official number........................Not known
Known date.......................................1960
Trim......................................................None
Also appears on.......................Not known

COMMENTS: This treatment, like Iris (D.125), has been seen only through a photograph. It is in the collection of Mr. and Mrs. Chet Barton of Whittier, California; Mr. Barton supplied the photo. Are there other Virginia Rose theme plates? This one is warmly attractive in browns, beiges, honeys, and umbers, and I assume the glaze is richly cream. The filigree also seems to be a different variety. Quite a find!

*The entire plate presents a warm, well-designed aspect.*

The center of the plate.

Close-up of the rim and filigree. Notice how the filigree stops to allow the embossing to show.

Left to right: The VR 11" platter, 9" plate, and 6" plate, all dated 1949.

The Swing nappy. The smooth roundness and the soft yellow edge make an almost perfect frame for the kitchen scene.

**VR#D.167**

PICTORIAL; colonial kitchen. Glaze: cream.

Name ..........................................."Colonial Kitchen"
Official number ....................................Not known
Known dates ....................................1948 – 1951
Trim ...............................................................Gold
Also appears on........................................Liberty,
  Nautilus Eggshell, Rhythm, Swing

COMMENTS: This decal is one of the most widely recognized and popular of all HLC treatments and is most readily seen on Swing. On only one piece each has the decal been noted on Liberty (creamer) and Nautilus Eggshell (fast-stand), but the existence of these pieces logically means Colonial Kitchen was available in full dinnerware sets. Small Virginia Rose sets can also be formed (the above dates are those of a set personally owned; the decal was probably available for a longer period) — so not only is it popular, it is quite easy to find. These two characteristics make Colonial Kitchen a very important decal. Because of the pictorial element, it has been used on large Rhythm plates, framed in ornate copper curls, and displayed as a wall decoration. A delightful, rather expensive Virginia Rose treatment.

### VR#D.170

PICTORIAL; colonial man and woman dancing to music produced by a flutist in the background; with trees, grass, usual garden scene. Glaze: cream.

Name.............................................."Colonial Quadrille"
Official number.......................................Not known
Known date.........................................................1947
Trim..................................................................Gold
Also appears on .....Georgian Eggshell, Liberty, very
common on the shapes of other manufacturers

COMMENTS: This is a commercial decal because it appears regularly on the ware of many potteries; it is one of the most common and easily recognized decals. Harker, for example, makes extensive use of it on the Royal Gadroon shape. The pictured 9" plate is the only Virginia Rose piece with this decal and there is a slight chance it might be a specialty item. But if it were meant to hang on the wall, would it not be more elaborate, more like the Liberty and Georgian Eggshell versions shown? If it is a regular dinnerware design, what would appear on the teacup?

*The magnificent 10" plate.*

*Detail of the central figures. This is a very common decal used by many potteries.*

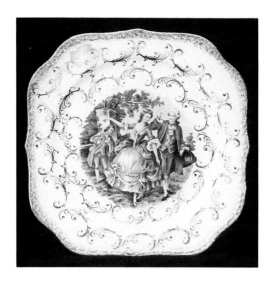

*Decal seen on a very ornate 8" square Georgian Eggshell plate, dated 1944. This piece also bears the Royal China overstamp.*

*The 10" Liberty plate, with an ornate rim band, dated 1944.*

104

*Large specialty bowl viewed from above. While labeled a "specialty," actually this piece could accompany any set bearing this common decal.*

### VR#D.170a

PICTORIAL; same design as #D.170; with elaborate filigree of baskets and flowers. Glaze: cream.

Name.............................."Colonial Quadrille Bowl"
Official number.....................................Not known
Known date.....................................................1945
Trim.....................................................Gold flecks
Also appears on.........Georgian Eggshell, Liberty,
    many shapes of other potteries

COMMENTS: A stunningly decorated specialty bowl, all gilt and drama. The gold filigree presents many stylized baskets overflowing with flowers and leaves. The golden flecked trim is also unusual. This piece was obtained through the kindness of Rick Gault of Louisiana. The central dancing couple can be commonly found, so this bowl could ostensibly be used with many sets. The main interest here is the Royal China secondary gold stamp. Only three other VR treatments (to date) bear an additional overstamp: Ribbons (D.72), Petit Point Rose (D.215), and Golden Temptress, (D.67). Royal China is a decorating firm and purchased the VR blank from HLC. What beautiful results.

*Detail of backstamp. This one, like the Georgian Eggshell 8" square plate, has the Royal China overstamp.*

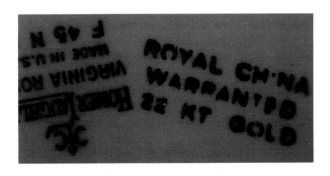

*Detail of the filigree: a vase of flowers, on a "bug-eyed Medusa."*

### VR#D.172

PICTORIAL; yellow, black, medium, two; with gold filigree around rim. Glaze: cream.

Name ............................"Grecian Melody"
Official number ...................Not known
Known date .....................................1949
Trim...................................................None
Also appears on ...................Not known

COMMENTS: A bright yellow canary perches on a stylized flower stalk curving from a black patterned cornucopia. Other stylized flowers and leaves, yellows, grays, pale blues, tumble from this curve-footed container portrayed in the Greek style. A very rare and unusual decal, delicately constructed. Around the edges of this large bowl are six sets of gold filigree roses in the same manner used on the Golden Rose series (D.65). Everything fits: the canary bird, the colors, the filigree, the cream glaze. Rick Gault of Louisiana must be thanked for this lovely Virginia Rose bowl.

*Looking down into the beautiful specialty bowl.*

*Extreme detail of the bright yellow canary.*

*The central decoration with the dark flower-sprouting cornucopia.*

*The small fruit bowl with a true white glaze.*

*The beautifully red poinsettia with green-gray leaves.*

## VR#D.175

POINSETTIA; deep red, small, one; with gray-green leaves. Glaze: white.

Name ..............................."Christmas"
Official number..............Not known
Known date.............................1939
Trim ...........................................Silver
Also appears on.............Not known

COMMENTS: Four lovely fruit bowls were found in a local mall about three years ago — taped securely together and priced $5.00. A very good buy for a friendly, unusual decal. This is a rare use of the poinsettia on Homer Laughlin dinnerware. Unfortunately, this treatment has not been seen again. The Christmas plant, with scarlet bracts under tiny yellow (here grayish) flowers is a welcome change from all the daisies and roses. The use of gray leaves instead of the more familiar green allows this set to be used at other times, so perhaps it was not meant solely for December 25th.

*9" plate. Note the especially warm glaze. While officially light yellow, the pieces in my possession tend to be closer to a warm tan.*

## VR#D.176

POPPY; orange-yellow, mauve, large, three to five with buds, pink; blue-gray leaves. Glaze: light yellow.

Name ................................."California Hillside"
Official number ..............................Not known
Known date .................................1936
Trim...........................................................None
Also appears on ...................................Century

COMMENTS: California Hillside is a well-created design. New collectors often believe Virginia Rose is all roses and small blue daisies, and here is a striking exception, poppies. The lines of the flowers are bold, yet shadowy, while the coloring and shading, the luminescent quality are reminiscent of a floral watercolor done in the field. This treatment should have been very popular, but there is very little seen on the market today. There are 18 pieces in my personal collection, mainly 10" plates, but one 7" plate, and a rim soup. Unfortunately teacups and saucers have not been seen. If the lady who bemoaned the fact that she viewed beloved Virginia Rose only with roses saw these lovely poppies, she certainly would have appreciated the appropriateness of these exquisite, nodding, pastel poppies!

*The Century square fruit bowl.*

*Extreme detail of the floral poppies.*

### VR#D.180

POPPY; red, medium-large, one or two; with many white daisies and purple violets; green leaves. Glaze: light yellow.

Name ............................................................"Flanders One"
Official number ..................................................Not known
Known date ................................................................1933
Trim.............................................................................None
Also appears on.....................Carnival, Georgian Eggshell,
    Cannonsburg, W.S. George, some Hull (see below)

COMMENTS: Surprising how many Virginia Rose treatments pique the interest. This is a commercially produced design and there are three Virginia Rose versions of Flanders:

    D.180: Flanders One: Two sprigs (decals), no trim. Date: 1933
    D.180a: Flanders Two: Two sprigs, silver trim. Date: 1936
    D.180b: Flanders Three: One sprig, silver trim. Date: unknown

    All three have been located, but in very small numbers, so it is strongly possible it was not very popular as a treatment. Yet I find it charming and personable. The wide date span hints that the versions were not available concurrently. Warm, red-orange poppies blend smoothly with white yellow-centered daisies yellow, and pale woodland violets, a combination one would hesitate to recommend, but here it works. Harvey Duke (see Duke, p.418) presents the rarely decaled Carnival teacup in Flanders. Also, in my possession are two very large deep yellow glazed service plates with no mark. The embossing is such as to admit two handles. An example appears in Jo Cunningham's book (Cunningham, p.23, upper right).

*A Georgian Eggshell sugarbowl.*

*15" Cannonsburg platter with cream glaze.*

    To be an informed collector is to have retentive eyes. Yet how easy it can be to overlook the obvious. Our Flanders decal is not solely the property of Virginia Rose; it appears with regular frequency on Hull's Little Red Riding Hood series. According to Brenda Roberts, a non-Hull wallpocket bearing this decal was made by Chic Pottery in Zanesville, Ohio, and decorated by Arthur Wagner. Did Mr. Wagner design the decal or just purchase it from a commercial source? At least three, and perhaps more, manufacturers used the red poppy.

Photo courtesy of Gary Geiselman.

*D.180a casserole and lid. This version has silver trim.*

Photo courtesy of Gary Geiselman.

*D.180b: silver trim with one decal (sprig).*

*Creamer in D.180: the no trim version. Flanders is considered rather scarce, especially for a treatment with three versions.*

*Cannonsburg 4¼" pitcher. These small charming pitchers often are collected items themselves.*

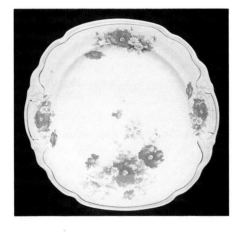

*One of the large yellow service plates mentioned in the text.*

*Detail of the poppy as it appears on the side of the Georgian Eggshell sugar.*

### VR#D.183

PUSSY WILLOW; orangy-white, medium large, one; with catkins branch, tiny flowers in pink, blue, and orange; tiny leaves. Glaze: light yellow.

Name.............................."Spring Promise"
Official number...........................VR#394
Known dates .......................1939 – 1940
Trim....................................................Silver
Also appears on ...................Not known

COMMENTS: What a fantastically refined and fragile decal and how unusual! The birch and the willow announce the coming of spring, with flocking robins and nodding daffodils in the yards and fields. How artistically conceived, the arching verticalness of the pussy willow branch contrasts sharply with the horizontal curve of the delicate birch catkins. To give the treatment a solid base, clusters of spring flowers anchor the branches firmly to the plate. The 9" oval baker gives the official number VR#394, but this number does not appear on either the 1937 or the 1952 list — so we assume it had a short run. Far too short for such a brilliant treatment.

*Left to right: 9" oval vegetable that has the official number; 7" plate; oatmeal bowl; rim soup; teacup and saucer. This beautifully sprawling decal is sadly constricted on the small pieces.*

*A set of plates: Left to right: the rare 8", 6", 10" and 7". Gary Geiselman also has several 9" plates, so this treatment had the full complement.*

*The creamer (left) has a bad lip chip. Rear: the rim soup, and the sugar with lid (right)*

*Casserole also has the official mark under the lid.*

*9" Virginia Rose plate with Bonsai Quince decal; treatment on Stetson dinnerware was called Acacia.*

*Striking Paden City Bak-Serve casserole.*

*Paden City's Bak-Serve pieces.*

## VR#D.184

QUINCE; orange, small, many: with feathery green leaves, and striped orange and black panels. Glaze: cream.

Name ..............................."Bonsai Quince"
Official number ......................Not known
Known date ........................................1947
Trim......................................................Gold
Also appears on ....Paden City Bak-Serve, Stetson

COMMENTS: In my garden there is a bonsai housed in a roughly glazed shallow rectangular pot. Each spring it is bedecked with nodding red-orange blossoms very similar to those appearing on this 9" plate. It is a miniature flowering quince — a much loved plant. This plate, too, is much loved by its owner: so much so I could not purchase it in order to get this photograph. Taken by the owner, it is excellent, and does justice, I am sure, to the original.

Orange is a rare color on dinnerware; perhaps the color seems to clash with everyday foods. Paden City did use the treatment on an extensive line of kitchenware. While not very common, these pieces are relatively cheap. The oven casserole shown was purchased in Brandon, Florida, for only $10.00 — less than the price of modern-day Pyrex, and much more beautiful. Also a large set of Stetson dinnerware has been noted at a very good price. This Stetson shape is Oxford; the exact shape used by the Mt. Clemens pottery, but here the shape name is not known (see Duke, p.796). Upon learning the Stetson name for this treatment was "Acacia," another strong look was taken at HLC's Acacia treatment on Swing and Nautilus Eggshell (see Jasper p.110). Though similar, HLC's and Stetson's lines are each distinctive, so the moniker "Bonsai Quince" holds.

### VR#D.186

ROSE (double); pale pink, small, two to three with tiny pinkish flowers; feathery light green foliage. Glaze: cream.

Name......................................"Heather Rose"
Official number................................VR#437
Known date ...............................1945 – 1958
Trim.........................................................Gold
Also appears on...............Nautilus Eggshell, Georgian Eggshell

COMMENTS: Four pieces were all I had in my collection and all were dated 1945. Then three additional pieces were purchased from Shirley Freeman. The casserole had the official number on the inside lid, and all three were dated 1958. This type of lucky circumstance occurs occasionally. Since #437 appears on the 1953 list, we also learn it was taken originally from a Georgian Eggshell design, and without viewing this eggshell shape, we listed it. Several months later, a graceful Georgian Eggshell teapot was seen in a Tarpon Springs, Florida, antique shop priced $45.00. Not over-priced, certainly, but it had a rather bad crack. The store owner allowed me to take a photograph. Nearly a year later, a single teacup was purchased from Lynn Fredregill of Texas which showed Heather Rose teacups with the inner ring. Snippet by curious snippet, information is gained. This decal is easily mistaken for Calais, a common treatment on Republic.

*Creamer. Notice the heather-like leaves.*

*Stately Georgian Eggshell teapot dressed in Heather Rose. This was very expensively priced and thus was photographed on the shelf in a Tarpon Springs, Florida, shop.*

*A very impressive casserole and lid. Remember in the older sets, the oval covered "casserole" was always termed "a covered dish." The name "casserole" was reserved for the round covered piece.*

*Nautilus Eggshell: the oval vegetable (rear) and round 9" nappy.*

*Photo courtesy of Allyn Rosa.*

*Turn this photograph over to see a perfect Viking ship, or a Venetian gondola!*

**VR#D.188**
ROSE (double); red, yellow, small, many: with black and green leaves. Glaze: light yellow.

Name..............................."Viking Rose"
Official number.................Not known
Known date..................................1935
Trim ...............................................None
Also appears on................Not known

COMMENTS: The elongated quarter-moon shape of this rose design is extremely fragile and delicate. The only example seen is the sauceboat with two decals. Turn the photograph upside down and the decal bears a strong resemblance to a stern-bowed Viking ship or a Venetian gondola. The photograph was supplied by Messrs. Geiselman and Rosa who inform me the decal on the reverse is quite different.

*The sugar and creamer flank the teacup and saucer with a 6" plate behind. Note the sugar/creamer set does not have the white rose decal.*

**VR#D.190**
**VR#D.190a**
ROSE (double); white, large, one; with green leaves, gold filigree. Glaze: cream.

Name ..............................."White Rose"
Official number.................Not known
Known dates...................1947 – 1954
Trim ...............................................None
Also appears on.......Cavalier, Rhythm

COMMENTS: Problem here! The rose when it appears on Virginia Rose lacks vitality. Strangely, this problem does not seem to occur on Cavalier or Rhythm. In a set of 47 VR pieces, half have the decal showing a serious fading. Perhaps the rose was an unfortunate last-minute addition bringing some interest to an all-filigree design. This treatment also totally ignores the embossed rose, the signature mark of this shape. A rather crude, ill-done treatment.

There is a second version White Rose Two (D.190a) represented by a single plate, date 1954. The rose is an exact duplication, the filigree presenting a different face. The clustered rose filigree is Woodland Gold (D.62) and it appears in orderly spacing near the rim. The rose decal is in excellent condition but we wonder if it too will prove unstable.

*The coupe soup with a faded central rose.*

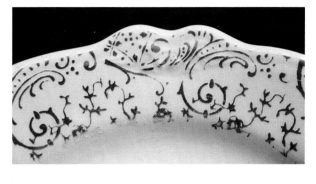

*Detail of filigree edging. Notice how the fussiness of the design completely overshadows the embossed rose. Not a very good idea in my estimation.*

*Close-up showing Golden Rose filigree, VR embossing, and the central decal of White Rose.*

*D.190a, 9" plate. Same stunning white rose, but with the filigree of Golden Rose.*

## VR#D.192

ROSE (double); pink, yellow, medium to large, one to two; with buds, smaller white daisies, tiny blue and yellow flowers; dark shiny green leaves, many small pale green leaves on winding stems. Glaze: cream.

| | |
|---|---|
| Name | "Louise" |
| Official number | VR#390 |
| Known dates | 1938 – 1940 |
| Trim | Silver |
| Also appears on | Not known |

COMMENTS: Each decal of this treatment is full, yet lacy in its aspect. Not quite just another VR floral pattern because of the focused detailing, and the trailing arrangement on the plate. A 15" platter was the only example ever seen until Jeanne Smiley sent two 9" plates, the important 6" plate, and the oval vegetable with the official number, but it was named by Sears, and appears in their 1940 catalog. Also an example of Louise appears in the morgue collection (p.168).

For a discussion of the possible confusion between the Louises and the Muriels, please see page 71, D.107.

*6" (left) and 9" plates.*

*The oval vegetable. Note this treatment has 3 sprigs.*

*Detail of the elaborate and naturalistic decal.*

*Mark on the oval vegetable which includes the official number, VR-390.*

*Sugar with lid and creamer. This set could really be used with either Louise or her little sister.*

*Teacup with inner ring and saucer.*

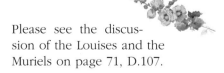

Please see the discussion of the Louises and the Muriels on page 71, D.107.

### VR#D.193

ROSE; pink, small, one; with blue, yellow daisies, tiny pale blue flowers; pale yellow-green leaves. Glaze: cream.

| | |
|---|---|
| Name | "Little Louise" |
| Official number | Not known |
| Known dates | 1940 – 1941 |
| Trim | Silver |
| Also appears on | Not known |

COMMENTS: Little Louise is a good example of the confusion which can arise in decal identification. Only seven pieces are in my collection, three 6" plates, two saucers, a teacup. Mention has been made about the slight and confusing decal changes often occurring on pieces of varying size. The larger plates give the best overall impression of any treatment, number of sprigs, varying decals used, etc. Frankly, this treatment could be Louise, but there are several reasons why it has been placed by itself. (1) Louise has prominent white daisies, here there are none; (2) Louise uses dark olive green rose leaves, here also absent; (3) the two Louises have different 6" plates, but both treatments share the smaller decal. But the general grouping and lacy appearance were apparent. Until Jeanne Smiley sent the 6" plate in Louise, there was a nagging question about whether these two were the same, but now we realize, without a doubt, two Louises exist in the world of Virginia Rose.

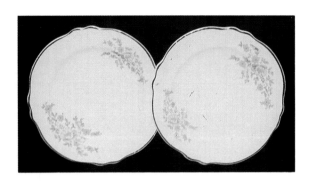

*Two 6" plates.*

*Detail of delicate rose and daisy decal.*

### VR#D.194

ROSE (double); pink (one with mustard outer petals), medium to small, three; with one mustard narcissus, many dark blue flowers, pink, yellow buds; light green leaves. Glaze: cream.

Name ...................................................."Baroque"
Official number ..................................Not known
Known date ...................................................1949
Trim...............................................................None
Also appears on ..............see Esperanza section

COMMENTS: A fantastically elaborate treatment. The rich ornamentation of this small fruit bowl exceeds even that of the Colonial Quadrille versions (D.170 and D.170a) or Grecian Melody (D.172). With this small bowl we see a chocolate-sweet richness of gold and burnished bronze and spiked traceries culminating in an arched floral design named Esperanza. Look straight into this bowl and see the perspective inside a painted baroque dome, the colorful, ornate interior architecture of a German abbey's cathedral. Quite a feat for a small Virginia Rose fruit bowl. Where are other examples of Baroque? Can you imagine the glorious richness of the platters or 10" plates? And how would the teacups be designed — with Esperanza inside? Wonder, wonder, wonder!

*Photo courtesy of Gary Geiselman.*

*A fruit with a highly ornate treatment. The central floral design is Esperanza (see Esperanza section p.169).*

*Teacup and saucer. Green trim is very rare.*

**VR#D.196**

ROSE (double); orange-red, large, one; with bud, yellow-orange flowers; chartreuse leaves. Glaze: cream.

Name ......................"Madame Gautier One"
Official number.........................Not known
Known date .........................................1935
Trim.................................................Green
Also appears on.........................Not known

COMMENTS: This treatment's very rare green trim color could not be overlooked if it were on the 1937 official number list. However, it does not appear, so it is likely the color combination did not find much public favor. The old-fashioned bourbon rose is realistically portrayed and droops with its own fullness. Only seven pieces have surfaced, and all have the 1935 date. The green trim version is quite special with its off-beat quality.

*Notice the rich color and detailing in this plump, heavy-scented old rose.*

*9" oval vegetable (baker). This piece is dated 1935 and has the flat bottom.*

**VR#D.196a**

ROSE (double); same as D.196

Name ...................."Madame Gautier Two"
Official number .......................Not known
Known date .........................................1935
Trim.................................................Silver
Also appears on .......................Not known

COMMENTS: The only difference between the two Gautier treatments is the trim color. With the substitution of silver trim for green, the style and effect are much lessened. Both versions have the same date, so the public was confronted with either-or choice. Look carefully at the color of the rose; could this be the beginning of the Fiesta red?

9" oval vegetable (baker): flat bottom.

### VR#D.198

ROSE (double); red, yellow, tiny, two; with blue daisy, miniscule flowers; tiny green leaves. Glaze: cream.

Name ..........................................."Florets"
Official number....................Not known
Known date....................................1946
Trim ................................................Silver
Also appears on .........Brittany, Nautilus
Eggshell (both with other decoration)

COMMENTS: A treatment of the middle-age of Virginia Rose which should not be confused with Flowers and Filigree (D.97), minus the silver over the rose embossing. A somewhat boring treatment, but there are points of interest. In a set of 34 pieces, only the 13" platter bears the usual VR stamp; all the rest are stamped just HLC. This is the only time noted that Virginia Rose has the regular stamp. But, it must be admitted, there are several instances where no backstamp appears. Another point, this small floral spray was popular enough to have two other shapes use it, with additional decoration, maroon paneling for the Brittany, and crisscross filigree for the Eggshell Nautilus.

Nearly two years after Florets was originally acquired, it was seen again, this time at a rough-and-ready outdoor flea market in Largo, Florida, displayed on a dirty carpet remnant. There lay a Daisy Chain casserole and 9" pie plate in top condition, shimmering in the hazy, silver sun. Price was $8.00 for both. This proves that the pieces were unknown to the dealer and that bargains still exist.

*Teacup and saucer. Note the inner cup ring which is worn but still noticeable.*

*Left to right: 11" platter, 6" plate, 9" plate, and fruit bowl.*

*Same small floral decal appears on a Brittany creamer, one of the many maroon banded designs.*

*Decal of clean and precise central decal.*

The same floral group is seen here on the edge of a Nautilus Eggshell 6" plate combined with an elaborate gold band resembling a needlework design.

Daisy Chain is a bonafide "new" HLC shape. Here it appears wearing VR's Florets treatment. At rear is a Daisy Chain 9" pie plate.

**VR#D.200**
**VR#D.200a**

ROSE (double); yellow, pink, tiny, three; with pink buds, miniscule blue flowers; leaves with tendrils, verge filigree. Glaze: cream.

| | |
|---|---|
| Name | "Rose Melody" |
| Official number | Not known |
| Known date | 1933 |
| Trim | Silver |
| Also appears on | Not known |

COMMENTS: Tiny swags of roses, buds, and pale blue flowers drape between the rose embossings. The tips of the swags trail toward the neighbor on either side in a delicate attempt to mingle. The verge detail of this very early treatment boldly separates the edge from the center and affords a defined space for the presentation of any food. It appears on other Virginia Rose items. The collection's 14 pieces all bear the 1933 date, but the treatment fails to appear on the official listing; mention of a silver verge line could not be overlooked. One of many "rose and flower" decals, Rose Melody might not have caught the public's interest.

This example, VR#109 D.200a, was found in the morgue, another version of Rose Melody without the verge design.

119

*Notice how the verge design encloses and empha-sizes the decaled border.*

*Extreme close-up of the rose decal.*

### VR#D.205

ROSE (double, single); pink, small to medium, three to four; with masses of blue, yellow, pale pink flowers; leaves and stems. Glaze: cream.

| | |
|---|---|
| Name | "Nosegay" or "Elaine" |
| Official number | VR#423 |
| Known dates | 1941 |
| Trim | None |
| Also appears on | Not known |

COMMENTS: Sold by Sears, Roebuck, 1940, under the name "Elaine," this softly feminine decoration was, according to Darlene Nossamen, introduced by Homer Laughlin in 1938. It has one of the later official numbers, so perhaps the 1940 date is closer to the truth. As mentioned at the beginning of the book, to draw conclusions about HLC dinnerware, numbers, names, and dates is, at best, an educated guess. This seems to be a treatment seen more often in small sets; why some decals can be found singly, and others discovered only in sets is another dinnerware mystery. Nosegay is a pleasantly soft, delicately muted design, one of the truly pretty treatments, and benefits strongly from the lack of a defining metallic trim.

*Creamer and sugarbowl with lid.*

*The Nosegay decal on the 9" plate. The grandeur of the blue larkspur is lost on the small pieces.*

*Teacup and saucer. On the small pieces, the sweep of the pink rose decal is not as evident.*

## The Armand Family
### VR#D.210, D.210a, D.210b

ROSE (double, single); pink, yellow, white, medium, two to five with pink buds, medium and small white daisies; gray-green leaves, stems. Glaze: light yellow.

COMMENTS: The Armand group has been a favorite ever since a set of 105 was purchased seven years ago for $40.00. This consisted of the treatment now known as Armand One and since then a few other pieces have been added: the OvenServe casserole and underplate, and 10 coupe soups. The coupe soup is rather scarce in Virginia Rose — the rim soup is the standard flat soup dish. Armand is also one of the VR lines possessing the rare Kitchen Kraft shakers; Spring Wreath D.158 is another, as are JJ#59 and VR#128. This fact makes it one of the most complete treatments available. My pieces only have dates 1944 – 1946, but since Armand appears on both the 1937 and the 1952 official lists, we must expand the dates; it was available at least 16 years. Also in 1952 a total of four Armand versions was produced: our original, VR#235, 3 sprigs, silver edge trim; VR#257, 2 sprigs, no line; VR# 325, 1 sprig, no line; and finally, VR#440, again with 3 sprigs, but now with a gold edge trim. Even though we know four versions of Armand exist, only three can be added to our list; as of this date they are the only ones seen. Like Fluffy Rose, but to a lesser extent, Armand has always been in popular demand. This treatment possesses a certain élan, taking it out of the ordinary class of roses and daisies; the teacup has the uncommon inside ring. Besides the very rare KK shaker, a thinner rounded mug/saucer set, known as a St. Dennis cup, is also available in Armand. The saucer has the HLC stamp with date 1949, and the set should be considered very scarce; it belongs in the generic category. Of intense interest is the appearance of the Armand decal on the rather mysterious OvenServe/Daisy Chain shape (see Appendix C, p. 182, for further information). It shares this distinction with three other VR treatments.

Details of the three Armands follow below and on page 123.

*Left to right: the very scarce St. Dennis cup, 9" plate, regular teacup and saucer, the server, and creamer.*

| | |
|---|---|
| Name | "Armand One" |
| Official number | VR#235 |
| Known dates | 1937 – 1953 |
| Trim | Silver |
| Also appears on | Kitchen Kraft, Liberty, OvenServe, OvenServe/Daisy Chain, Republic |

| | | |
|---|---|---|
| VR#235 | 3 sprigs, silver edge line | |
| VR#257 | 2 sprigs, no edge line | |
| VR#325 | 1 sprig, no edge line | |
| VR#429 | 3 sprigs, no edge line | |
| VR#440 | 3 sprigs, gold edge line | |

COMMENTS: This version is the one most easily located and bears three sprigs (decals) in three different sizes. It is usually encountered in single pieces or small groupings. Even though entire sets are rarely found, it will not be difficult to gather a nice representation of Armand One. A spectacular find in Ellenville, Florida, was a large, mint set of Armand One on Republic. It was marked by the piece and would have cost over $600.00 if every piece had been purchased. As it was, the five pieces bought for photographic purposes came to $49.00. It was, however, a magnificent sight. Since only this treatment sports the silver trim, identification, even of the smaller pieces, is without problem. Again, the full complement of decals appears only on the larger pieces.

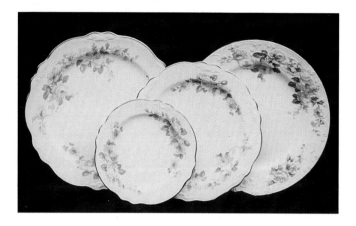

*Left to right: 9" plate, 6" plate, the scarce 8" plate, and OvenServe 9" plate or casserole underplate. Notice the smaller plates usually have fewer decals (sprigs) than the large plates or the platters. Since the 6" plate has silver trim, we know it is Armand One, VR#235.*

*OvenServe saucer.*

*Generic pieces to accompany the Armand series: Left 8" OvenServe casserole (no lid); server; 10" Kitchen Kraft pie plate; St. Dennis cup; Kitchen Kraft shaker. The shaker must be considered one of the rarest of pieces.*

*The 9" Liberty plate, dated 1947. Since this plate has 3 sprigs and no edge line, it technically should belong to the Armand Three version (see descriptive material), but for convenience it is placed here.*

*As a shape, Republic predates Virginia Rose by many years. Introduced in the early 1900s, it was produced until the late 1940s. Two sizes of sugar/creamer sets were offered; this is the smaller, called "individual." All these pieces are dated 1948.*

*Armand Two is much more difficult to find than Armand One. Here is one of the few pieces ever seen, a 13" platter.*

*The sauceboat dated 1934.*

(Armand family, cont.)
ROSE (double, single); Same as D.210.

Name ....................."Armand Two"
Official number...............VR#257
Known dates ...........1934 – 1957
Trim.......................................None
Also appears on .........OvenServe

COMMENTS: As always, the versions can be interchanged on the table, but since only the OvenServe has been noticed both with and without silver trim, it is the only other shape mentioned. My collection has very little of Armand Two (actually only seven pieces), but its sauceboat is dated 1934, one of the earliest VR pattern dates, and one of the collection's two 9" plates is dated 1957; this second version has a longer date span. The possibility arises that Armand Two was produced first, and technically might really be Armand One. But this possibility will be side-stepped to keep from getting lost in a morass of technicalities.

*Gold trimmed Armand VR#440 (D.210b). Courtesy of Roger Rozeboom.*

Name ..............................................."Armand Three"
Official number ...........................................VR#440
Known dates.......................................1945 – 1957
Trim ................................................................Gold
Also appears on...................................Not known

COMMENTS: The rarest version, the only known set at this point is a collection owned by Roger Roseboom of Nebraska who says his wife's grandmother also owned a set. The Roseboms bought theirs at auction and have been slowly adding to it for years and they almost have a setting for twelve. Not one piece of Armand Three has been seen on the East Coast, but, naturally, it might be lurking in attics or cellars. There is a possibility (for Homer Laughlin was known for the practice) that the gold trim version was offered for sale only in the middle sections of the country. But this assumption could be wrong because Roger also mentioned that the silver-edged version is available in his area. Whatever the situation, we are thankful to receive this information. No other shapes have been seen with three Armand sprigs and gold trim, but it seems logical that the kitchenware lines were produced to compliment this version. It is important to state and restate how researchers are dependent upon the kindness of collectors.

One dealer, Jack Hamlin, informed me Armand is the third most popular Virginia Rose treatment, but this was several years ago, and now perhaps Armand could be reduced in ranking to fourth. This list no doubt should read: Moss Rose, Fluffy Rose, Patrician, Armand, but then possibly Nosegay. No matter the sequence, Armand is one of the most important of the Virginia Rose treatments. Naming the top five (or six, or ten) is an interesting pastime, but can lead to quibbling, so I'll say simply that Armand is one of the top ranking designs. I would not care where this treatment places in popularity for it remains important simply because I like it.

## VR#D.212

ROSE (double); pink, medium, two; with rose leaves and bud, yellow floral spray, blue florets. Glaze: cream.

Name ................."Sunday Offering"
Official number ...........Not known
Known date ............................1955
Trim .................Apple-green wash
Also appears on ..........Not known

COMMENTS: Initially, Bountiful (D.119) and Apple (D.96) were thought to be the only lines with a color-washed edge. But here is another. Pictured is a 9" oval baker with a central floral decal and a diffused border of apple-green wash, a color very close to a Granny Smith. The bouquet, dominated by two full pink roses, is very similar to those flower blankets placed decoratively on church altars. I have seen many such offerings in ancient Anglican parish churches hidden away in tiny English villages. There is an earnest simplicity about this treatment and the color-wash makes it unique.

*9" oval baker, dated 1955. The studio photograph accounts for the darker glaze.*

*A 9" plate with the teacup and saucer. Note the treatment becomes a band encircling the hollowware.*

## VR#D.215
## VR#D.215a

ROSE (petit point); pink, medium, one; with various other petit point flowers, blue, yellow; green leaves. Glaze: cream.

COMMENTS: The "petit point" approach has given rise to one of the most popular of all treatments. Petit Point Rose appears on six HLC shapes, all avidly sought, available, but certainly not common. The style has been translated to include cottages, fruit, and country folk by many other manufacturers, and even though there are minor variations, this must be considered a commercial decal. Popularity must rest upon a homey, old-fashioned country quality; a style so visible in today's country kitchen interiors, that many collectors specialize solely in it. At one time, collectors thought this treatment only had gold trim, but plates with silver trim have been located and with an earlier date. In my collection, there are 30 pieces divided into:

10 with gold trim, bearing the gold Cunningham & Pickett stamp. Interestingly these 10 pieces have the date span 1948 – 1957;

17 with gold trim, bearing no marks;

3 with silver trim and the regular HLC Virginia Rose mark, date 1943.
There are two versions of this pattern but neither can be assigned an official number.

D.215     Petit Point Rose One, silver trim, date 1943
D.215a     Petit Point Rose Two, gold trim, date 1948 – 1957

Petit Point Rose appears on Century, Kitchen Kraft, Liberty, Nautilus, Nautilus Eggshell, Harker ware and others. Because of the specialty of this treatment, collectors might be tempted to overpay in order to add to their pieces and some dealers charge more than usual. With care, however, Petit Point Rose can be acquired at normal prices. For example, at an Ocala, Florida, mall, my three 10" pieces with fair silver trim cost $4.00 each.

A final note: Look closely at a decal on one of the larger plates and see a grid so detailed that a needle artist could reproduce this charming design on placemats or other table decoration.

*Photo courtesy of Gary Geiselman.*

*Sugarbowl with lid and the OvenServe spoon. Both use the band version of the decal.*

*A fantastic Nautilus 14" platter. We apologize for the blue cast, but the photograph was taken several years ago, and the piece has since been (sadly) broken.*

*Kitchen Kraft items: the cake plate and small covered jar.*

*Nautilus Eggshell creamer.*

*Large coffee cup and saucer produced by Harker.*

*Detail showing the needlepoint quality of the decal.*

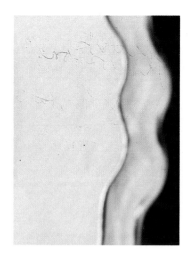

*Usually Petit Point Rose comes with gold trim. Here the rarely seen silver trim is shown.*

*Note the difference in trim colors. Rear D.215 silver, front D.215a gold.*

### The Evelyn Family
### VR#D.217, 217a, 217b

ROSE (single); mauve pink, medium, one to two; with medium blue daisies, small orange-yellow flowers, pale green; gray leaves, stems. Glaze: pale cream.

Name ...........“Evelyn” or “Wild Pink Rose”
Official number ..............................VR#233
Known date .............................1934 – 1952
Trim......................................................Silver
Also appears on........................Not known

COMMENTS: At the International Academy, Tampa, Florida, where I work as the librarian, we have an administrative assistant, Evelyn Caro, for whom this treatment is named. Ms. Caro is energy packed and extremely knowledgeable — and she must be because everyone depends upon her. Having brought some photographs of dinnerware for her to view, she exclaimed how much she liked this one and thus it was named. Evelyn (the china, not the lady) is also an example of how chinaware knowledge comes in tiny bits and is dependent on circumstance. For several years, the only pieces of this treatment owned were a 10" and a 7" plate both with the date 1942, and it was classified as a middle-period design. By chance, in a junk shop, a 6" plate — in terrible condition — was found with the date 1934. For a two-bit purchase price, this treatment moved back to the early years of Virginia Rose and with these years of availability probably was rather popular with the public. With access to a 1934 Montgomery Ward catalog, we find it was known by another name, Wild Pink Rose. How different life was in 1934. The catalog states “...this enchanting Wild Rose pattern sells for as high as $4.69 (for a 32-piece set). The 32 pieces are handy for small families, or as a breakfast set.” I was born in 1931, and my family ate breakfast all during my school years. Do families eat breakfast together today? Is there a need for a breakfast set in 1997?

*Thanks to Jeanne Smiley for the loan of this Evelyn sugarbowl, VR#256 (D.217a).*

*Detail of decal.*

*These 9" and 6" plates, (D.217a), plus two rim soups, are the only Evelyn pieces in my collection.*

*Original 1934 Montgomery Ward advertisement showing VR#233 (D.217) with silver trim.*

(D.217 "Evelyn" cont.)

Six months after I thought Evelyn was "put to bed," Jeanne Smiley sent me a sugar-bowl to photograph: it was Evelyn with no trim and the date was 1952. Immediately this treatment expanded its time, from an early 1934 until 1952, 18 years before the public.

With the discovery of the morgue collection, and an official number, knowledge about Evelyn exploded. For example:

| | | |
|---|---|---|
| D.217 | VR#233 | 2 sprigs, silver trim, 740 |
| D.217a | VR#256 | 2 sprigs, no trim |
| | VR#367 | 2 sprigs, no trim, (3rds) |
| | VR#371 | 2 sprigs, no trim (Butler Brothers) |
| D.217b | | 3 sprigs, silver trim |

The last example listed was found in the morgue with the handwritten number, R-5177 on the reverse. What can be deduced? The number 740 appearing after the first VR listing gives the idea that Evelyn was a commercial decal. The fact the 3-sprig version (D.217b) had no official VR number and had a handwritten R-5177 leads to the belief the commercial decal first appeared on the Republic shape, and there is a very good chance D.217b was a prototype and was never produced (see the morgue section, p.158). But, of course, this is pure conjecture. Evelyn has risen to be one of the treatments with many variations. The expansion of these facts was made possible by Joanne Jasper's discovery of the morgue collection of Virginia Rose.

The shading on the dark pink roses is very refined, and the graceful inward arc makes the central area less blank, still leaving an undecaled space for the food. Like its name-sake, Evelyn, is a very pretty treatment.

### VR#D.220

ROSE (single); pastel blue, pink, large, three; with bud; pale gray leaves, on twigs. Glaze: cream.

Name..............."Pastel Wood Rose"
Official number............Not known
Known date............................1932
Trim .........................................Silver
Also appears on ....................Wells

COMMENTS: One of the earliest examples of Virginia Rose, this set is over 60 years old and in mint condition. The set is the only representative of the treatment in the collection. About three years ago, they were found in the same mall booth, but separated; the dealer might not have known they went together. Having been reunited, I believe their value increased. The underplatter is the usual 11" example. The decal is very delicate and is worthy of appearing on a fine French Toiles de Jouy. Even though of this decal was used on Wells dinner sets, no other pieces on VR have been unearthed; it might have been an early specialty set. An extremely desirable, but elusive decoration.

*One of the loveliest of all known Virginia Rose sets: the covered 5" jug and covered 7½" jug on an 11" platter. These make up a very rare batter set.*

*Notice the delicacy and pastel shading in the Pastel Wood Rose decal.*

*Jade creamer and open sugarbowl. Pastel Wood Rose is also rare on this shape.*

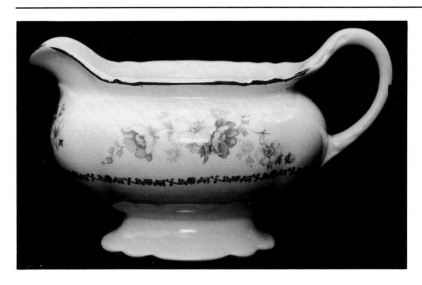

*The Virginia Rose creamer, the only example known. Note the small decal under the lip, a rather unusual placement.*

*Close-up of the silver filigree band.*

## VR#D.223

ROSE (single); pink, white, small, three; with tiny yellow flowers; gray/green leaves, filigree of miniscule oriental roses. Glaze: light yellow.

Name.................."Melody Bouquet"
Official number.............Not known
Known date.............................1935
Trim .........................................Silver
Also appears on ....Filigree appears on other Virginia Rose treatments, Century.

COMMENTS: Only one piece of Melody Bouquet has been found, the creamer seen in the photograph. But with a creamer, there must have been a sugar-bowl, and teacups, saucers, most likely plates, maybe an entire set. The filigree adds a finished note and appears, somewhat liable to being overlooked, on a number of Century treatment variations. The roses used are the typical Virginia Rose type but with a graceful arching line.

## VR#D.227
## VR#D.227a

ROSE (single); white, pale pink, medium, three to five; with grayish green leaves. Glaze: light yellow.

Name..................................."Moss Rose" or "Pinks"
Official number ...............................JJ#59
Known dates.......................1934 – 1965
Trim ..............................................Silver
Also appears on ..............Kitchen Kraft, Orleans,*
OvenServe, Debutante, OvenServe/Daisy Chain

COMMENTS: For many collectors and dealers, this treatment represents Virginia Rose. So ubiquitous is this design, it has become the most popular, the most available of all VR treatments, and because of this, considerably more can be written about Moss Rose. This interest and demand drive the prices of individual pieces quite high in spite of their obtainability. It actually can seem more common because it is confused often with Fluffy Rose, a treatment nearly its equal in all categories. Moss Rose, or Pinks, was produced for exclusive sale in the national chain of J.J. Newberry stores. Until very recently it was thought the butterdish was manufactured only in Moss Rose and Fluffy Rose — they have never been seen wearing other VR decals, but now Bouquet (D.107) is known to have a Jade butterdish, and there might be more! Whenever the elusive generic pieces are found, egg cup, mug, shakers, they are most often JJ#59, and always quite expensive.

*A 7½" jug, and its companion 5" jug. These pieces are sometimes called the milk and syrup jugs.*

* A dealer e-mailed me an astounding photograph of Moss Rose on a Orleans platter. This came while book was in production, so commentary will have to wait.

(D.227 "Moss Rose" cont.)

Because of its production length, there are several Moss Rose shape differences arousing enthusiastic response among Virginia Rose collectors. A distinct difference appears among the 9" oval vegetable dishes (bakers). Two completely different molds were used and surprisingly, they were manufactured concurrently. The major difference is in the bottoms of the pieces; I label them "flat" or "ridged." Eight 9" bakers exist in my collection, five are flat, three are ridged, and the dates range from 1935 to 1957. There are also other mold differences. The ridged variety is ⅛" higher, wider, and longer, while the flat ones are much heavier. Aside from different molds, two other variations exist: (1) the size of the large decal; and (2) the trim treatment on the baker handles. (Note: handle differences can also be seen on platters.) Some of the central decals are noticeably larger, more distinct, and much brighter in color. The trims can simply run along the edge, or outline each embossed section of the handle. Randy Dunn first brought this to my attention. This variation could be overlooked unless one has an extensive number of handled pieces, i.e., bakers or platters. Attention to such detail can separate the serious collector from those who flit, moth-like, from interest to HLC interest! When one collects dinnerware, details are dangerous to disregard.

Jack Hamlin reports the appearance of the Moss Rose decal on non-HLC pieces: ashtrays and candy dishes. If this is so, this most typical of VR decorations could be considered commercial, but since Mr. Hamlin did not produce any proof (photograph or actual piece), the fact cannot be verified. Perhaps other readers can help?

A rather unusual piece of Moss Rose is the 7" nappy. This rare item was not listed in Joanne Jasper's *The Collector's Encyclopedia of Homer Laughlin China*, but does appear in the revised edition. Was this diminutive bowl made for other VR treatments? Yes, it does appear in Sarasota Cosmos (D.22), and Fluffy Rose 5 (D.231d) so hopefully readers can provide information about whether the 7" nappy exists with other decorations.

A new discovery! Thanks to Gary Gieselman, we can include a photograph of the JJ#59 decal on the Debutante shakers, a rarity indeed. (Gary will not part with them.) We can only wonder if other VR decals will be found on the Debutante shaker. This information makes the careful scanning of salt-and-pepper sale shelves doubly important.

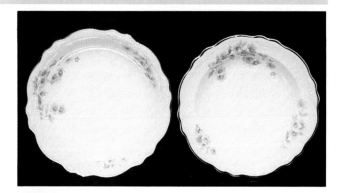

*Notice the difference between the rim soup (right) and less common coupe soup (left).*

*Left to right: 9" oval baker, creamer, 11" platter, and rim soup. In front, the small fruit bowl and the rather scarce oatmeal bowl.*

(D.227 "Moss Rose" cont.)

Rita Bee of California told of these shakers appearing in her home state. So the hunt is out. Ms. Bee also submitted the photograph of the very rare, handled bread tray. This is 8½" round and is dated August 1937. (See Huxford p.159, pl.291.)

Finally, Jo Dee Rice sent two photographs of the Kitchenware pie plate in JJ#59. There are mysterious, subtle differences; one is deeper and has an intricate embossed line directly under the outside rim. This is a one-of-a-kind example, and we thank Ms. Rice for sharing it with us. (Note: It was later discovered this embossed pie plate was the mysterious, rare OvenServe/Daisy Chain shape; see Appendices, p.182, for a discussion of the line.)

Not only is Moss Rose the embodiment of the shape, it is one of the earliest (1934), and was available for a wide expanse of time, a full 32 years, until 1966. The dates on my own personal collection stop at 1965. I have several pieces of Moss Rose and two pieces of Fluffy Rose with that date, but Jack Hamlin states he has several pieces of JJ#59 dated 1966, but again, unfortunately, no proof. It is important to repeat, as far as it is now known, only JJ#59 and VR#128 were available after 1960. No other treatments have been discovered with a date later than 1959. There is, of course, a good chance this popular design extends into the 1970s, but even stopping at 1966, it has as a proven span one of the longest, not only for Virginia Rose, but for all decaled HLC shapes. Only Fiesta, Homer Laughlin's premier shape, has a slightly longer production run: 1936 until 1969 — 33 years. If any reader has examples of Moss Rose dated after 1965, please pass on the information. Check each piece of your Virginia Rose collection. Perhaps, just perhaps, we of the decaled persuasion can give the Fiestaware owners a tiny shove into reality!

The morgue yielded the only known version of Moss Rose, VR#152, (D.227a) with a rich, gold-flecked trim (see p.168).

Moss Ross is as comfortable and unassuming as an old friend, no blatant surprises — as reliable and sturdy as Ma Perkins of radio days, as gently resourceful as Stella Dallas. Not much zip or glamour — just peaceful gentility. No wonder this single treatment, Moss Rose, ranks as one of the most enduring of all American dinnerware patterns.

9" oval vegetable (baker): flat and ridge bottom.

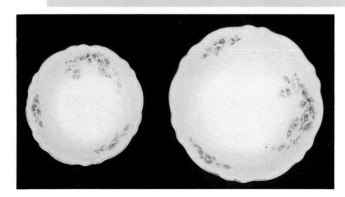

*The rare 7" nappy and the 9" version. The latter is probably the most common size of round vegetable bowl.*

*Right: the Swing shakers wearing the Moss Rose decal. Left: the only known set of Debutante shaped shakers in Moss Rose. From the collection of Gary Geiselman.*

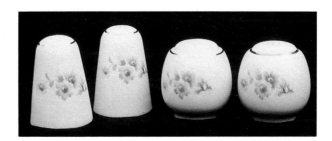

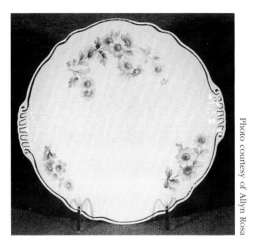

*Photo courtesy of Allyn Rosa*

*Very rare 8" handled tray, identical to the 12" cake plate.*

*Photo courtesy of Jo Dee Rice.*

*Two versions of the Moss Rose Kitchen Kraft pie plates (see text for explanation).*

*Two versions of the 9" baker. The one on the left has larger, brighter decals, and trim outlined handles. The right bowl has much smaller, duller decals and the handle trim simply runs along the edge.*

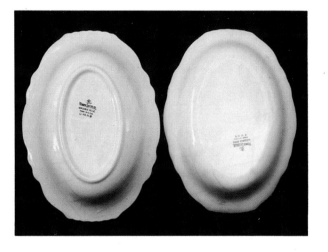

*Two very different molds were used to produce these bowls. The "ridged" bottomed example at left is more delicate, flared, and slightly larger. The "flat" bottom bowl at right lacks the graceful curve, and is much heavier. Judging from the date marks, it seems both versions were produced at the same time.*

*Detail of the Moss Rose decal.*

*Detail of pie plates. Note the embossing under the rim at left. This marks the pie plate as Daisy Chain.*

## The Fluffy Rose Family
### VR#D.231, D.231a, D.231b, D.231c, D.231d

ROSE (single, ruffled); white, pale pink, medium large, several; with pale green leaves and stems. Glaze: light yellow.

The manner in which the Fluffy Rose family is approached must be slightly different from the other treatments. This treatment is a very close second in popularity and availability to Moss Rose (JJ#59), but unlike the latter, Fluffy Rose was a commercial decal, and appeared both on other HLC shapes (Georgian, Kitchen Kraft, OvenServe, Republic, Yellowstone), and the wares of other manufacturers. These facts contribute to its interest, its complexity, and its collectibility.

Moss Rose was a J.J. Newberry exclusive, and as such, supposedly did not appear on any other shapes except Virginia Rose and its attendant KK and OvenServe pieces. Nor did it appear in many versions. Conversely, Fluffy Rose endorsed variety, and was produced in six different variations, each with its own official HLC number. The company's Virginia Rose production list briefly describes each treatment and makes clear any links with other treatments. VR#128 was the first version to be produced, and thus is the premier member of the Fluffy Rose family; all other versions are linked to #128. Please see section in the appendices covering these official company lists.

Here is a listing with the official terminology:

| | | | |
|---|---|---|---|
| Fluffy Rose 1 | D.231 | VR#128 | 2 sprigs (decals), silver trim |
| Fluffy Rose 2 | D.231a | VR#178 | 1 sprig, silver trim |
| Fluffy Rose 3 | D.231b | VR#299 | 1 sprig, no line (trim) |
| Fluffy Rose 4 | D.231c | VR#312 | 2 sprigs, silver line (trim?) |
| Fluffy Rose 5 | D.231d | VR#332 | 2 sprigs, no line (trim) |

The final version has not yet been seen and does not have a D# assigned, yet it can be listed here.

Fluffy Rose 6(?) D.231e(?) VR#368: 6 sprigs, no trim. This is listed as a specialty treatment with the designation W-128. With six individual versions, Fluffy Rose ranks with Meadow Goldenrod as having the most variations.

To the casual observer, all Fluffy Roses are the same, but those truly involved in Virginia Rose find the differences fascinating, and, as proof, the company considered the versions as separate entities, and numbered them individually.

Each of the Fluffy Roses has some interesting specific characteristics, so these will have individual commentary.

9" oval vegetable (baker): flat and ridge bottom.

*Left to right: creamer, rim soup, 9" plate, 10" plate, and teacup and saucer.*

### VR#D.231

Name . . . . . . . . . . ."Fluffy Rose 1"
Official number . . . . . . . .VR#128
Known date . . . . . . . .1933 – 1956

COMMENTS: According to known records, Fluffy Rose 1, the first of the versions, predates its only real competitor, Moss Rose, by one year. Many dealers try to link the round Republic butterdish with VR, and continually we read of "rare round Virginia Rose butterdishes." Prices for these pieces soar. Remember, however, the Republic butterdish lists at about one-half the VR price. Yet, for an avid Virginia Rose collector, perhaps the acquisition of a round Republic butterdish wearing the Fluffy Rose decal is worth $250.00, the average price asked.

(D.231 "Fluffy Rose 1" cont.)

There are also rumors of a Republic teapot bearing the Fluffy Rose decal. This would be quite an addition to any Virginia Rose collection specializing in this family and well worth a substantial price.

In my own personal Fluffy Rose collection, this version accounts for about 95% of the pieces, a good indication that VR#128 was the most important of the group. My set includes the scarce 10½" platter, unmarked and flat-bottomed. Rick Gault owns the rare flat sided Kitchen Kraft casserole with lid in #128. He offered to send it for photographing, but we declined because of the rarity of the piece (see Huxford, p.158, pl.291). The Jade butterdish, the mug, and the egg cup are available with some frequency, but not as often as those pieces wearing JJ#59. There are one or two critics who maintain Fluffy Rose and Moss Rose are two versions of the same treatment. This is, of course, untrue, but such opinions epitomize the exciting confusion regarding connections between the two most popular Virginia Rose treatments.

The generic pieces. Left to right: rim casserole (missing lid), 9" Kitchen Kraft pie plate, St. Dennis cup, mug, Kitchen Kraft cake plate, Cable double egg cup, Kitchen Kraft small mixing bowl.

The "round VR butterdish" is in reality the cheaper Republic butterdish.

Detail of the Fluffy Rose decal.

The heavier unmarked Georgian 10" plate wearing Fluffy Rose.

Yellowstone creamer.

A small 4½" Grecian vase. These are unmarked with unglazed base and can be found with many decals.

A 12" ornate, unmarked lamp base. These can often be quite expensive because they are good quality.

Close-up of decal on chop plate.

Photo courtesy of Allyn Rosa.

14¼" plate. This magnificent and rare Fiesta chop plate was discovered by and belongs to Gary Geiselman; it has no back mark.

Back of chop plate.

*9" Yellowstone plate, dated 1934. From the collection of Geiselman and Rosa.*

### VR#D.231a

Name...................................."Fluffy Rose 2"
Official number................................VR#178
Known dates ............................1937 – 1952

COMMENTS: Only six examples can be found in my personal collection, all 9" plates. Like five of the other Fluffy Rose treatments, #178 appears concurrently for 16 years and one wonders why the company thought it necessary to offer the various versions at the same time. Donna Pope of Arizona and Alvin Daigle of North Dakota are the dealers who supplied this version.

*One of a set of six 9" plates, VR#178 (D.231a).*

### VR#D.231b

Name........................................."Fluffy Rose 3"
Official number...................................VR#299
Known dates ...............................1937 – 1952

COMMENTS: Simply a VR#178 with no trim. For almost four years, a 6" plate in this treatment puzzled me; with only one decal and no trim, it did not fit in with the #128, yet not enough was known to solve the "problem." I have never seen another piece of this version and it must be considered extremely rare. Imagine my distress when it was dropped and fragmented while being washed. This unfortunate incident happened before being photographed, and the readers will have to believe me as to its existence. I did, however, keep all the splinters, just to remind myself to be extremely cautious when washing plates — or teacups — or any dinnerware!

*Official stamp: VR-312.*

*Official stamp: VR-128.*

### VR#D.231c

Name..........................."Fluffy Rose 4"
Official number......................VR#312
Known dates ..................1937 – 1952

COMMENTS: This is the "problem" version. Jeanne Smiley of Virginia sent me the only piece ever seen, a 9" oval vegetable with the gold official stamp, VR-312. Minute examination with naked eye and magnifying glass can discern no difference between #128 and #312. Included are side-by-side photographs. Before this single example was received, it was thought the use of the term "silver edge" was different from #128's term "silver edge line," but this belief was unfounded. The two bowls are identical, yet one is stamped VR-128, and another VR-312. Any ideas?

*Two 9" oval vegetables. See if you can discover any differences; I could not. The one on the left is stamped VR-312; the one on the right, VR-128.*

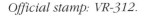

*One of two VR#332 (D.231d) bowls, with the plate shown below, the only examples seen.*

### VR#D.231d

Name..........................."Fluffy Rose 5"
Official number......................VR#332
Known dates ..................1937 – 1952

COMMENTS: The final version to be held-in-hand is a re-working of the 2 sprigs #128, but without any silver trim. The collection consists of two small 7" nappies, and a beautiful 10" plate, the latter supplied by Jeanne Smiley. Trimless versions of any treatment have a soft, diffused appearance that works well with a gently colored decal. My personal opinion? #332 is actually more attractive than the silver-edged version. Since the five known versions belonging to the Fluffy Rose family are so similar, many of the lesser known types must be lurking in collections, masquerading as their more illustrious sister, VR#128. Those readers/collectors who have prodigious numbers of Fluffy Rose would benefit by a careful perusal, with notes taken of any variants and date marks. Important information for them as collectors and very important for continuing Virginia Rose research.

*The somewhat scarce VR 10" plate, courtesy of Jeanne Smiley.*

### VR#D.235

ROSE; pink, large, one: with dark green leaves, shadow effect. Glaze: light yellow.

Name ........................................"Rhythm Rose"
Official number.............................Not known
Known dates...............................1940 – 1946
Trim..............................................................Gold
Also appears on .................Brittany, Cavalier, Kitchen Kraft, Nautilus, Rhythm, and on the ware of Cannonsburg; Taylor, Smith, Taylor; Universal

COMMENTS: There are some treatments and some decals so important it is felt they must appear on the Virginia Rose blank. While not particularly admired personally, Rhythm Rose is such a treatment. For years, I knew it somehow had to be on VR, but it escaped me, and none of my contacts had discovered it either. Then, quite by chance, in a far booth in a most ramshackled indoor flea market, two mint 9" plates were discovered. Every collector has experienced the same type of find. Why was this large market even considered as a place to hunt for Homer Laughlin? It is located on heavily trafficked Route 19 in Holiday, Florida, and is devoted mainly to cheap clothing, local garden produce, booths selling birds, mice, snakes, computer games, and vivid, ugly artificial flowers: we have all experienced such a sales emporium. Since I was there, I rambled around the aisles lined with link-fence divided booths, and at the farthest end, a point where turning about was the only option, was a second-hand furniture area, watched over by hawk-eyed, elderly woman. There were, however, some bowls and plates on several tables, and I entered to examine them, followed closely by the wary caretaker. As I turned to leave, sparkling behind dirty glass in a crude '30s china cabinet, were two 9" Virginia Rose plates wearing Rhythm Rose. So familiar was this decal that I experienced no rush of excitement. The woman strode over as the plates were freed from their prison. "Ten dollars each," she croaked. I paid and fled.

*When first seen, this Universal's Ballerina coupe soup looked exactly like Rhythm, and was nearly ignored.*

*The Nautilus creamer adds a narrow forest green strip that is missing on the saucer. Wonder why?*

*Cannonsburg platter.*

138

(D.235 "Rhythm Rose" cont.)

To name this treatment was simple. Rhythm Rose is a very popular and well-known name to all HLC collectors, so it should be "Rhythm Rose on the Virginia rose shape." While quite common on the Rhythm shape, and appearing with regularity on the Kitchen Kraft line, this treatment must be considered rare on Virginia Rose and Brittany .

Incidentally, this rose appears stark in the center of a Brittany plate I own. Unusual because Brittany most often has some type of rim decoration, the most common being a maroon band with tiny flowers. On Nautilus and Cavalier the pink rose is accompanied by a colored band in forest green and yellow. But as far as Virginia Rose is concerned, I wondered if this were the actual "first rose" appearing on the shape. Are there other VR examples hiding in other bustling farmers' markets, some bearing the date 1932, or even as Joanne Jasper once believed, 1929? Finding this treatment proved the important collector adage: Hunt everywhere!

Soon after, a new discovery enlightened me further. Again, by chance, I noted a rather shallow round bowl, and nearly did not pick it up so sure it was Rhythm. But I did, and it was Universal's Ballerina E20 with its name on the backstamp — a simple "Rose." Looking up Universal potteries in Harvey Duke's reference work, I learned Ballerina's two most common decaled treatments were "Moss Rose" and "Thistle." This bowl was not marked "Moss Rose" but it is to be wondered if this is its true name, though it does look more like a tea rose. Since Universal Potteries did not come into existence (under that name) until 1934, can we assume Universal used the decal first, but how strange that Virginia Rose's most prevalent, and popular treatment also is called "Moss Rose."

If nothing else, we now know this rose decal was commercial, and as such will appear on the work of potteries other than HLC. To this date it has been seen in a small shop in Hernando, Florida, gracing 36 pieces of Cannonsburg, and at Smiley's, Micopany, Florida, on a substantial set of Taylor, Smith, Taylor. The latter has a wide forest green, gold filigree band, very much like HLC's Lady Greenbriar. The discovery of the shadowed pink rose on the Virginia Rose piqued my interest, and suddenly the treatment is seen everywhere. Strange how one simple find expands the view.

*A Rhythm 7" plate and coupe soup stand behind a Cable egg cup.*

*9" VR plate, Rhythm Rose.*

**The Wild Rose Family**
**VR#D.240, D.240a, D.240b**

ROSE (single); pink, pink-white, medium large, one to two; with buds; pale green leaves. Glaze: cream.

Name ..................................................................................................."Wild Rose 1"
Official number..............................................................................Not known
Known dates...............................................................................1947 – 1955
Trim ......................................................................................................Silver
Also appears on........Century, Kitchen Kraft, Nautilus Eggshell, Yellowstone

COMMENTS: Versions 1 and 2 of Wild Rose are good examples of the intricacies of assigning official HLC numbers (please refer to Appendix H, p.195). With the known dating, we certainly assume these two would appear on our 1952 list, and indeed this version might. Yellowstone has the same treatment with gold trim, so we looked for two entries with two sprigs, one with silver, one with gold trim; these two must have the same Yellowstone number as their source. Several entries were located with Y-137 as the antecedent, but not one mentioned gold trim. We were stumped! These roses are soft and fill the space fully with a ruffled, delicate charm. Wild Rose is very feminine without being over-refined, delicate without being overdone.

*D.240 teacup and saucer. Note the inside ring on teacup.*

*Kitchen Kraft pie plate, with 6" plate and creamer.*

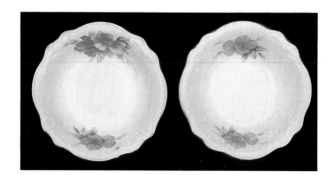

*Two differences exist between the two versions of Wild Rose: the inner teacup ring, and the fact that all the gold trimmed fruit bowls lack the larger rose decal. Left: silver trimmed. Right: gold trimmed.*

*Beautiful detailing marks the decal.*

Rear: Kitchen Kraft 8" covered casserole. Front: Nautilus Eggshell casserole and lid.

*9" plate, teacup and saucer, and fruit bowl.*

*With a delicate pale green washed edge, this 15" platter is shown courtesy of Evelyn Honeycutt.*

Note: "Piecemealing" at its most welcome! Jeanne Smiley, about five months later, sent another Wild Rose platter dated 1937. Every tiny smidgen of information adds immeasurably to VR knowledge, and I also thank Ms. Smiley.

### VR#D.240b

ROSE (single); same description as D.240 except different glaze. Glaze: light yellow.

Name ............................"Wild Rose Platter"
Official number ........................Not known
Known dates ...........................1936 – 1937
Trim ...............................Apple green wash
Also appears on: .................Kitchen Kraft,
   OvenServe, Yellowstone

COMMENTS: This impressive 15" platter, while not as large as the 18" Bountiful (D.119), still presents the unusual wash edge treatment, here in a delicate apple green. Besides the wash, this piece has another interesting factor: its date. Both D.240 and D.240a are dated in the late 1940s, and suddenly this platter is discovered with the date 1936! While not iron-clad proof, we can surmise the other Wild Rose versions were also available some ten years earlier. But we will have to wait before we change the known dates, and more proof is required. This again illustrates the "piecemealing" procedures of collecting and identifying dinnerware.

### VR#D.245
### VR#D.245a

ROSE; yellow and orange, small, one to five; with many prominent buds; black, green leaves, twining stems. Glaze: light yellow.

Name ................"Wild Brambles One"
Official number ................Not known
Known date ................................1935
Trim.............................................Silver
Also appears on ...............Not known

COMMENTS: An early stylish treatment of a wild bramble rose. The soft rusty-orange and creamy yellow contrast beautifully with the glaze. An easy treatment to identify due to the black rose leaves and the general "brambly" look, the kind of wild rose found in an English hedgerow. Note the many hairy buds, the curving, sprawling stems. A cursory look reminds one of Medieval Rose (D.113) but Wild Brambles is very naturalistic. Thanks to Diane Kelly for sending this fantastic Virginia Rose platter.

There is also a second version of this treatment, Wild Brambles Two, having two decals (sprigs) and no trim. This version does have an official HLC number, VR-132, which does not appear on the 1937 list. Discovered in the HLC morgue, its illustration can be seen on page 168.

*Close-up of the finely detailed bramble roses.*

*15" platter.*

*Teacup (with inner ring) and saucer, silver rimmed.*

*Silver trimmed sauceboat, courtesy of Lynn Fredregill.*

*Detail of faded decal.*

### VR#D.258

VIOLET; purple, very large, one bunch; with dark green leaves. Glaze: light yellow.

Name ............."Woodland Beauty One"
Official number ....................Not known
Known date ....................................1950
Trim.................................................None
Also appears on....................See below

COMMENTS: A huge bunch of realistic violets framed with large shiny leaves nearly fills the well of this 9" plate, the only example of this treatment in the collection. Very prominent and remarkably executed, but, one wonders, does it make a suitable or welcome decoration on a dinner plate? This treatment has technically not yet been located on other HLC shapes, if the guidelines are strictly followed. Debutante and Rhythm have the large violet decal, but they also sport a second smaller bunch and this becomes a third version. Since Virginia Rose's Woodland Beauty also exists with gold trim, does the two-bunch grouping also appear on VR? This seems very possible because both Debutante and Rhythm were produced after Virginia Rose, and if these later shapes borrowed the treatment, it would be logical the two-bunch version did exist.

*9" plate D.258 with the violets filling the entire center.*

*Detail of the richly colored violets.*

**VR#D.258a**

VIOLET; purple, very large, one bunch with dark green leaves. Glaze: light yellow.

Name .................."Woodland Beauty Two"
Official number .......................Not known
Known date ........................................1952
Trim ....................................................Gold
Also appears on........................See below

COMMENTS: The gold trim on this version adds a touch of elegance. Some Virginia Rose treatments are quite attractive with no edging, others look a little pale. To attempt to locate the official number of the two Woodland Beauties, I studied the 1953 list. There are two candidates, VR#434 (no trim) and VR#443 (gold trim). Both are based on a Ravenna treatment, RV-7833. There is no two-sprig variation mentioned, but it might have been discontinued, or, perhaps, it never did exist on Virginia Rose. Does any reader possess any Ravenna pieces or know of any bearing these Virginia Rose violets? If the connection can be made, we have the numbers of two more VR treatments.

*Debutante 6" plate, dated 1952, also with two decals.*

*D.258a. The gold trimmed sugarbowl. The violet decal is reworked to fit the piece's shape.*

*Rhythm coupe soup with two sprigs (decals), dated 1957. Perhaps there is a Virginia Rose version with two violet bunches.*

*13" platter with off-center decal and gold trim.*

*Waterlilies are rarely depicted on dinnerware. This massive 15" Hudson platter has an awkwardly positioned decal of a group of waterlilies.*

**VR#D.270**

WATERLILY; white, pink tips, large, one; with floating buds, lilypads, representation of water. Glaze: cream.

Name ...................."Waterlily," "Lotus"
Official number.......................VR#398
Known date ...............................1937
Trim................................................Silver
Also appears on ...............Not known

COMMENTS: A very beautiful and rare design. Water flowers rarely appear on American dinnerware due to the difficulty in representing water. Only one other piece in my collection tackles the inherent problems of depicting reflective water, a fascinating 15" Hudson platter. Here on Virginia Rose, it is cleverly accomplished as a naturalistic, pinky-white lily floats on the surface of a quiet pond shimmering with underwater reflections. A set of 25 was obtained with the help of Kim Hanz, Rochester, Michigan, a lady well-regarded in American dinnerware circles. The dating is problematic; although all the pieces are dated 1937, VR#398 does not appear on the valuable 1937 official list. It could have been produced late in that year, or, more likely, my list is incomplete. However it is not listed on the 1957 account either, so we must assume it was no longer available. Perhaps it proved too unusual for regular customer popularity.

9" oval vegetable (baker): flat bottom.

*The 9" baker and small fruit bowl.*

*Detail of the decal. Beautifully executed in delicate colors, and presenting the illusion of water.*

*9" and 6" plates.*

**VR#D.275**
**VR#D.275a**

WHITE; no decoration. Glaze: cream.

Name...................................................."Snow"
Official number............................Not known
Known dates..............................1948 – 1957
Trim...........................................................None
Also appears on ..............Plain undecorated
    versions are available in many HLC
    shapes as blanks or deliberate offerings.

COMMENTS: Were these Virginia Rose pieces offered for commercial sales or are they blanks that escaped the factory? Not many undecorated items have been found, certainly not enough to make a set. Yet as I write this, other pieces are being discovered — six fruits in an Ocala, Florida, collection; 6" plates belonging to an acquaintance in New York City; an oatmeal and an oval vegetable in South Dakota; and six mugs found in Oneonta, New York, at a rural auction, purchased in a box lot for $6.00. Gladly, the buyer sent me one. So, even though not much undecorated Virginia Rose is seen, it certainly was offered on the dinnerware market. There is a sculptural, dramatic quality about the three hollowware pieces in my collection, especially the two shown in the photograph. A coupe soup is seen in Jo Cunningham's book (p.197), and my personal experience with Snow stops there. Unless some reader has been lucky enough to assemble a full set, the treatment or lack of treatment must be considered beautiful, but rare.

*The Marigold creamer, dated 1948, also shown in pure simplicity. White Marigold is even more rare than white Virginia Rose!*

*A deliberately designed photograph. The sun was rising, and bathed the left side, throwing the acanthus embossing into high relief.*

*Note: Just as some collectors consider the pure white Zeisel Hallcraft piece the ultimate standard of the line, the sculptural and unadorned creamy white Virginia Rose nears perfection. Not many pieces are seen, but this urn-like sugarbowl and lid, with no decoration to deflect the eye, shows the cleverness of the attached handles. The dramatic 7" jug has additional embossing on the handle and spout which is also often overlooked on decorated pieces. A sauceboat, plates in several sizes, and a 13" platter are known to exist, and this proves white Virginia Rose pieces are not just escaped blanks.*

D.275a. A studio photograph of an unadorned Virginia Rose 8" plate, trimmed in silver. Courtesy of Gary Geiselman.

### VR#D.275a
Name ...................................."Silver Snow"
*See D.275 for description.*

This version was supplied by Gary Geiselman through this photograph. The date is 1949, so it is impossible to state which version came first; more pieces will have to be discovered. If there was an accompanying verge silver line, it would be a version of Double Gold Band (D.127). The treatment has been named Silver Snow and I cannot help but wonder if there is a third version with gold trim. The longer Virginia Rose is studied, the more one can predict the possibility of certain treatments. The prime example of this was Bluebirds (D.11) and there was a nagging feeling that these popular birds would be discovered on Virginia Rose. Have the same feeling with a single gold trim version also, but we will have to wait for the proof. There seem to be very few pieces of Silver Snow.

### The Carolyn Series
### VR#D.278, D.278a, D.278b, D.278c

We end our Virginia Rose review by discussing a new, but unmistakable, version of the shape. In 1956, HLC began producing dinnerware of a heavier weight, aimed primarily at the commercial market, and 1960 was the year the company "officially" started offering several lines to the public. Some of these early commercial shapes and items are no longer being produced, making them highly collectible.

As dinnerware flooded into America from foreign factories, to survive, Homer Laughlin turned from the retail to the commercial trade. Of all its former lines, HLC decided that only three would make the transition from retail to institutional, albeit modified. These were Theme which became Vintage; Brittany renamed Banquet China and accompanied by the Debutante shakers; and Virginia Rose changed her name to Carolyn.

The Carolyn line is also known as the Carolyn/Princess line, but any Virginia Rose person can easily separate the Carolyns from the Princesses. While there are a number of treatments on the Carolyn shape, we will mention only nine, and assign them D(ecoration) numbers. Please remember, this Carolyn list is not complete.

D.278    White, pure white body.
D.278a   Styleline Gold (BCC-828), white body, edge trim light mustard color.
D.278b   Gold Trim, white body, gold edge line.
D.278c   Capitol (BC-762), white body, trim light mustard with additional fine black inner trim.
D.278d   Maroon Band, maroon band edged in green.
D.278e   Styleline Black, (BCC-847), black trim.
D.278f   Mulberry, rich cream glaze, no edge trim, thin black line at verge, wide deep mulberry band.

*Carolyn Gold Trim: 11" platter, 7" plate, and teacup.*

*An AD cup and saucer in Carolyn Styleline Gold. The regular saucer (left) is Carolyn Capitol.*

(Carolyn Series cont.)

D.278g    Mustard, white glaze, no trim, wide mustard yellow band.

D.278h    Red Baker, pure white glaze, no trim, very thin red line near edge, figures of baker, small boy, and tiny dog in red.

Of all the available pieces of Carolyn, the platters in all sizes seem the most available, and the most recognizable. My collection boasts 18 Carolyn platters, from 7" to 12". Unfortunately, the larger platters, 13" – 18", are no longer available.

I asked Jonathan O. Parry, current HLC art director, if the Carolyn shape weren't based on Virginia Rose. His initial response was negative, describing Carolyn as a popular industry standard of the 1960s with less appeal now. I wanted Carolyn to be the modern Virginia Rose, with less detail and more rounded outlines, but still charming Virginia Rose with a hint of maturity in its heavier profile. About five days after my conversation with Mr. Parry, he wrote about speaking with William Pickin Sr., sales director for HLC in 1960, who confirmed my theory of Virginia Rose as inspiration for Carolyn — an old friend with a pleasant new sleekness.

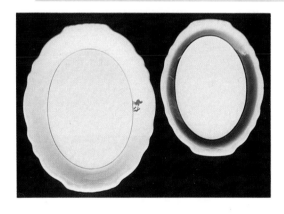

*A small platter in Carolyn Mulberry presents a rich, finished appearance (left). The much larger Red Baker is very plainly sophisticated.*

*Carolyn Mustard 14" platter. The glaze is clear and very shiny.*

---

**VR#D.283**

SOLID COLOR; no decal. Glaze: tan.

| | |
|---|---|
| Name | "Honey Chip" |
| Official number | Not known |
| Known date | Not known |
| Trim | None |
| Also appears on | Not known |

COMMENTS: Another acquisition courtesy of Rick Gault. He purchased this unusual piece at an auction held during the 1996 East Liverpool convention. The price was high for a 6" plate, but it was worth the cost. At first, the plate was assumed to be experimental and this might still be correct, but Jo Rice reports having seen a sugarbowl and lid in an East Liverpool store. It was not for sale and it would be nice to know if it were dated. What is obvious? That someone at HLC dipped some Virginia Rose in this glaze for a purpose yet unknown. Rick related a conversation he had with a fellow auction goer about this piece, and it seems other plates are known to exist. Experimental or a special set, this little plate is an important part of my personal collection.

*6" plate purchased at an auction held at the East Liverpool Pottery Convention, 1996. It is a warmer, more caramel-colored version of HLC's Amberstone.*

# Virginia Rose Specialty Bowls

From the onset of research and organization, the category of specialty bowls proved persistently problematic. Officially Homer Laughlin titled them "salad nappies," and they were no longer produced after 1952. There is one example dated 1959 (D.303) so this statement has exceptions. But should they be named and numbered? Should they be placed with the regular dinnerware or form a separate division? With the stenciled bowls, the difficulties were even more involved. Although only three varieties of Virginia Rose stenciled bowls are known, the floral or fruit decals appearing in the bowl center are abundantly different. Some of these, unfortunately, are known only through photographs.

Arbitrarily, three categories were assigned to Virginia Rose specialty bowls:
1. Stenciled, with floral or fruit central decals.
2. Marilyn bowls (similar to Georgia Eggshell Marilyn), with floral central decals.
3. Miscellaneous bowls not fitting into the above two
    categories, and listed among the dinnerware.

## Stenciled Bowls

Three varieties of stencils, three colors in each. The central decal comes in wide variety — some, possibly, not yet known.

I. The HLC #W1700 series: three-leaved clover design.
    a. Medium blue        #W1700
    b. Emerald green       #W1701
    c. Red/brown           #W1702

The numbering is a logical conjecture, because, as Mrs. Jasper states, these were identified in a 1950s sales brochure with the #W1700 designation. HLC usually numbered color variation consecutively. These bowls come up with a variety of center decals, having been seen with groups of fruit, Rhythm Rose, the very prevalent Esperanza (see p.169), and others.

If a photograph is available in this book, a special D(ecoration) number is noted.

|         | Known Bowl                                      | Date |
|---------|-------------------------------------------------|------|
|         | Medium blue with fruit decal (see J.J., pl.63)  | NK   |
|         | Emerald green with floral decal (see J.J., pl.63) | NK |
| D.300   | Emerald green with Esperanza decal              | 1947 |
| D.301   | Red/brown with Rhythm Rose decal                | 1951 |
| D.302   | Red/brown with rose floral decal                |      |

D.300. Stenciled emerald green with Esperanza decal.

D.301. Stenciled red/brown with Rhythm Rose. This large full blown pink rose is most familiar on the Rhythm shape, but also has appeared on VR dinner-ware (see D.235).

D.302. Stenciled red/brown with rose floral decal.

II. The SAL series: cross-hatching and stylized daisy design.
     a. Medium blue      SAL 75
     b. Emerald green   SAL 73
     c. Red/brown      SAL 74

The SAL group is also decorated with a floral center but, in this case, usually Rhythm Rose. If a photograph is available in this book, a special D(ecoration) number is noted.

| | Known Bowl | Date |
|---|---|---|
| D.303 | Emerald green with Rhythm Rose decal | 1959 |
| | Red/brown with Rhythm Rose decal (see J.J., pl.64) | NK |

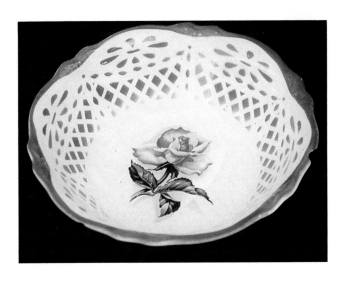

*D.303. Stenciled emerald green with Rhythm Rose decal.*

III. Full Clover series.
     a. Medium blue
     b. Emerald green
     c. Red/brown

The Full Clover series has not yet been numbered, but they, too, have central decals. If a photograph is available in this book, a special D(ecoration) number is noted.

| | Known Bowl | Date |
|---|---|---|
| D.304 | Medium blue with floral decal | 1945 |
| D.305 | Emerald green with floral decal | 1949 |
| D.306 | Red/brown with floral decal | 1944 |

*D.304. A worn example of stenciled medium blue with floral decal.*

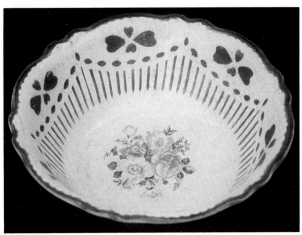

*D.305. Stenciled emerald green with identical floral decal as D.304.*

*D.306. Stenciled red/brown, again with the identical floral of D.304.*

# The "Marilyn" Bowls

Named for the Georgian Eggshell treatment, Marilyn. There is a wide band of soft, pastel color, edged in gold filigree, and, like the stenciled bowls, having a central decal, here called Esperanza. The Georgian Eggshell comes in four colors, pink, pale blue, soft yellow, and mint green. To date, only the pink and blue versions have been discovered on the VR bowls.

If a photograph is available in this book, a special D(ecoration) number is noted.

|  | Known Bowl | Date |
|---|---|---|
| D.307 | Pink, narrow verge filigree, Esperanza decal | 1950 |
| D.308 | Blue, narrow verge filigree, Esperanza decal | 1943 |
| D.309 | Blue, wide verge filigree, floral decal | 1949 |

*D.307. Pink border with Esperanza central decal.*

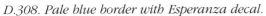

*D.308. Pale blue border with Esperanza decal.*

*D.309. A narrow pale blue border, wider filigree and floral central decal identical to the Clover Series.*

## Miscellaneous

There are presently four bowls in this category and for convenience are listed among the dinnerware with their own D(ecoration) number.

| | |
|---|---|
| D.57 | Agnes |
| D.170a | Colonial Quadrille Bowl |
| D.3a | Fall's Beauty Bowl |
| D.172 | Grecian Melody |

There are 17 known treatments on Virginia Rose specialty bowls. Fourteen appear in this book, 10 in this section, and four among the dinnerware. Three versions can be seen only in Mrs. Jasper's book. Again, the appeal goes out to the readers. If other varieties of VR specialty bowls are known, please share this information.

# The Morgue Collection

Only a select few visitors to the Homer Laughlin factory are allowed into the morgue. Sharon and Bob Huxford were so favored and an entire section of their book, *Collector's Encyclopedia of Fiesta*, deals with the treasures located in the "dark secretive room."

Joanne Jasper also gained access but her description of the morgue is somewhat different than the Huxfords', so it is felt there are two such mysterious places. Mrs. Jasper speaks of broken windows, seeping water, and fusty accumulations of dirt and grime, a below ground cellar. The Huxfords' morgue is "in the uppermost niche of the office building." No matter if there are two such repositories, they are both exciting treasure-troves.

During the 1996 East Liverpool Pottery Convention, Joanne and a friend gained entrance, and, located, washed, photographed, and carefully boxed for a more peaceful storage a series of Virginia Rose plates. Some of these plates were probably prototypes never put into full production. Some are variations of known treatments. Yet even more importantly, all have official HLC numbers either on the back, or written in the well of the plate. Some have numbers below VR-105 (the first number appearing on the 1937 list) so it can be assumed these treatments came and went before the 1937 date — nor do they reappear on the 1952 list. They could have been revived during the intervening years, possible, but doubtful. The dates of only a few are presently known.

Since these treatments have been seen by Joanne in person and by me via the photographs, they must receive D(ecoration) numbers. The following criteria was decided:

- if the treatment is exactly the same as one already known, it will receive the same number.
- if the treatment located in the morgue is a variation of a treatment known to exist, it will receive the same number with an additional letter (example: Wild Brambles 2, D.245a). This variation will be mentioned and numbered in the original discussion and a reference made to the morgue photograph (see p.168).
- if the treatment is completely new, never seen outside the morgue, it will be named and receive a special number. These special numbers will commence at 400, e.g. Jewelled Rose, VR#DM.402. The morgue plates will be illustrated directly after this page. Remember, except for the "DM" designation, these pieces will be treated exactly the same as all others in the book. The "M", of course, denotes "morgue."

## VR#DM.400

BAND (verge); blue triangular form divided by floral swags yellow background. Glaze: light yellow.

| | |
|---|---|
| Name | "Hollander" |
| Official number | VR#122 |
| Known date | Not known |
| Trim | Silver |
| Also appears on | Not known |

COMMENTS: Known only through a photograph taken in HLC's morgue, this treatment reminds the viewer of the older Kwaker trim designs. One of the few Virginia Roses sporting a verge decoration, it is quite smart-looking and rather modern. Teacups and sugarbowls are needed to discover how the verge decoration translates to the hollowware. We do have an idea in the example of Band of Plenty (D.8), (see page 22).

### VR#DM.401

FLOWERS; pink, pale blue, medium to small, many; with tiny florets. Glaze: light yellow.

| | |
|---|---|
| Name | "Head of Class" |
| Official number | VR#101 |
| Known date | Before 1937? |
| Trim | Silver |
| Also appears on | Not known |

COMMENTS: Just another Virginia Rose floral design — but some fascination surrounds this treatment. It does not appear on the 1937 list and it holds the earliest VR number yet found. It is possible HLC started the Virginia Rose's numbering system with 100, making Head of Class the second design on the shape. It is a pretty set of decals but with no exceptional artistic features. Perhaps the art staff was trying out new floral designs and hoping to catch the eyes of potential customers.

There is another point to discuss here. Gold Rose's official number was VR#115 (D.61) and some pieces in my collection bear the date 1932. This can lead us to surmise the possibility of VR numbers before VR#115 being dated before 1932. It is extremely important for me to view the date of Head of Class, but this entails a trip to the factory and permission to enter the morgue.

### VR#DM.402

FILIGREE; gold, covering rose embossing, edging and line. Glaze: light yellow.

| | |
|---|---|
| Name | "Jewelled Rose" |
| Official number | VR#114 |
| Known date | Not known |
| Trim | Gold |
| Also appears on | Not known |

COMMENTS: The entire embossed rose is covered in gold, not just outlined, and this gives the effect of jewelry. The appearance is richer than Gold Rose (D.61) and much more so than Patrician (D.75). It is a wonder this treatment never became popular. But was it ever put into production? Jewelled Rose is another treatment that might push back the date when VR was thought to be introduced. The date is very early because Gold Rose, VR#115, first appeared in 1932, and the numbers tended to be assigned in consecutive order.

### VR#DM.403

ANEMONE; yellow, pink, lilac, large, three; with leaves, buds. Glaze: light yellow.

Name ................."September Charm"
Official number....................VR#452
Known date ...................Not known
Trim............................................Silver
Also appears on...................Rhythm

COMMENTS: Seeing this late Virginia Rose treatment was like suddenly coming across an old friend. My aunt had a set of Rhythm bearing large, anemone-like flowers and it was never imagined VR would bear the same treatment! September Charm seems too modern, too perfectly suited for a pure rounded shape. Since her death, my aunt's set has been packed away. After viewing the morgue photograph, I hunted about, located, and scrubbed what remained of the Rhythm set. The VR official number is very late and does not appear on any list in my possession, although the Rhythm set bears the date 1955. Which came first, Virginia Rose or Rhythm? Unanswerable! But with September Charm, another family link has been forged.

*Three sprig Evelyn, D.217b.*

*Two sprig Evelyn, D.217a.*

**VR#DM.404**

ANEMONE; yellow, pink, blue, medium, six; with buds, tendrils, leaves. Glaze: light yellow.

Name ........................................."Margaret"
Official number.......................A-740 BS(?)
Known date ............................Not known
Trim.........................................Silver
Also appears on ...........................Rhythm

COMMENTS: Are these really anemones? I like to think so. They are very difficult flowers to grow and blanket the spring woods gardens surrounding English country homes. Margaret is, no doubt, a true prototype because the number is not stamped on the reverse, it is handwritten in ink. Perhaps an authority at the company can enlighten both the readers and me. Margaret is a bright, fresh, gently colorful treatment oriented to country living and appears appealingly and with regularity on the Rhythm shape.

*Rosy Ring (left) and Curtains (right).*

**VR#DM.405**
**VR#DM.406**

COMMENTS: These two morgue treatments are listed together because they involve verge decoration. The official numbers are known for both yet they do not appear on any listing, so perhaps they were prototypes, or simply did not have customer appeal. Rosy Ring (VR#120, DM.405) is a rather pedestrian design, and the tiny dabs of lop-sided flowers along the rim are not really attractive. Conversely, Curtains (VR#121, DM.406) is different; the swag motif is very attractive, understated, and unusual. I yearn to know how these curtains were translated onto the smaller hollowware. Both treatments have silver trim.

### VR#DM.407

IMPATIENS; red, yellow, small to tiny, many; with tiny blue florets, pale leaves. Glaze: light yellow.

Name ......................."Temptation"
Official number................VR#105
Known date .........................1937
Trim......................................Silver
Also appears on..........Angelus (?)

COMMENTS: Temptation is almost identical to Four O'Clock Delight (D.123). In fact, it still might be resolved as a version of that shape. The viewer might be so quick to place the two treatments together that the small, plump pink rose in the center decal is overlooked. Temptation appears as the first entry on the 1937 list, and is followed by "A-313" which, if the rules run correctly, means it was taken from an Angelus decoration. However this does seem an unusual transfer, the richly colored impatiens seem to be an unlikely candidate for an Angelus design. Unless I be accused of impulsiveness, I questioned the appearance on Angelus.

### VR#DM.408

PEONY; pink, large, two; with smaller yellow, white flowers; pale green elongated leaves. Glaze: light yellow.

Name ......................................."Peony"
Official number ......................VR#155
Known date ................................1937
Trim .............................................Silver
Also appears on...........................Jade

COMMENTS: Known only through the morgue specimen, Peony fills the plate with a lacy, soft, feminine grace. Its inclusion on the 1937 list proves an early appearance and gives the origin as Jade (J#9). We'd like more of this treatment to be located, both on Virginia Rose and Jade!

**VR#DM.409**

ROSE; pink, yellow, medium-large, seven; with lily-of-the-valley, green rose leaves. Glaze: light yellow.

Name ............................."White Pearls"
Official number .................Not known
Known date ........................Not known
Trim.................................................Silver
Also appears on ................Not known

COMMENTS: Another bouquet from the morgue marked simply R 6120. The tightly packed roses seem a strange treatment for Republic. More proof is needed so anyone who has some of the White Pearls decoration on the earlier shape, please inform! Because there is no official VR number, we can assume this decoration was never produced on Virginia Rose. How would this rose bouquet be divided to appear on smaller VR pieces?

**VR#DM.410**

FLOWERS; red, yellow, medium-large, many; with buds; various green leaves. Glaze: light yellow.

Name..............................................."Vellum"
Official number ...............................VR#143
Known date .............................Not known
Trim...........................................Gold flecks
Also appears on .............................Century

COMMENTS: Graceful gladoli dominate this exuberant and warmly colored treatment. Notice the artistic effect of the arching leaves contrasting the upward thrust of the tall coral gladoli. The gold flecking is also unusual, although not as rare as once thought since the morgue treasures were located. Vellum can be found on Century; in fact, I have known of two large sets being offered for sale in the past year. For an idea how this design translates to Century, see Jasper, p.77.

**VR#DM.411**
**VR#DM.411a**

TULIP; pale pink, yellow, medium to large, two to three; with buds; various pale gray leaves. Glaze: light yellow.

COMMENTS: This treatment was found in two versions, Polly 1 and 2, the only difference being the trim. The parrot tulips are identical; three different sprigs arch around the edge.

| | | |
|---|---|---|
| DM.411 | VR#142 | 3 sprigs, silver trim |
| DM.411a | VR#151 | 3 sprigs, gold flecked trim |

**VR#DM.412**
FLOWERS; yellow, blue, orange-red, small, many; with tiny florets; leaves, twining branches. Glaze: light yellow.

| | |
|---|---|
| Name | "Wildflowers" |
| Official number | VR#141 |
| Known date | 1937 |
| Trim | Silver |
| Also appears on | Century |

COMMENTS: This well-proportioned, well-colored, sprightly treatment waits on a plate in the morgue. Its number, #141, appears on the 1937 list, so it was a 1930s offering. The decoration originated on Century. There is nothing aloof or sophisticated about Wildflowers and there is a slight resemblance to Bouquet (D.107). It is a simple floral tribute to the abundant meadows abutting gladed forests, tall grasses swaying in cool breezes, sprinkled with star-like wildflowers!

**VR#DM.413**

NASTURTIUM; red, yellow, blue, medium, one to three; with buds; dark green leaves, tendrils. Glaze: light yellow.

Name ........................................."Pepper Pot"
Official number ...............................VR#162
Known date ..............................Not known
Trim....................................................Green
Also appears on .......Kwaker, Yellowstone

COMMENTS: Unlike Bugles (D.147), Pepper Pot depicts naturalistic, sparkling nasturtiums, leaves, and stems brimming with the sharp bite of pepper. My Nan, long a believer in natural foods and spurning spices, snipped generous handfuls of nasturtium leaves and stems to flavor stews and salads. The flowers can also brighten a green salad and the buds are an inexpensive substitute for capers. Quite a lot to offer from a simple annual flower. I own about 10 pieces on Kwaker and on Yellowstone have a rather rare set of bouillon cups. Finally, not to be overlooked, the rare green trim.

*The very rare Yellowstone bouillon cup.*

*Kwaker sauceboat, teacup and saucer.*

**VR#DM.414**

COSMOS; pale blue, pink, medium, one to two; with small yellow flowers; well-lobed leaves, embossing covered with silver. Glaze: light yellow.

Name.................................................."Feathers"
Official number..............................VR#153
Known date..............................Not known
Trim......................................................Silver
Also appears on ........................Not known

COMMENTS: As said once before, the 1930s abounded in cosmos designs; these flowers were very popular on American dinnerware. The addition of the Patrician-like filigree makes for a unified design. I like Feathers! When attending art school, we were told to squint our eyes at a design to notice the unity and balance. Feathers passes this test admirably. The glint of the metal adds a jewel-like note. Is this design superior to Helene (D.30)?

**VR#DM.415**

ROSE; white, pink, medium, two to three; with blue corn-flowers, chicories; sprawling twigs. Glaze: light yellow.

Name.................................."South of France"
Official number .................................VR#387
Known date............................................1937
Trim .......................................................Silver
Also appears on...........................Not known

COMMENTS: Very similar to English Rose (DM.417), this treatment is more delicate, the shape of decals more feminine, the aspect Victorian. The casual observer would confuse the two. One wonders why Homer Laughlin produced so many treatments puzzling in their similarity. According to the company's records, South of France was produced exclusively for Neisner Brothers.

*Large Rhythm platter.*

### VR#DM.416

ROSE; pale pink, pale yellow, tiny to small, many; with buds; feathery gray leaves, embossing covered with silver. Glaze: light yellow.

Name ..............................."Rose Cream"
Official number.................Not known
Known date ................................1941
Trim...............................................Silver
Also appears on......................Rhythm

COMMENTS: Here is another Virginia Rose treatment appearing on the more modern-looking Rhythm. Without the silver filigree, the plate would look too open and blank, like a lady without make-up. The edging is needed to complete the charm. With no known VR number, it is not known if Rose Cream was produced; it appears in my collection only on a single large platter. Probably not a common pattern.

### VR#DM.417

ROSE; pink, white, medium, two; with many tiny flowers in blue, yellow, pink; various leaves. Glaze: light yellow.

Name ..........................."English Rose"
Official number .......................VR#430
Known date.......................Not known
Trim ..............................................Silver
Also appears on...............Not known

COMMENTS: Another rose treatment inspired by the Victorian period (see DM.415). It is a late production as attested by the official number. Not appearing on the 1952 list, it must have been discontinued by then. The proximity of the red and white roses brought to mind the English War of the Roses — Lancaster White Rose battling the York Red Rose — a brutal time with the throne of England in the balance. Dishes fire up my imagination!

## VR#DM.418

FLOWERS; pink, white, blue, orange, small to medium, many; with buds; dark green leaves. Glaze: light yellow.

Name ........................"Marsh Bouquet"
Official number ................Not known
Known date ................................1950
Trim..............................................Silver
Also appears on....................Marigold

COMMENTS: It must be noted that Mrs. Jasper occasionally photographed the reverse of plates not having the VR number written on the front. With the aid of a magnifying glass, I could make out some dates, Rose Cream (DM.416) and this treatment. We knew that Marigold gave the Springtime decoration to Virginia Rose (D.4) and now the morgue turns up another contribution. Marsh Bouquet is marked M-212, exactly the same as the Marigold — thus this certainly could be a prototype, never placed in normal production. Even for the sisterhood between the two embossed shapes, there is a strong competition between the two, sparring between themselves but presenting a unified front to the outside world. Strangely, Virginia Rose borrowed from Marigold and not vice versa.

*Notice the small outer decals on the plate are the only ones appearing on the creamer.*

**VR#DM.419**

FLOWERS; white, two shades of pink, yellow, tiny to small, many; with leaves.

Name..........................................."Esther"
Official number.......................VR#118
Known date .................................1937
Trim.............................................Silver
Also appears on .....................Century

COMMENTS: Esther appears on the 1937 list with the added notation C-74, so it is known the treatment originated with Century. Pleasant, decorative, and perfectly balanced. Try the squinted eye approach mentioned under Feathers (DM.414), and you will see how unified is the design. The swell of the floral decal fits well and enhances the curve of the embossed rose. Charming without being bold, conservative yet not staid.

**VR#DM.420**

ROSE; pink, tiny, many; with feathery leaves. Glaze: light yellow.

Name ................................"Jeanette"
Official number ...................VR#119
Known date.............................1937
Trim ..........................................Silver
Also appears on..................Hudson

COMMENTS: How similar to Republic's Jean (see J.J., p.33) and yet different. Jeanette appears on the 1937 list and informs, by the additional note H-135, it was copied or adapted from a Hudson design. There is a formal slant to this treatment, quite suitable to dinner parties of the important kind. I remember seeing a decoration very much like Jeanette on a Haviland set once in an elegant antique shop in the Soho district of New York City. Perhaps HLC borrowed it, placed it elegantly on Hudson, and then experimentally transferred it to Virginia Rose. Who knows? The world of dinnerware is shrouded in mysteries.

*D.245a Wild Brambles Two, a variation with two sprigs and no trim.*

*D.135 Wedgwood, a rather rare treatment on Virginia Rose.*

*D.227a Moss Rose Two with gold-flecked trim.*

*D.192 Louise, named by Sears and presented in their 1940 catalog.*

*D.25 Upright Meadow Goldenrod appears rather awkward on flat-ware, possibly more suited to taller hollowware pieces.*

# Esperanza, A Special Category

There is one decal, widely and differently used on Homer Laughlin ware, that cannot be placed in a regular category. The decal can, however, be described in the usual manner:

ROSE; (double), pink (one with mustard outer petals), medium to small, three; with one mustard narcissus, many dark blue flowers, pink, yellow buds; light green leaves.

This decal has been named Esperanza (Hope) because it appears everywhere in many different guises. What makes the above seemingly usual description an exception? Simply that it never appears alone on any Virginia Rose piece. It does appear on Republic; the photograph below depicts a 10" plate, no trim, marked E 48 M 5. On Virginia Rose, it appears only in conjunction with another decorative form, e.g., filigree, color borders or bands, combinations of the two, etc. Many VR specialty bowls have Esperanza as the central floral decal and one lusciously decadent treatment named Baroque (D.194) also uses it as the central motif. Esperanza is common on Georgian Eggshell, and Nautilus Eggshell, but again, usually with another decorative scheme.

Another interesting facet of Esperanza is its wide use on a multitude of other ware: lamp bases, vases of all styles and sizes, bowls, ashtrays, Scio pottery, Cannonsburg's Westchester shape, candy dishes, etc. Commercially-supplied decals present an inherent problem; the unwary collector might assume a lamp base decorated with a decal appearing on some HLC ware was produced by the Homer Laughlin Company. This is rarely true. Commercial decals can catch the collector unprepared. Do not assume a lamp base wearing Esperanza (or Fluffy Rose, for that matter) was manufactured by Homer Laughlin. These are commercial decals available to any pottery willing to purchase them.

Esperanza is a commercial decal, widely used by Homer Laughlin and other companies, and appearing by itself on Republic and with other decorative additions on Georgian Eggshell, (the Marilyn series), Nautilus Eggshell, and Virginia Rose.

*An untrimmed 10" Republic plate, dated 1948.*

Photo courtesy of Allyn Rosa.

*Stately and magnificent unmarked vases wearing Esperanza. They are 10" tall, and would be at home in a duplex apartment foyer on Central Park East in Manhattan.*

*Republic 9" oval vegetable, this time richly trimmed.*

*Detail of the Esperanza decal.*

*Shown as the central floral decal on the Georgian Eggshell shape. Left: the pale green bordered 8" square plate, dated 1942, and right, a 6" pink border plate, dated 1940.*

*Esperanza in the bottom of a Georgian Eggshell cream soup.*

*Three lovely Esperanza vases and a lamp base, 9¾", (far right). Only one piece has a mark: the 5" plump round vase (second from left), marked Old South in gold script.*

*The delightful duck candy dish, 8½" x 6". Marked USA Vitreous China.*

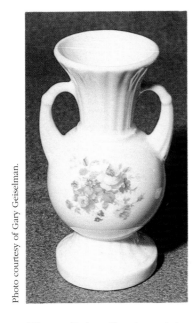

Photo courtesy of Gary Geiselman.

*These little Grecian type vases are not difficult to find, and come in a variety of decorations. Here Esperanza is the decal.*

*Esperanza on an 8" pale blue bordered Virginia Rose specialty bowl. These are usually called "Marilyn bowls."*

*Nautilus Eggshell: creamer, dated 1941, and matching fruit bowl, dated 1943.*

*Same as above, except pale pink.*

171

# *Curiosities*

Always when one is dealing with collectibles, there occasionally arise pieces that fit no category or are the results of very intriguing mistakes. They are rare, so rare, in fact, that after several years of intense interest in Virginia Rose, only two were found. They must be mentioned if for no other reason than to alert those collectors intent on knowing everything about this exciting shape.

These two are rare examples of the Virginia Rose mark being placed on the bottom of other shapes. If it happened twice, I am sure there are more Marigold, Liberty, Republic, etc. dishes masquerading as Virginia Rose. This makes collecting even more exciting, turning over Marigold plates to find a Virginia Rose mark.

Lori Cunningham, Dade City, Florida, wrote me a short letter informing me of a deep, small bowl (36s) with Marigold embossing, yet stamped Virginia Rose. She graciously sold the piece to me. By careful manipulation of the camera, both the mark and the half-marigold embossing can be seen. Could an entire set of Marigold Springtime or a large shipment of the coveted 36s bowl be thus incorrectly stamped?

The second example was harder to photograph and the Virginia Rose stamp was faded, gracing the reverse of a Liberty 6" plate with a dramatic, yet softly colored, magnolia decoration. This small plate is in the Liberty collection of Lynn Fredregill of Texas and could be acquired only as a loan.

Readers, keep casting about for these anomalistic Virginia Roses.

*The Marigold 36s bowl, with Springtime decal, marked Virginia Rose, 1947.*

*Front of 6" Liberty plate with white magnolia and bud. This decal is very common on Rhythm.*

*Bottom of the Liberty plate taken to show edge. Dated 1950 and stamped Virginia Rose. Courtesy of Lynn Fredregill, Humble, Texas.*

# Price Guide

This price listing is a guide only and cannot and must not be viewed as a final authority. Many factors must be considered, the section of the country, the type of shop, mall, or store, the knowledge of the dealer, the desire of the customer, even, at times, the season. There are too many variables swirling about these dollar signs. Virginia Rose has long been limited, in many people's minds, to just a few treatments, and the lesser known ones can hardly be priced as high as those with numerous devotees waiting anxiously to add pieces to their collections.

All prices refer to mint condition and all Homer Laughlin pieces known to exist in any Virginia Rose treatment are listed. Even though I have never seen the VR AD cup or saucer, nor know of anyone who has seen an example of these extremely elusive items, they do appear on the list, mainly as a matter of tradition.

The following guide attempts to distinguish between the VR treatments and to do this, four categories have been established.

**A.** Those treatments which are very popular, widely collected and readily available. They are Armand, Colonial Kitchen, Fluffy Rose, Moss Rose, and Patrician.

**B.** Treatments whose popularity waxes and wanes, or is affected by regionality and availability. They are Bouquet, Gold Rose, Golden Rose, Meadow Goldenrod, Nosegay, Petit Point Rose, Tulips in a Basket, and, to some extent, filigree designs patterned after Patrician.

**C.** Includes all other treatments.

**D.** The fourth category consists of treatments so rare and so avidly desired that many collectors would pay any price to purchase them. For this edition we limit these "super" treatments to Sunporch, Mexicali, and Mexicana. Politely they could be labeled ND (price not determined), but honestly, unfortunately, the policy is probably one of anything goes.

The vitreous Carolyn series is still too new to be on the regular price list. Whenever found, however, the prices tend to be very reasonable, and it is suggested the pieces be purchased!

| Piece | A | B | C |
|---|---|---|---|
| Baker, oval vegetable, 7" (rare) | $20.00 | $18.00 | $16.00 |
| Baker, 8" (scarce) | 18.00 | 16.00 | 14.00 |
| Baker, 9" (flat bottom) | 16.00 | 14.00 | 12.00 |
| Baker, 9" (ridge bottom) | 14.00 | 12.00 | 10.00 |
| Baker, 10" | 16.00 | 14.00 | 12.00 |
| Bowl, 36s (scarce) | 22.00 | 20.00 | 18.00 |
| Casserole/lid | 75.00 | 60.00 | 45.00 |
| Covered butter (Jade) (scarce) | 125.00 | 90.00 | 75.00 |
| Platter, 10¼" (scarce) | 22.00 | 18.00 | 14.00 |
| Platter, 11½" | 16.00 | 14.00 | 12.00 |
| Platter, 13" | 22.00 | 18.00 | 14.00 |
| Platter, 15¼" (scarce) | 30.00 | 26.00 | 22.00 |
| Platter, 18" (rare) | ND | ND | ND |
| Tray/handles 8" (bread) (very rare) | ND | 60.00 | 50.00 |
| Tray/handles 12" (cake) (very rare) | ND | 70.00 | 60.00 |
| Egg cup, Cable (scarce) | 40.00 | 35.00 | 30.00 |
| Egg cup, Double (very rare) | ND | ND | ND |
| Nappy, round vegetable, 7" (rare) | 20.00 | 18.00 | 16.00 |
| Nappy, 8" | 14.00 | 12.00 | 10.00 |
| Nappy, 9" | 16.00 | 14.00 | 12.00 |

| Piece | A | B | C |
|---|---|---|---|
| Nappy, 10" (salad nappy) | 18.00 | 16.00 | 14.00 |
| Fruit | 5.00 | 4.00 | 3.00 |
| Oatmeal | 8.00 | 7.00 | 6.00 |
| Plate, 6" | 5.00 | 4.00 | 3.00 |
| Plate, 7" | 7.00 | 6.00 | 5.00 |
| Plate, 8" (scarce) | 14.00 | 12.00 | 10.00 |
| Plate 9" | 9.00 | 8.00 | 7.00 |
| Plate 10" | 14.00 | 12.00 | 10.00 |
| Plate, deep (rim soup) | 9.00 | 8.00 | 7.00 |
| Coupe soup | 14.00 | 12.00 | 10.00 |
| Cream soup (rare) | 30.00 | 25.00 | 20.00 |
| Cream soup liner (very rare) | ND | ND | ND |
| Sauce boat | 18.00 | 16.00 | 14.00 |
| Sauce boat liner/pickle | 10.00 | 9.00 | 8.00 |
| Fast-stand sauce boat (rare) | 25.00 | 22.00 | 20.00 |
| Teacup | 8.00 | 7.00 | 6.00 |
| Saucer | 4.00 | 3.00 | 2.00 |
| AD cup (very rare) | ND | ND | ND |
| AD saucer (very rare) | ND | ND | ND |
| Coffee mug (scarce) | 40.00 | 35.00 | 30.00 |
| Mug, St. Dennis (rare) | 50.00 | 45.00 | 40.00 |
| Sugar/lid | 16.00 | 14.00 | 12.00 |
| Creamer | 12.00 | 10.00 | 8.00 |
| Shakers, pair (Swing) (scarce) | 120.00 | 100.00 | 80.00 |
| Shakers, pair (Debutante) (very rare) | ND | ND | ND |
| Shakers, (KK), pair (rare) | 150.00 | 125.00 | 100.00 |
| Jug, 5" (scarce) | 100.00 | 80.00 | 70.00 |
| Jug, 7½" (scarce) | 125.00 | 110.00 | 100.00 |
| Jug, covered 5" (rare) | 130.00 | 120.00 | 110.00 |
| Jug, covered, 7½" (rare) | 150.00 | 140.00 | 130.00 |

The list consists of 50 separate pieces. The scarce category means the item can be found with diligence and perseverance and the prices might fluctuate. Pieces belonging to the rare category should be purchased whenever possible, especially if the cost is below the listed price. These are items easy to resell. The very rare category means the pieces have only been seen once or twice, or, like the AD cup/saucer, are known only by HLC records.

## Prices for Items with Virginia Rose Decals

Beware the advertisement offering a round Virginia Rose butterdish in the Fluffy Rose treatment (VR#128). They have been touted as rare with a price of $200.00 or more. This butterdish belongs to the Republic shape, and the price should not be more than $40.00. Yet, if the collector wishes to expand, this butterdish would make a nice addition to be displayed beside the regular Jade butter in Moss Rose (JJ#59) or Fluffy Rose.

The Fluffy Rose decal, being a commercially produced decoration, is quite prevalent on vases, large and small; lamp bases; ashtrays; etc. See D.231 in the treatment section of this book for photographs of some of these pieces. The small vases are reasonably priced at $10.00 to $15.00, while the lamp bases can command up to $100.00. It is wise to hunt for these auxiliary pieces at flea markets and thrift stores, as only the decal makes them of interest to the Virginia Rose collector.

Other manufacturers produce wares bearing Virginia Rose decorations. The avid collector's interest should be honed to recognize these pieces and purchase when reasonable. The American Limoges platter duplicating the VR Rose Quilt treatment (D.103) was purchased for $2.00, and Field Ox-Eye (D.35) can be collected on a wide variety of Cannonsburg and Paden City pieces. Since the prices for the work of these companies is much less than for Homer Laughlin, they can be added at little cost.

Esperanza is a decal appearing on many, many non-HLC items (see the chapter entitled Esperanza). A tall lamp base in this decal can cost between $50.00 and $75.00, but a lovely 1940s ashtray or candy dish might be priced at less than $10.00. Esperanza has been noted on a large variety of small vases and many of these are beautifully proportioned. Prices fluctuate considerably. My small round porcelain vase (see p.170) was bought for $8.00; others of the exact type were seen in an antique shop priced $30.00 to $40.00 each. Prices paid for all peripheral pieces depend completely upon the collector's needs and desires.

The purchase of non-Homer Laughlin pieces to augment the Virginia Rose collection, while not necessary, is satisfying and adds another dimension to an already fascinating hobby!

## Pricing for Kitchen Kraft and Ovenserve with Virginia Rose Decals

As of this writing, the following Virginia Rose treatments are accompanied by Kitchen Kraft and/or OvenServe pieces:

| | |
|---|---|
| Daisies (D.13) | Sunporch (D.150) |
| Red Beauty (D.16) | Spring Wreath (D.160) |
| Columbines (D.20) | Armand (D.210) |
| Liberty's Dogwood (D.42) | Petit Point Rose (D.215) |
| Rose Sparkle (D.77) | Moss Rose (D.227) |
| Olivia (D.111) | Fluffy Rose (D.231) |
| Mexicana (D.144) | Wild Rose (D.240) |

Others might surface at any time and it is wisely acknowledged that the kitchenware listed above was primarily planned for shapes other than Virginia Rose: Mexicana, Sunporch, and Petit Point Rose are examples in point. But this does not affect their use. Not all the items available in the kitchenware lines have been discovered with VR decorations. The most alluring example of this is the OvenServe fork. Not one has been located with a Virginia Rose treatment.

We list Moss Rose (JJ#59) and Fluffy Rose (VR#128) separately due to their popularity. All prices are suggestions, and refer to pieces in top condition.

| | JJ#59:VR#128 | Others |
|---|---|---|
| Bowl, 6" mixing (Kitchen Kraft) | $25.00 | $15.00 |
| Bowl, 8" mixing (Kitchen Kraft) | 30.00 | 20.00 |
| Bowl, 10" mixing (Kitchen Kraft | 35.00 | 25.00 |

| | JJ#59:VR#128 | Others |
|---|---|---|
| Bowl, stack set and lid (Kitchen Kraft) | ND | 70.00 |
| Casserole/lid, 8" (Kitchen Kraft) | 40.00 | 25.00+ |
| Casserole/lid (straight-sided) (Kitchen Kraft) (rare) | 75.00 | 40.00 |
| Casserole, small (OvenServe) | ND | 20.00 |
| Pie plate, 8" (Kitchen Kraft) | 15.00 | 10.00 |
| Pie plate, 10" (Kitchen Kraft) | 20.00 | 15.00 |
| Pie plate, 9" (OvenServe) | 20.00 | 15.00 |
| Pie plate, 10" (OvenServe) | 25.00 | 20.00 |
| Cake plate (Kitchen Kraft) | 50.00 | 30.00 |
| Underplate, 9" (OvenServe) | 10.00 | 8.00 |
| Underplate, 6" (OvenServe) | 10.00 | 8.00 |
| Platter, (Kitchen Kraft) | 75.00 | 50.00 |
| Cup (OvenServe) (scarce) | ND | 15.00 |
| Saucer (OvenServe) (scarce) | ND | 8.00 |
| Shaker* (Kitchen Kraft) (each) (rare) | 75.00 | 40.00 |
| Server (OvenServe) (scarce) | 40.00 | 20.00 |
| Spoon (OvenServe) (scarce) | 40.00 | 20.00 |
| Fork (OvenServe) (very rare) | ND | ND |

*These shakers are now being found as single units. Salt or pepper, it does not matter; they are still rare and the price is suggested at $150.00 a pair!

# Suggested Prices for Daisy Chain

Daisy Chain, while appearing on the OvenServe shape, is a separate Homer Laughlin shape with its own series of official numberings, i.e., DC-117, (see p.182). But all Daisy Chain pieces seen are still stamped "OvenServe," and the collector must be aware of the presence or lack of rose embossing which distinguishes the two shapes. Only three Daisy Chain pieces are known to exist: the very recognizable round casserole, its lid, and the 9" pie plate. Perhaps other kitchenware pieces will be discovered. Presently there are only six known Virginia Rose treatments also appearing on the Daisy Chain shape, and it is assumed, perhaps rashly, that both DC pieces were as readily available.

| | | |
|---|---|---|
| Armand (D.210) | Fluffy Rose (D.231) | |
| Columbines (D.20) | Medley of Fruits (D.112) | |
| Florets (D.198) | Moss Rose (D.227) | |

| | JJ#59:VR#128 | Others |
|---|---|---|
| Casserole/lid | $50.00+ | $30.00+ |
| Pie plate, 9" | 20.00 | 15.00 |

# Appendices

## Appendix A
## Availability of Virginia Rose Treatments

The statement bears repeating and repeating: many dealers and many collectors understand "Virginia Rose" to mean both the shape and the treatments — usually Moss Rose (JJ#59) (D.227), and, to a lesser extent, Fluffy Rose (VR#128) (D.231). A reader can disagree with all else that appears between these covers, if only this myth is dispelled!

Granted, and here I strongly concur, Moss Rose is the most prevalent, the most accessible, the most prominent, the most collected, and, oftentimes, the most expensive of all Virginia Rose treatments. This decoration is seen a vast majority of the time.

Fluffy Rose, easily confused with Moss Rose, claims another 20 percent or so of dealer/collector interest. There are some who insist these two are simply versions of the same decal, but this view is quite incorrect. Often the two are mixed wantonly since they are of the same ancestry and mingle well. These two treatments can account for nearly 70 percent, possibly more, of the Virginia Rose seen in the malls and shops and advertised in sundry papers and periodicals. But there is life after we pass over these two treatments. Many others, striking or common, are available in shops and malls, sometimes seen in small sets, or most often in a piece-by-piece situation. These Virginia Rose examples can be built into nice usable collections. Hunt them down; the thrill, after all, is in the chase, not necessarily the capture.

Let us list those treatments, other than the two mentioned above, that, while not really easy to locate, can be pursued with a reasonable chance of success and "bringing to heel."

Patrician (VR#124) (D.75) is the third most available design. But if you are collecting it, purchase as soon as found! While it does appear in small sets, these are not daily, or even monthly, occurrences. There are more collectors buying than there are pieces for sale. It is usually sought by the younger urbanites who have nice disposable incomes, so Patrician tends to be expensive, maybe at times, more costly than Moss Rose. Remember, Patrician has yet to be seen on the kitchenware lines. This treatment is available, but on a limited scale.

After Patrician, the hunt runs into troublesome terrain. Armand (VR#235) (D.210) is rarely seen in sets. Only one set has ever been personally seen for sale, and I captured it immediately. So it does happen. Kitchen Kraft in Armand is readily available and teacups, saucers, and small plates are not difficult to find, if you persist. Not many months ago, 15 teacups were stacked in a Bradenton, Florida, mall at $3.50 each, not a bad price, but there were no saucers. A good sized dinner set can be assembled with steady plodding. I have seen sugars and creamers, vegetable bowls and platters offered for sale singly, but never a casserole, 36s bowl, or the butterdish. It can be assumed these were manufactured but in small numbers. The complete line of Kitchen Kraft, including the shakers, and a number of pieces in OvenServe are available. Be aware only Fluffy Rose and Armand have been seen on the St. Dennis cup. Keep your eyes open.

Bouquet (W#137) (D.107) presents a different situation. This treatment can be seen on many unusual individual pieces but they are rare to scarce. Bouquet egg cups, the butterdish, the small open jug and the 36s bowl are known and this makes ferreting out pieces more fun. Shirley Freeman reports seeing the small jug in Oklahoma. I have seen two jug sets for sale and networking has brought two others to my attention. No mug has been noted yet, but other generic pieces, and the large salad nappy and casseroles are all available in spurts and starts. There is a gentle anomaly here because this treatment was a Woolworth exclusive and this chain was certainly as prevalent as those belonging to Newberry. So why are there more of Newberry's Moss Rose or does it just seem so? Perhaps large quantities of Bouquet are waiting to be discovered. Again, as in Patrician, if Bouquet is a personally important pattern, buy whenever it is seen. It would be correct to state, Bouquet is not especially hard to find, and the variety of pieces is wider than Armand, and perhaps even Patrician. But, as of this writing, no Kitchen Kraft or OvenServe has been discovered.

Meadow Goldenrod (VR#135) (D.24) presents even a more unusual case. It has six variations, although only four have been cataloged, which easily combine and this can help or hinder the collector. If there are restrictions, for example, a collector will consider only those trimmed in silver, then gathering Meadow Goldenrod can be frustrating. I have no experience with complete sets being sold, but Meadow Goldenrod appears by the piece with enough frequency to make it a good choice. In one huge mall on Route 19, Holiday, Florida, two Meadow Goldenrod casseroles (one silver trimmed, one untrimmed) were seen languishing in separate booths.

Colonial Kitchen is the most common treatment seen on Swing. Once I saw a set of 175 Swing pieces at an outdoor fair. On Virginia Rose (D.167) it is most often seen in small sets for four or six, very expensively marked. Here the high visibility of the decal propels the price skyward. For a tea service or breakfast set, Colonial Kitchen is a good choice, but the serving pieces common in other treatments seem to be missing here. I have never even heard of a butterdish, a casserole, large platters, oval vegetables, mugs, or Kitchen Kraft items — so they might not exist. Only an 8" nappy has been seen. If you want a treatment with a reasonably wide choice of the hollowware, do not choose Colonial Kitchen.

The same situation haunts Tulips in a Basket (VR#285) (D.252). Like Meadow Goldenrod, there are various versions and thus, this treatment is actually more available, but the poor viability of the decal makes nice pieces harder to find. About one-fourth of the tulip decals I have seen have the red faded to a yellowish orange. The hunt for Tulips in a Basket in good condition can be long, protracted, and foggy.

Blue Dresden's (D.90) flatware, especially the large dinner plates, is very common. Hardly a mall can be visited without seeing some samples. Sets made up of ordinary pieces are quite common also, but remember, prices should be slightly lower, and be sure you appreciate the differences in style and weight before you invest. The treatment does have a clean, understated tile-like charm, but it could not be called beautiful. Casseroles and the rare 7" jug flash into view with regularity, but Blue Dresden is hardly a popular treatment.

A word of caution: beware of meteoric appearances. An example is Spring Promise (D.183). This treatment was unknown to me until January 1996. Then a small mixed set of eight was purchased through Gary Geiselman, then Evelyn Honeycutt sent some photographs which included an example. Finally, an entire set of 34 came to my notice, all within a few short months. The meteor syndrome in action — once unknown, suddenly highly visible, and, just as suddenly slipping back into the dark. If Spring Promise, a very beautiful decal, continues to be seen at markets, and in advertisements, then it will merit availability consideration. At this point, it should still be considered rare.

Nosegay (VR#423) (D.205) is another example. Mentioned in Joanne Jasper's Homer Laughlin book, this feminine treatment was first seen several years ago when a cream and sugar were purchased for $25.00 at a huge outdoor Florida festival. Then a set of 25 was acquired in 1994. After this, it has never been seen again. Not one of my excellent contacts has mentioned Nosegay. In the price guide, Nosegay was listed among those that wax and wane in popularity. It is charming, has a special type of visibility through Mrs. Jasper's book, but should a collector plan to acquire a set for 10, plus serving pieces? Well, one can always hope.

The eternal collector can surely count on seeing considerable Moss Rose, Fluffy Rose in slightly less abundance, and Patrician, Armand, and Bouquet appearing frequently enough to keep interest piqued. Meadow Goldenrod, in all its versions, is a reasonable choice in the availability chase while highly popular Colonial Kitchen treatment is always eagerly in demand. The filigreed Golden Rose is also available in fits and starts, but its conservative old-fashioned quality may suppress enthusiasm. Tulips in a Basket and Blue Dresden are regularly noted but these do have inherent problems for collectors.

A true Virginia Rose aficionado will not let my musings deter the quest. This shape is out there, sometimes presenting its charms freely and frequently, sometimes shyly hiding among dust and litter. Hunt and you will be rewarded! Sunporch, that rarest of treatments? Jeanie Milburn of Maryland has a few Virginia Rose pieces with the fantastically rare Sunporch decal, and John Moses of New York has at least one plate. All these known pieces have no trim. Dream on about finding a set for eight in a blue-trimmed Sunporch treatment!

# Appendix B
## Summary of Mold Differences

This fact bears repeating: the more narrow the collecting subject, the deeper the collector can delve, and the information and interest become vertical rather than horizontal. This brings us to the subject of mold differences. Virginia Rose, having been manufactured for many years and in such abundance, has a series of different molds. These would, of course, slightly change the VR blanks, and the most quizzical aspect of this fact is mold differences cannot be separated into date periods. All differences were being produced at the same time. It must be noted mold differences, no matter how extreme, never imply a different version.

The most important and obvious differences occur in the 9" oval vegetable. There are two radically different molds in this piece, flat bottom and ridge bottom. The only treatment to present both these differences is Moss Rose, JJ#59 (D.227), and a possible explanation is because so many 9" oval vegetables in this treatment have been studied. We cannot dogmatically say other treatments did not have both bottoms. Since not every treatment seen has included this piece, the listings are far from complete. However, when known, this important mold difference has been noted at the end of the informative material, in this book, i.e., 9" oval vegetable (baker), flat bottom (or ridge bottom). It is a personal opinion that the differences are radical enough to be mentioned in the suggested price list; the flat bottoms are preferable, so they are priced nominally higher. For a more detailed discussion of these two differences, see D.227.

There are also other mold variations, not as dramatic, but nonetheless important, and, like the bottom differences, they occur in all date spans. These variations generally occur in the plates, the platters, and some fruit and oatmeal bowls, and are not differentiated in the suggested prices. For convenience the variations have been numbered and photographs supplied for identification.

Variations in plate molds:

1. No inner ridges, two well-spaced outer ridges
2. One inner ridge, no outer ridges
3. Two inner ridges, no outer ridges
4. Three inner ridges, no outer ridges
5. Four inner ridges, no outer ridges

Variations in platter (dish) molds:

1. Flat
2. Ridge but no ring
3. Ridge with single ring

If the collector wishes to designate the mold of any piece, it is suggested the following form be used:

Patrician, 10" plate (plate mold 2)     Moss Rose, 15" platter (platter mold 3)

Naturally, not all collectors will wish to be this precise, but the choice is there for anyone devoted to fine detail.

*Mold #1. Notice the graceful curve and the lack of a hard line ridge foot.*

*Detail showing gentle swell leading into the two ridges*

*Left: Mold #2. All the following have the ridge foot with a number of inner rings. This mold has one delicate ring close to the foot.*

*Right: Detail of mold #2*

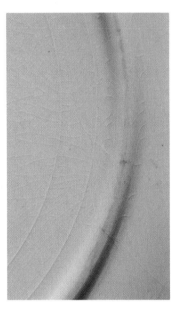

*Left: Mold #3. Two inner rings.*

*Right: Detail of mold #3.*

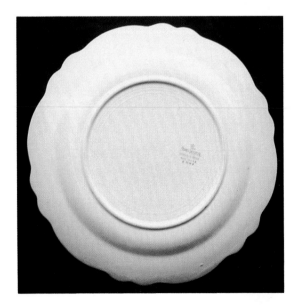

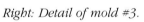

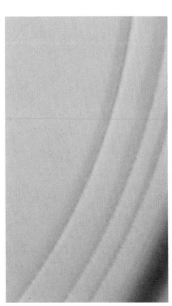

*Left: Mold #4. Three inner rings, the third more widely spaced.*

*Right: Detail of mold #4.*

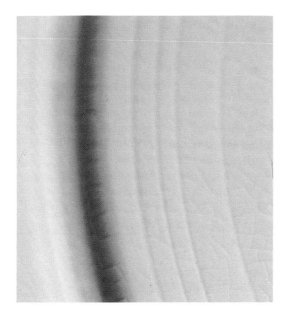

Dish mold #1. Flat.

Detail of mold #5. Four inner rings.

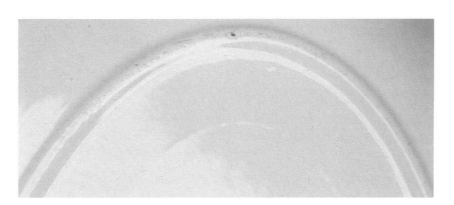

Detail of dish mold #3. A slightly less prominent foot with one delicate inner ring.

Detail of dish mold #2. Obvious ridge foot, but no inner ring.

# *Appendix C*
## *Virginia Rose, Handy Andy, and OvenServe/Daisy Chain*

Are you lucky enough to have examples of Homer Laughlin's Daisy Chain shape? For a number of years, some of the most assiduous of HLC collectors have been struggling with an intriguing question: Handy Andy versus OvenServe versus Daisy Chain. Which is what and how do they differ?

First, some background. In Huxfords' Fiesta book (7th ed.), page 98, there wearing the Conchita decal (at least on the lid) is an unusual casserole on a metal base. This casserole is topped with a strikingly different lid. Notice, please, the vertical thrust at the center, with a bursting "fountain-like" finial edged in red. According to the Huxfords, "The casserole is marked Handy Andy on the base; and, although it is hard to see in the photo, there is an embossed design at the rim of the *lid* (italics mine) as well as around the outside of the underplate above it." Looking carefully and closely at the underplate (which Daisy Chain does not have), the conclusion is drawn that it is embossed in the usual OvenServe manner; but that lid! There is no mention of any embossing on the bottom part, the piece marked Handy Andy, and the reason is simple — these two pieces do not belong together!

Joanne Jasper is also working on this question. She wrote about it in *The Laughlin Eagle,* summer 1994, but since that time, no new information has bubbled from the cauldron of knowledge.

So the fateful question is posed: what is a Handy Andy, and just what is that tall erupting lid appearing on page 98 of the Huxford book? And what of the low buzzing rumor over a Homer Laughlin official listing of "Daisy Chain?" Mrs. Jasper has lists, records, accounts, but no actual proof. A catalyst was required, and by an act of wonderment, it came through the interest in Virginia Rose.

Florida summers are infamously humid – when shoes mold in dank, dark closets, and marshy, watery smells pervade the listless air. Not much is accomplished regarding collectibles from June to September: the wise are in the cooler North. Yet in Ellenton, a small community just across the freighter-laden Lower Tampa Bay from St. Petersburg, there is a charming, old-fashioned country-type mall, The Feed Store, filled with slatted wall dividers, cozy, moist corners, and many gently whirring fans to help brush aside the pervasive heat. It is filled, not only with the summer's heat, but with friendly folk, and possible treasures, awaiting the brave and persistent.

In late July near the end of meandering through this rambling place, I was bemoaning the fact that no treasure had been found. No items of interest had risen to bar my slow progress toward the exit. Suddenly, attention was focused upon a strange casserole seeming to wear the familiar Armand (D.210) treatment. What was a Virginia Rose decal doing on this strange casserole? Did this mean the Armand decal was commercial? The base also had the Armand decals, and there was a sudden rush of recognition. This was a Virginia Rose decaled example of Mrs. Jasper's mystery casserole. Unlike the Huxford example, both lid and base had the same embossed edging, and most importantly, the inside of the lid was stamped DC-713. The official HLC number cracked the code!

When this new casserole was brought home and placed side-by-side with a Handy Andy casserole, these observations were made:

**Handy Andy Casserole:**
- metal lid;
- the mark, OvenServe/Handy Andy;
- measurements: 3⅛" high, 8" round, with the inside bottom measuring 5" round;
- no notching inside the rim near the top;
- outside edge decoration consisting of three lines forming three "steps" and two similar lines at the foot.

**Daisy Chain Casserole:**
- a ceramic lid topped by an elegant sprouting finial, an eight petaled daisy design with another daisy motif at the center;
- the mark, OvenServe;
- daisy embossing around the edge of the lid, and the top of the bowl;
- measurements: 3" high, 8⅛" round, with the inside bottom measuring 6¼" round;
- fluted "U" embossing about the foot.

**Note:**

- The ceramic lid fits both bowls, while the metal lid fits only the Handy Andy base.
- While marked "OvenServe," the Daisy Chain casserole has no familiar rose embossing usually seen on OvenServe pieces.

Are you lucky enough to have the true Daisy Chain shape among your OvenServe pieces? Jo Dee Rice does, and this astute collector sent some detailed photographs. A new Homer Laughlin shape has been confirmed through an interest in Virginia Rose. To date, Daisy Chain was produced in only two pieces: the specially lidded casserole, and the 9" pie plate.

As far as presently known, the Daisy Chain shape (and it is a true shape with its own official numbering) appears wearing the Conchita decals, and shares seven treatments with these Virginia Rose groups.

> Virginia Rose #128 (Fluffy Rose, D.231)
> Virginia Rose #232 (Columbine, D.20)
> Virginia Rose #235 (Armand, D.210)
> Virginia Rose JJ#59 (Moss Rose, D.227)
> Virginia Rose #? (Medley of Fruits, D.112)
> Virginia Rose #? (Florets, D.198)

Known only through HLC's official listing, the yet unseen Virginia Rose treatment, VR#265.

The first six have been personally seen and verified. Now my mind tingles at the possibility that the Conchita treatment, since it appears on the Daisy Chain shape, also is on some Virginia Rose plates.

So again, search through your collection of OvenServe. Forget the stamped mark, and see if indeed, your "OvenServe" is really the unusual Daisy Chain.

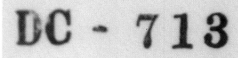

*Example of Daisy chain backstamp.*

---

### DAISY CHAIN SHAPE (OLD IVORY)
**3-Pc. Daisy Chain Set\* (1 Casserole Covd. 8" and Pie Plate 9½")**

| Pattern | Sel. | S | D.S. | Unc. | Description |
|---------|------|-------|-------|------|-------------|
| HAS-86 | Sch. | $ .58 | $ .61 | $ .65 | 3 sprigs (VR-128) silver edge line |
| HAS-150 | Sch. | .58 | .61 | .65 | 1 sprig (N-233) red edge line |
| | | | | | |
| DC-701 | Sch. | .58 | .61 | .65 | 3 sprigs (W-5923) red verge line |
| DC-703 | Sch. | .58 | .61 | .65 | 4 sprigs (K-8917) red edge line |
| DC-704 | Sch. | .58 | .61 | .65 | 6 sprigs (VR-265) red edge line |
| DC-705 | Sch. | .58 | .61 | .65 | Silver border stamp, red edge line |
| DC-707 | Sch. | .58 | .61 | .65 | 3 sprigs (M-167) red edge line |
| DC-709 | Sch. | .58 | .61 | .65 | 3 sprigs (M-167) blue edge line |
| DC-711 | Sch. | .58 | .61 | .65 | Silver stamp border, silver edge line |
| | | | | | |
| DC-713 | Sch. | .58 | .61 | .65 | 3 sprigs (VR-235) silver edge band |
| DC-714 | Sch. | .58 | .61 | .65 | 3 sprigs (O-19) silver edge band |
| DC-715 | Sch. | .58 | .61 | .65 | 3 sprigs (VR-128) silver edge band |
| DC-716 | Sch. | .58 | .61 | .65 | Asst'd sprigs (G-12) no line |
| DC-717 | Sch. | .58 | .61 | .65 | 6 sprigs (N-1449) silver edge line |
| DC-718 | 3rds | .40 | .42 | .46 | Silver stamp border, red edge line |
| DC-719 | Sch. | .58 | .61 | .65 | 2 sprigs (OS-149) silver edge line |

\*In all dinnerware listings, lids (sugarbowls, jug) or covers are counted as separate pieces.

*Note Daisy-like embossing under rim and unusual curved trim at base. The usual embossed rose and leaves are missing on OvenServe/DaisyChain.*

# Appendix D
## Alphabetical List of
## Virginia Rose Treatments with the D(ecoration) Numbers

(s) signifies Specialty item
* designates official HLC treatment names

| | |
|---|---|
| Agnes (s) ...............................D.57 | Flanders 2 ................................D.180a |
| Amherst .................................D.132 | Flanders 3 ................................D.180b |
| Apple .....................................D.96 | Florets ....................................D.198 |
| April ......................................D.146 | Flowers and Filigrees ...............D.97 |
| Armand 1 ...............................D.210 | Fluffy Rose 1 ...........................D.231 |
| Armand 2 ...............................D.210a | Fluffy Rose 2 ...........................D.231a |
| Band of Plenty 1 .....................D.8 | Fluffy Rose 3 ...........................D.231b |
| Band of Plenty 2 .....................D.8a | Fluffy Rose 4 ...........................D.231c |
| Banded Rose ..........................D.7 | Fluffy Rose 5 ...........................D.231d |
| Baroque .................................D.194 | Folly .......................................D.122 |
| Blue Dresden .........................D.90 | Four .......................................D.105 |
| Bluebirds ...............................D.11 | Four Flowers Bowl (s) ..............D.105a |
| Bonsai Quince ........................D.184 | Four O'Clock Delight ...............D.123 |
| Bouncing Betty ......................D.249 | Funny Face .............................D.149 |
| Bountiful (s) ...........................D.119 | Garden Door 1 ........................D.45 |
| *Bouquet ...............................D.107 | Garden Door 2 ........................D.45a |
| Bugles ...................................D.147 | Garden Ring ...........................D.33 |
| California Hillside ...................D.176 | Garden Theme ........................D.110 |
| Carolyn Series | General's Daughter .................D.40 |
|    Carolyn Mulberry ............D.278a | *Gold Rose .............................D.61 |
|    Carolyn Mustard .............D.278b | Golden Rose 1 ........................D.65 |
|    Carolyn Red Baker ...........D.278c | Golden Rose 2 ........................D.65a |
|    Carolyn White .................D.278 | Golden Temptress (s) ..............D.67 |
| Century's Three Daisies 1 ........D.87 | Grecian Melody (s) .................D.172 |
| Century's Three Daisies 2 ........D.87a | Greengage (s) .........................D.120 |
| Charms ..................................D.137 | Hallow's Eve ...........................D.92 |
| Charlotte's Rose .....................D.70 | Head of Class .........................DM.401 |
| Christmas ..............................D.175 | Heather Rose .........................D.186 |
| Christmas Plate (s) .................D.163 | Helene ...................................D.30 |
| *Colonial Kitchen ...................D.167 | Het Loo ..................................D.109 |
| Colonial Quadrille ..................D.170 | Hidden Meadow .....................D.98 |
| Colonial Quadrille Bowl (s) ......D.170a | Hollander ...............................DM.400 |
| Columbines ...........................D.20 | Honey Chip ............................D.283 |
| Curtains .................................DM.406 | Iris .........................................D.125 |
| Daisies ...................................D.13 | Jeanette .................................DM.420 |
| Double Gold Band ..................D.127 | Jesus Plate (s) .........................D.126 |
| English Rose ..........................DM.417 | Jewelled Rose .........................DM.402 |
| Esther ....................................DM.419 | June Morn (s) ..........................D.104 |
| Evelyn 1 .................................D.217 | Lesser Nosegay .......................D.206 |
| Evelyn 2 .................................D.217a | Liberty's Dogwood ..................D.42 |
| Evelyn 3 .................................D.217b | Little Louise ...........................D.193 |
| Fall's Beauty ...........................D.3 | Liza ........................................D.114 |
| Fall's Beauty Bowl ...................D.3a | Los Angeles (s) .......................D.165 |
| Feathers .................................DM.414 | *Louise ...................................D.192 |
| Field Ox-Eye 1 ........................D.35 | Madame Gautier 1 ..................D.196 |
| Field Ox-Eye 2 ........................D.35a | Madame Gautier 2 ..................D.196a |
| Flanders 1 ..............................D.180 | Margaret ................................DM.404 |

# *Appendix E*
## *List of Virginia Rose*
## *Official Homer Laughlin Company Numbers*

One of the joys of the scrupulous collector is adding another bit of information about a piece in the collection. While not absolutely necessary to enjoyment, the additional knowledge of any treatment's official HLC number adds the crowning fillip. It bears repeating that the number is most often located under the casserole lid, or the backside of the oval vegetable bowl. "Most often" is the term here, not "always." At malls and stores, even if a purchase is not at hand, all casseroles and oval bowls should be checked for the official mark to supply a dollop of cream to one's slice of peach pie for increased enjoyment.

Sixty-four official numbers have been located and appear within these covers, but hopefully, more will be added as collectors become aware and share their knowledge. Since this volume is to be considered a Virginia Rose working manual, no one should hesitate to pencil in added material.

| | | | | | |
|---|---|---|---|---|---|
| #101 | Head of Class | DM.401 | #231 | Flowers and Filigrees | D.97 |
| #105 | Temptation | DM.407 | #232 | Columbines | D.20 |
| #106 | Spring Song 2 | D.112a | #233 | Evelyn 1 | D.217 |
| #109 | Rose Melody 2 | D.200a | #235 | Armand 1 | D.210 |
| #114 | Jewelled Rose | DM.402 | #256 | Evelyn 2 | D.217a |
| #115 | Gold Rose | D.61 | #257 | Armand 2 | D.210a |
| #116 | Double Gold Band | D.127 | #269 | Wild Rose 2 | D.240a |
| #118 | Esther | DM.419 | #285 | Tulips in a Basket 1 | D.252 |
| #119 | Jeanette | DM.420 | #312 | Fluffy Rose 3 | D.231b |
| #120 | Rosy Ring | DM.405 | #324 | Ruby's Fall Cosmos 2 | D.31a |
| #121 | Curtains | DM.406 | #332 | Fluffy Rose 4 | D.231c |
| #122 | Hollander | DM.400 | #360(?) | Folly | D.122 |
| #124 | Patrician | D.75 | #376 | Hallow's Eve | D.92 |
| #128 | Fluffy Rose 1 | D.231 | #387 | South of France | DM.415 |
| #132 | Wild Brambles 2 | D.240a | #390 | Louise | D.192 |
| #133 | Upright Meadow Goldenrod | D.25 | #394 | Spring Promise | D.183 |
| #135 | Meadow Goldenrod 1 | D.24 | #396 | Tulips in a Basket 2 | D.252a |
| #136 | Band of Plenty 1 | D.8 | #398 | Waterlily | D.270 |
| #138 | Band of Plenty 2 | D.8a | #399 | Matinee Medallion | D.143 |
| #141 | Wildflowers | DM.412 | #404 | Meadow Goldenrod 3 | D.24b |
| #142 | Polly 1 | DM.411 | #411 | Meadow Goldenrod 4 | D.24c |
| #143 | Vellum | DM.410 | #412 | Tulips in a Basket 3 | D.252b |
| #151 | Polly 2 | DM.411a | #423 | Nosegay | D.205 |
| #152 | Moss Rose 2 | D.227a | #431 | Helene | D.30 |
| #153 | Feathers | DM.414 | #430 | English Rose | DM.417 |
| #155 | Peony | DM.408 | #437 | Heather Rose | D.186 |
| #162 | Pepper Pot | DM.413 | #440 | Armand 3 | D.210b |
| #172 | Silver Scrolls | D.79 | #452 | September Charm | DM.403 |
| #175 | Meadow Goldenrod 2 | D.24a | #456 | Wedgwood | D.135 |
| #178 | Fluffy Rose 2 | D.231a | CAC 186 | Spring Wreath | D.160 |
| #208 | Sarasota Cosmos | D.22 | W 137 | Bouquet | D.107 |
| #221 | Ruby's Fall Cosmos | D.31 | W245 | Marigold Springtime | D.4 |

## Appendix F
### Homer Laughlin Shapes Using Virginia Rose Treatments

The following listing does not take into account the variations of any treatment. Since these refer to number of sprigs and trim decoration (or lack of it), it is redundant to mention them.

Yellowstone and Century lead the list, tied with 16 entries. In rapid succession come Kitchen Kraft, 14; Republic, 11; Rhythm, 10; Liberty, nine; and Georgian Eggshell, nine.

A special point should be made for Kitchen Kraft and OvenServe (seven listings), for it must be assumed the treatments appeared first on Virginia Rose and then the artistic decision was reached to offer a companion line of kitchenware. But this assumption, as with many statements regarding American dinnerware, might be purely presumptuous! Some of the VR treatments, Daisies (D.13) for example, are so innocuous as to cause wonder why kitchenware was chosen to accompany them. In all other cases, the treatments could have traveled from Virginia Rose to the other shapes, or vice versa.

ANGELUS
  Temptation (?) . . . . .DM.407
BRITTANY
  Florets . . . . . . . . . .D.198
  Olivia . . . . . . . . . . .D.111
CAVALIER
  Bouncing Betty . . . . .D.248
  White Rose . . . . . . . .D.190
CENTURY
  California Hillside . . . .D.176
  Century's Three Daisies .D.87
  General's Daughter . . .D.210
  Golden Rose . . . . . . .D.65
  Marigold Springtime . . .D.4
  Matinee Medallion . . . .D.134
  Meadow Goldenrod . . . .D.24
  Melody Bouquet
    (filigree) . . . . . . . . .D.223
  Mexicana . . . . . . . . .D.144
  Petit Point Rose . . . . .D.215
  Sunday Morning
    (filigree) . . . . . . . .D.106
  Sunporch . . . . . . . . .D.150
  Upright Meadow
    Goldenrod . . . . . . . .D.25
  Vellum . . . . . . . . . .DM.410
  Wild Rose 1 . . . . . . .D.240
  Wildflowers . . . . . .DM.412
CHELSEA
  Bluebirds . . . . . . . . .D.11
  Meadow Goldenrod . . .D.24
  Red Beauty . . . . . . . .D.16
  Wild Hyacinth . . . . . .D.100
CORONET
  Gold Rose (technique) . .D.61
  Red Beauty . . . . . . . .D.16
DAISY CHAIN
  Armand . . . . . . . . . .D.210
  Columbines . . . . . . . .D.20

Florets . . . . . . . . . .D.198
Fluffy Rose . . . . . . . .D.231
Medley of Fruits . . . .D.118
Moss Rose . . . . . . . .D.227
DEBUTANTE
  Moss Rose . . . . . . . .D.227
  Woodland Beauty . . . .D.250
EMPRESS
  Bluebirds . . . . . . . . .D.11
FIESTA
  Fluffy Rose . . . . . . . .D.231
GENESEE
  Bluebirds . . . . . . . . .D.11
GEORGIAN
  Fluffy Rose . . . . . . . .D.231
  Medieval Garden (?) . . .D.116
GEORGIAN EGGSHELL
  Bountiful . . . . . . . . .D.119
  Bugles . . . . . . . . . . .D.147
  Colonial Quadrille . . . .D.170
  Flanders . . . . . . . . . .D.130
  Golden Rose . . . . . . .D.65
  Heather Rose . . . . . . .D.186
  Medieval Rose . . . . . .D.113
  Rose Cream . . . . . .DM.416
  Wedgwood . . . . . . . .D.135
HARLEQUIN
  Mexicali . . . . . . . . . .D.140
IVORA
  Olivia . . . . . . . . . . .D.111
JADE
  Garden Door . . . . . .D.45
  Peony . . . . . . . . . .DM.408
  Red Beauty . . . . . . . .D.16
KITCHEN KRAFT
  Armand . . . . . . . . . .D.210
  Daisies . . . . . . . . . . .D.13
  Fluffy Rose . . . . . . . .D.231
  Liberty's Dogwood . . . .D.42

Mexicana . . . . . . . . .D.144
Moss Rose . . . . . . . .D.227
Olivia . . . . . . . . . . .D.111
Petit Point Rose . . . . .D.215
Red Beauty . . . . . . . .D.16
Rhythm Rose . . . . . . .D.235
Shirley . . . . . . . . . . .D.117
Spring Wreath . . . . . .D.160
Sunporch . . . . . . . . .D.150
Wild Rose . . . . . . . .D.240
KWAKER
  Medieval Garden . . . . .D.116
  Medieval Rose . . . . . .D.113
  Olivia . . . . . . . . . . .D.111
  Pepper Pot . . . . . . .DM.413
LIBERTY
  Armand . . . . . . . . . .D.212
  Colonial Kitchen . . . . .D.162
  Colonial Quadrille . . . .D.170
  Golden Rose . . . . . . .D.65
  Liberty's Dogwood . . . .D.42
  Meadow Goldenrod . . .D.24
  Petit Point Rose . . . . .D.215
  Spring Wreath . . . . . .D.160
  Tulips in a Basket . . . .D.252
MARIGOLD
  Gold Rose (technique) . .D.61
  Marigold Springtime . . .D.4
  Marsh Bouquet . . . . .DM.418
  Patrician (technique) . . .D.75
  Snow (technique) . . . .D.275
  Wings (technique) . . . .D.50
NAUTILUS
  Field Ox-Eye . . . . . . .D.35
  Hallow's Eve . . . . . . .D.92
  Olivia . . . . . . . . . . .D.111
  Petit Point Rose . . . . .D.215
NAUTILUS EGGSHELL
  Colonial Kitchen . . . . .D.167

# Appendix G
## Alphabetical List of Virginia Rose Treatments by Edge Trim

### Silver Edge Trim

## Gold Edge Trim

Amherst .................................D.132
April......................................D.146
Armand 3 ............................D.210b
Bonsai Quince .....................D.184
Carolyn White......................D.278
Charlotte's Rose ....................D.70
Colonial Kitchen ..................D.167
Colonial Quadrille ..............D.170
Double Gold Band ...............D.127
Field Ox-Eye 2.....................D.35a

Flanders 3 .........................D.180b
Gold Rose ...........................D.61
Golden Rose 2 .....................D.65a
Heather Rose ......................D.186
Helene ..................................D.30
Hidden Meadow...................D.98
Iris .......................................D.125
Marigold Springtime ...............D.4
Petit Point Rose ..................D.215
Rhythm Rose.......................D.235

Ribbons ................................D.72
Spring Wreath .....................D.160
Tulips in a Basket 3 ..........D.252b
Wedgwood ..........................D.135
Wild Hyacinth .....................D.100
Wild Rose 2.........................D.240a
Woodland Beauty 2 ...........D.258a
Woodland Gold .....................D.62

## Red Edge Trim

Agnes.....................................D.57
Folly.....................................D.122
Garden Door 1 ......................D.45
General's Daughter................D.40
Mexicali ...............................D.140
Red-Ring.................................D.10
Shirley....................................D.94
Tulips in a Basket 1 ............D.252

## Orange Edge Trim

Hallow's Eve ..........................D.92

## Yellow Edge Trim

Medley of Fruits...................D.118

## Green Edge Trim

Bugles..................................D.147
Madame Gautier 1 .............D.196a
Pepper Pot .........................DM.413

## Flecks and Washes

Gold fleck:  Colonial Quadrille Bowl..............D.170a
Gold fleck:  Rose Quilt .........................................D.103
Gold fleck:  Moss Rose 2 .....................................D.227a
Gold fleck:  Polly 2 ...........................................DM.411a
Gold fleck:  Vellum ..........................................DM.410
Brown wash:  June Morn ...........................................D.104
Green wash:  Apple ...................................................D.96

Green wash:  Meadow Goldenrod Bowl.............D.24d
Green wash:  Parrot.............................................D.151
Green wash:  Sunday Offering ............................D.212
Green wash:  Wild Rose Platter ..........................D.240c
Teal wash:  Bountiful ........................................D.119
Teal wash:  Het Loo ..........................................D.109

## No Edge Trim

Armand 2 .............................D.210a
Baroque.................................D.194
Bluebirds................................D.11
Blue Dresden.........................D.90
California Hillside.................D.176
Century's Three Daisies 1.......D.87
Century's Three Daisies 2 .....D.87a
Charms .................................D.137
Christmas Plate ...................D.163
Evelyn 2 ..............................D.127a
Field Ox-Eye 1......................D.35
Flanders 1 ............................D.180
Fluffy Rose 3........................D.231b
Fluffy Rose 5........................D.231d
Four ......................................D.105
Four Flowers Bowl............D.105a
Funny Face ..........................D.149
Garden Door 2 ....................D.45a
Golden Rose 1......................D.65

Grecian Melody ...................D.172
Greengage............................D.120
Lesser Nosegay ...................D.206
Jesus Plate ...........................D.126
Liberty's Dogwood ................D.42
Los Angeles...........................D.165
Matinee Medallion ...............D.134
Meadow Goldenrod 1 ............D.24
Meadow Goldenrod 3...........D.24b
Medieval Garden ..................D.116
Mexicana ..............................D.144
MoonGlo ..............................D.117
Mums.....................................D.12
Muriel ...................................D.108
Nosegay.................................D.205
Olivia....................................D.111
Oriental Garden....................D.162
Red Beauty 1 .........................D.16
Red Pig..................................D.143

Rose Sparkle ...........................D.7
Roulette ...............................D.114
Sentinel.................................D.121
Signs of Spring .......................D.1
Snow ....................................D.275
Spider Rose ............................D.55
Summer's Garden .................D.155
Sunny Morning.....................D.106
Sunporch...............................D.150
Upright Meadow Goldenrod....D.25
Viking Rose .........................D.188
White Rose 1 ........................D.190
White Rose 2.........................D.190a
Wild Brambles 2 .................D.245a
Wild Rose 1 ..........................D.240
Wings ....................................D.50
Woodland Beauty 1.............D.258

# *Appendix H*
## *Virginia Rose Official Homer Laughlin Company Lists*

The following two lists, years 1937 and 1952, are extremely important for any Virginia Rose researcher. Much can be ascertained from a concentrated study of the lists although there are gaps which can alternately intrigue and infuriate. To help the reader, we will trace the Fluffy Rose series because it is a straightforward search and reasonably simple to reconstruct.

The original Fluffy Rose is VR#128; it was introduced in 1933 (or perhaps 1932), but still was being offered in 1937. From the entry under the official number, we get a very brief description, 2 sprigs (decals) with a silver edge line (trim), but, importantly, we also learn the decal set was obtained from a commercial source under the number 3831. This commercialism accounts for the Fluffy Rose decal appearing on vases, lamps, and ashtrays not manufactured by Homer Laughlin.

Since VR#128 is the premier treatment, we read down the list and notice VR#178 uses the Fluffy Rose decal only once (1 sprig) but continued the silver edge. Next we note VR#299 uses one Fluffy Rose decal, but with no trim. VR#312 (this is the problem one; please see section of book under D.231c) again has 2 sprigs with the silver edge. It must be noted the terms "edge" and "line" are interchangeable. The penultimate entry, VR#332, reverts to 2 sprigs (exactly like VR#128) but with no trim. The Fluffy Rose entries conclude with VR#368 marked W-128 Spec, decorated with 6 sprigs and no trim. Please remember the full number of decals will only appear on the larger plates, the bowls, and platters; the 6" and 7" plates, and the saucers and teacups will probably have three decals, yet this is enough to distinguish VR#368 from the other treatments with never more than two decals on the smaller pieces.

When we turn to the 1952 list, it is noted VR#128 is still being produced; in fact all the Fluffy Rose treatments are still available except the specialty one, VR#368. In this way, it is known all these treatments had the time span of, at least, 1937 to 1952.

This list can be useful for identifying treatments on other shapes as well. The abbreviations are:

| | |
|---|---|
| Y – Yellowstone | RV – Ravenna |
| C – Century | CO – Coronet |
| H – Hudson | M – Marigold |
| W – Wells | N – Nautilus |
| J – Jade | |

Thus, if a person has a VR oval vegetable stamped with the official number VR#344, the Marigold treatment M-167 is immediately known. The section "Also appears on" can also make use of the listings, as again in VR#344 we know this decal appears on Marigold.

The frustration arises when the reader notices many entrees with the same "other shape" designation, i.e., Y–137. So many Virginia Rose treatments could be known if only we had one example of Yellowstone #137. However, imagine the relief when a Yellowstone oval vegetable stamped Y-137 is finally discovered. There are also other surmises that intrigue, e.g., VR#355 and VR#370 could be the same except with gold substituting for silver. But beware of hasty conclusions, and remember free-standing numbers, 1348, 707, mean the decal(s) used were obtained through a commercial source.

Used judiciously, these two official annual lists can advance the study of the Virginia Rose shape and its treatments.

COMMENTS:

Any person doing American dinnerware research is continually frustrated by the lack of official information. This dearth of historical material can be understood when it is realized the china manufacturers could not foresee the future collector mania surrounding their wares. A shape or treatment was produced, offered to the purchasing public, and then simply withdrawn when interest lagged. Very few records were kept and today the researcher must hunt and make do with fragmentary material, basing many conclusions on logical conjecture. We are extremely lucky to have the treatment lists of 1937 and 1952, and the 1952 item list.

On the May 1, 1952 item list:

- Necessary to remember, the sizes are given in the trade version, but these are reasonably easy to interpret. We know there were five sizes of plates, thus Plate 4" must be the 6" plate, and the Plate 8" is the 10" plate.
- Note the Onion Soup using the Regular Nautilus lug oatmeal, and the existence of a square 8" plate, but on the Marigold shape. This is quite fascinating, and needs more investigation.
- There is an oblong butterdish, but, very confusingly, the ditto mark seems to imply this was made in the Virginia Rose shape; the Jade shape is not mentioned. This, no doubt, was an oversight, or perhaps there is a butter in the actual Virginia Rose shape. This too needs more investigation.
- Remember, also, the uses of trade terminology:

  Dish – platter                Nappy – round vegetable bowl

  Baker – oval vegetable bowl    Deep plate – rim soup

- In 1951, the Virginia Rose line consisted of 38 pieces; in 1952, 10 items were deleted making 28 available pieces. Quite a limitation. The cake and bread plates were no longer offered and these are now thought to be the two sizes of the tray-with-handles.
- The piece now known as the specialty bowl, so prevalent through the 1940s and first years of the 1950s and here labeled the salad nappy, was also discontinued. These seem to have been reissued toward the end of the decade because one of the SAL series has the date, 1959 (see section on Specialty Bowls).
- There are individual pieces not seen on either list; the huge 18" platter (see D.119), the rounded Swing shakers, the covered jug in two sizes, and the AD cup and saucer. Since the first three mentioned have been seen and collected, they must have been discontinued prior to 1951. As discussed in the Introduction, because of the total lack of sightings of the last mentioned AD cup/saucer, I hypothesize they were never put into production.
- Finally, there are those rare items which, obviously, were never really meant to be numbered among the average Virginia Rose set, e.g., the Debutante shakers, the Fiesta double egg cup, the St. Dennis cup, even the coffee mug, are not recorded. It cannot be ascertained when or how often they were decorated with a VR decal but they must be included as possibilities

# Official Homer Laughlin Company List, 1937

## Virginia Rose Shape (Light Yellow Glaze)

| Pattern | Sel. | S | D.S. | Unc. | Mat. | Description |
|---------|------|------|------|------|------|-------------|
| VR-105 | Sch. | 9.50 | 10.00 | 10.50 | 11.50 | 7 sprigs, A-313, silver edge line |
| VR-106 | Sch. | 9.50 | 10.00 | 10.50 | 11.50 | 7 sprigs, 3894, silver edge line |
| VR-115 | R.K. | 9.50 | 10.00 | 10.50 | 11.50 | Gold stamp and lines |
| VR-116 | Sch. | 7.75 | 8.25 | 8.75 | 9.75 | Gold edge and verge line |
| VR-117 | Sch. | 8.00 | 8.50 | 9.00 | 10.00 | Gold band and verge line |
| VR-118 | Sch. | 9.00 | 9.50 | 10.00 | 11.00 | 6 sprigs (C-74) silver edge line |
| VR-119 | R.K. | 12.50 | 13.00 | 13.75 | 14.50 | Border (H-135) gold lines |
| VR-124 | R.K. | 10.00 | 10.50 | 11.25 | 12.00 | Silver stamps and lines |
| VR-125 | Sch. | 7.75 | 8.25 | 8.75 | 9.75 | Silver edge and verge line |
| VR-128 | Sch. | 8.75 | 9.25 | 9.75 | 10.75 | 2 sprigs, 3831, silver edge line |
| VR-131 | Sch. | 7.75 | 8.25 | 8.75 | 9.75 | Gold stamps and edge line |
| VR-134 | Sch. | 8.00 | 8.50 | 9.00 | 10.00 | 2 sprigs (W-7133) no lines |
| VR-135 | Sch. | 8.00 | 8.50 | 9.00 | 10.00 | 2 sprigs (Y-137) no line |
| VR-136 | R.K. | 11.00 | 11.50 | 12.25 | 13.00 | 7 sprigs, verge border, 3893, silver edge line |
| VR-139 | Sch. | 7.50 | 8.00 | 8.25 | 9.50 | 6 silver stamps and edge line |

| Pattern | Sel. | S | D.S. | Unc. | Mat. | Description |
|---------|------|------|------|------|------|-------------|
| VR-140 | Sch. | 9.00 | 9.50 | 10.00 | 11.00 | 6 sprigs, 625, silver edge line |
| VR-141 | Sch. | 8.75 | 9.25 | 9.75 | 10.75 | 3 sprigs (C-117) silver edge line |
| VR-155 | Sch. | 8.75 | 9.25 | 9.75 | 10.75 | 2 sprigs (J-9) silver edge line |
| VR-156 | Sch. | 8.00 | 8.50 | 9.00 | 10.00 | Litho blue edge and band |
| VR-157 | Sch. | 8.00 | 8.50 | 9.00 | 10.00 | Green edge and band |
| VR-158 | Sch. | 8.00 | 8.50 | 9.00 | 10.00 | Red edge and band |
| VR-159 | Sch. | 8.00 | 8.50 | 9.00 | 10.00 | Dark blue edge and band |
| VR-163 | Sch. | 7.75 | 8.25 | 8.75 | 9.75 | Silver edge and verge |
| VR-170 | Sch. | 9.00 | 9.50 | 10.00 | 11.00 | 7 sprigs, 3993, silver edge line |
| VR-172 | R.K. | 10.00 | 10.50 | 11.25 | 12.00 | Assorted silver stamp and edge |
| VR-173 | R.K. | 9.50 | 10.00 | 10.50 | 11.50 | Assorted gold stamps and edge |
| VR-174 | Sch. | 8.00 | 8.50 | 9.00 | 10.00 | 6 silver stamps, edge and verge lines |
| VR-175 | Sch. | 8.50 | 9.00 | 9.50 | 10.50 | 2 sprigs (Y-137) silver edge line |
| VR-178 | Sch. | 8.00 | 8.50 | 9.00 | 10.00 | 1 sprig (VR-128) silver edge line |
| VR-181 | Sch. | 8.00 | 8.50 | 9.00 | 10.00 | 1 sprig (RV-1) silver edge line |
| VR-185 | R.K. | 10.00 | 10.50 | 11.25 | 12.00 | Sorted gold stamps edge and verge |
| VR-187 | 3rds | 6.50 | 7.00 | 7.25 | 8.50 | Silver stamp (Y-56) no lines |
| VR-188 | 3rds | 6.25 | 6.75 | 7.00 | 8.25 | 6 silver stamps (VR-131) no line |
| VR-195 | Sch. | 8.75 | 9.25 | 9.75 | 10.75 | 3 sprigs (Y-146) silver edge line |
| VR-199 | Sch. | 9.50 | 10.00 | 10.50 | 11.50 | 7 sprigs (VR-140) silver verge stamp and edge |
| VR-203 | Sch. | 9.50 | 10.00 | 10.50 | 11.50 | 7 sprigs (VR-106) gold verge, stamp and edge |
| VR-204 | Sch. | 9.50 | 10.00 | 10.50 | 11.50 | 6 sprigs (C-74) gold verge stamp and edge |
| VR-205 | Sch. | 10.00 | 10.50 | 11.25 | 12.00 | 7 sprigs (VR-106) asst'd gold stamp and edge |
| VR-212 | Sch. | 8.75 | 9.25 | 9.75 | 10.75 | 2 sprigs (W-5923) silver edge line |
| VR-214 | 3rds | 6.50 | 7.00 | 7.25 | 8.50 | 6 gold stamps (VR-131) no line |
| VR-218 | Sch. | 7.50 | 8.00 | 8.25 | 9.50 | Silver edge line |
| VR-219 | Sch. | 8.75 | 9.25 | 9.75 | 10.75 | 3 sprigs (Y-146) silver edge line |
| VR-231 | R.K. | 11.00 | 11.50 | 12.25 | 13.00 | 7 sprigs, 1348 asst'd silver stamps and edge |
| VR-232 | Sch. | 8.75 | 9.25 | 9.75 | 10.75 | 3 sprigs, 707, silver edge line |
| VR-233 | Sch. | 8.75 | 9.25 | 9.75 | 10.75 | 2 springs, 740, silver edge line |
| VR-234 | Sch. | 8.75 | 9.25 | 9.75 | 10.75 | 3 sprigs, 619 silver edge line |
| VR-235 | Sch. | 8.75 | 9.25 | 9.75 | 10.75 | 3 sprigs, 1226 silver edge line |
| VR-241 | R.K. | 10.50 | 11.00 | 11.75 | 12.50 | 12 silver stamps, verge band, edge line |
| VR-242 | R.K. | 10.50 | 11.00 | 11.75 | 12.50 | 12 silver stamps, verge border, edge line |
| VR-251 | R.K. | 10.25 | 10.75 | 11.50 | 12.25 | 7 sprigs (VR-231) silver edge, verge border |
| VR-254 | Sch. | 7.75 | 8.25 | 8.75 | 9.75 | Asst'd silver stamps |
| VR-255 | Sch. | 7.75 | 8.25 | 8.75 | 9.75 | Asst'd silver stamps |
| VR-256 | Sch. | 8.25 | 8.75 | 9.25 | 10.25 | 2 sprigs (VR-233) no line |
| VR-257 | Sch. | 8.25 | 8.75 | 9.25 | 10.25 | 2 sprigs (VR-235) no line |
| VR-258 | Sch. | 8.75 | 9.25 | 9.75 | 10.75 | 2 sprigs (VR-235) silver edge |
| VR-259 | Sch. | 7.75 | 8.25 | 8.75 | 9.75 | Asst'd silver stamps |
| VR-260 | Sch. | 7.75 | 8.25 | 8.75 | 9.75 | Asst'd silver stamps |
| VR-261 | Sch. | 7.50 | 8.00 | 8.25 | 9.50 | Silver (Y-56) stamps |
| VR-262 | Sch. | 8.50 | 9.00 | 9.50 | 10.50 | Asst'd silver stamp and edge |
| VR-263 | Sch. | 10.25 | 10.75 | 11.50 | 12.25 | 6 sprigs, 1438 blue edge, verge, red con. line |
| VR-265 | Sch. | 10.50 | 11.00 | 11.75 | 12.50 | 7 sprigs, 1439, tan edge, green verge and con. line |
| VR-266 | Sch. | 8.50 | 9.00 | 9.50 | 10.50 | 2 sprigs, (VR-234) silver edge line |
| VR-269 | Sch. | 8.50 | 9.00 | 9.50 | 10.50 | 2 sprigs (W-7133) silver edge line |
| VR-270 | Sch. | 9.00 | 9.50 | 10.00 | 11.00 | 6 sprigs (VR-237) silver edge line |
| VR-271 | Sch. | 9.00 | 9.50 | 10.00 | 11.00 | 6 sprigs (VR-238) silver edge line |
| VR-273 | Sch. | 8.00 | 8.50 | 9.00 | 10.00 | Asst'd gold stamps |
| VR-274 | Sch. | 8.25 | 8.75 | 9.25 | 10.25 | 2 sprigs (J-3) no line |
| VR-275 | Sch. | 7.50 | 8.00 | 8.25 | 9.50 | 1 sprig (RV-1) no line |
| VR-276 | Sch. | 7.75 | 8.25 | 8.75 | 9.75 | Asst'd silver stamps |

| Pattern | Sel. | S | D.S. | Unc. | Mat. | Description |
|---|---|---|---|---|---|---|
| VR-279 | Sch. | 10.25 | 10.75 | 11.50 | 12.25 | 6 sprigs (VR-263) red edge, verge and con. line |
| VR-283 | Sch. | 7.75 | 8.25 | 8.75 | 9.75 | Asst'd silver stamps |
| VR-284 | Sch. | 7.75 | 8.25 | 8.75 | 9.75 | Asst'd silver stamps |
| VR-286 | Sch. | 7.75 | 8.25 | 8.75 | 9.75 | Asst'd silver stamps |
| VR-279 | Sch. | 7.50 | 8.00 | 8.25 | 9.50 | 1 sprig (W-7723) no line |
| VR-299 | Sch. | 7.50 | 8.00 | 8.25 | 9.50 | 1 sprig (VR-128) no line |
| VR-302 | Sch. | 8.00 | 8.50 | 9.00 | 10.00 | 1 sprig (W-7723) silver edge line |
| VR-304 | Sch. | 7.50 | 8.00 | 8.25 | 9.50 | Silver edge only |
| VR-307 | Sch. | 8.00 | 8.50 | 9.00 | 10.00 | 1 sprig (W-5723) silver edge line |
| VR-309 | Sch. | 8.00 | 8.50 | 9.00 | 10.00 | 1 sprig (W-1733) silver edge |
| VR-311 | Sch. | 7.50 | 8.00 | 8.25 | 9.50 | Bright gold edge line |
| VR-312 | Sch. | 8.75 | 9.25 | 8.75 | 10.75 | 2 sprigs (VR-128) silver edge |
| VR-316 | Sch. | 8.25 | 8.75 | 9.25 | 10.25 | 3 sprigs (VR-234) no line |
| VR-318 | Sch. | 7.50 | 8.00 | 8.25 | 9.50 | 1 sprig (J-4) no line |
| VR-320 | Sch. | 7.25 | 7.75 | 8.00 | 9.25 | 6 silver stamps, no line |
| VR-322 | Sch. | 7.50 | 8.00 | 8.25 | 9.50 | 1 sprig (W-5923) no lines |
| VR-324 | 3rds | 7.00 | 7.50 | 7.75 | 9.00 | 2 sprigs (Y-146) silver edge |
| VR-325 | Sch. | 7.50 | 8.00 | 8.25 | 9.50 | 1 sprig (VR-235) no line |
| VR-326 | Sch. | 7.50 | 8.00 | 8.25 | 9.50 | 1 sprig (W-7133) no line |
| VR-329 | Sch. | 7.25 | 7.75 | 8.00 | 9.25 | Asst'd silver stamps, no line |
| VR-331 | Sch. | 7.50 | 8.00 | 8.25 | 9.50 | Gold edge line only |
| VR-332 | Sch. | 8.25 | 8.75 | 9.25 | 10.25 | 2 sprigs (VR-128) no line |
| VR-333 | Sch. | 9.25 | 9.75 | 10.25 | 11.25 | 4 silver verge lines, silver edge |
| VR-336 | 3rds | 6.50 | 7.00 | 7.25 | 8.50 | 2 sprigs (Y-137) no line |
| VR-337 | 3rds | 6.50 | 7.00 | 7.25 | 8.50 | 6 sprigs (CAC-6) no line |
| VR-338 | 3rds | 6.50 | 7.00 | 7.25 | 8.50 | 6 sprigs (Q.O. 10) no line |
| VR-340 | Sch. | 8.50 | 9.00 | 9.50 | 10.50 | 6 sprigs (VR-271) no line |
| VR-341 | Sch. | 8.00 | 8.50 | 9.00 | 10.00 | 2 sprigs (W-5923) no line |
| VR-343 | Sch. | 8.75 | 9.25 | 9.75 | 10.75 | 3 sprigs, 1305, gold edge line |
| VR-344 | Sch. | 8.75 | 9.25 | 9.75 | 10.75 | 3 sprigs, (M-167) silver edge line |
| VR-345 | Sch. | 8.75 | 9.25 | 9.75 | 10.75 | 3 sprigs (M-167) celestial blue edge line |
| VR-346 | Sch. | 8.75 | 9.25 | 9.75 | 10.75 | 3 sprigs (VR-343) silver edge line |
| VR-348 | Sch. | 8.00 | 8.50 | 9.00 | 10.00 | 2 sprigs (Y-146) no line |
| VR-350 | Sch. | 7.75 | 8.25 | 8.75 | 9.75 | 1 sprig ( CO-100) no line |
| VR-351 | Sch. | 8.75 | 9.25 | 9.75 | 10.75 | 3 sprigs, 1287, silver edge line |
| VR-352 | Sch. | 8.00 | 8.50 | 9.00 | 10.00 | 2 sprigs (Y-155) no line |
| VR-353 | Sch. | 8.75 | 9.25 | 9.75 | 10.75 | 3 sprigs, A-1740, silver edge line |
| VR-354 | Sch. | 8.25 | 8.75 | 9.25 | 10.25 | 3 sprigs (VR-353) no line |
| VR-355 | Sch. | 8.75 | 9.25 | 9.75 | 10.75 | Silver stamps, edge and wave line |
| VR-356 | 3rds | 7.00 | 7.50 | 7.75 | 9.00 | 3 sprigs (Y-155) silver edge line |
| VR-358 | 3rds | 6.50 | 7.00 | 7.25 | 8.50 | 4 sprigs (W-1726) no line |
| VR-359 | 3rds | 6.50 | 7.00 | 7.25 | 8.50 | 3 sprigs (E-4213) no line |
| VR-360 | Sch. | 8.75 | 9.25 | 9.75 | 10.75 | 3 sprigs (M-167) red edge line |
| VR-361 | Sch. | 7.75 | 8.25 | 8.75 | 9.75 | 1 sprig (CO-101) no line |
| VR-362 | Sch. | 8.75 | 9.25 | 9.75 | 10.75 | 3 sprigs (CO-117) gold edge line |
| VR-363 | Sch. | 8.25 | 8.75 | 9.25 | 10.25 | 1 sprig (CO-100) silver edge line |
| VR-364 | 3rds | 6.50 | 7.00 | 7.25 | 8.50 | 3 sprigs (Y-51) no line |
| VR-365 | Sch | 8.75 | 9.25 | 9.75 | 10.75 | 2 sprigs (J-6) silver edge line |
| VR-367 | 3rds | 6.50 | 7.00 | 7.25 | 8.50 | 2 sprigs (VR-233) no line |
| VR-368 | 3rds | 6.50 | 7.00 | 7.25 | 8.50 | 6 sprigs (W-128 Spec) no line |
| VR-369 | Sch. | 8.75 | 9.25 | 9.75 | 10.75 | 2 sprigs (CO-527) silver edge line |
| VR-370 | Sch. | 8.75 | 9.25 | 9.75 | 10.75 | Gold stamps, edge and wave line |
| VR-371 | Butler Bros. | | | | | 2 sprigs (VR-233) no line |

| Pattern | Sel. | S | D.S. | Unc. | Mat. | Description |
|---------|------|------|-------|-------|-------|-------------|
| VR-375 | Sch. | 8.25 | 8.75 | 9.25 | 10.25 | 3 sprigs (N-234) no line |
| VR-376 | Sch. | 8.75 | 9.25 | 9.75 | 10.75 | 3 sprigs (N-234) orange color edge line |
| VR-377 | Sch. | 8.25 | 8.75 | 9.25 | 10.25 | 1 sprig (CO-101) silver edge line |
| VR-378 | R.K. | 10.25 | 10.75 | 11.50 | 12.25 | Gold edge, verge band and stamps |
| VR-379 | Sch. | 9.00 | 9.50 | 10.00 | 11.00 | 6 sprigs (CO-542) silver edge line |
| VR-380 | Sch. | 8.75 | 9.25 | 9.75 | 10.75 | 2 sprigs (N-1409) gold edge line |
| VR-381 | 3rds | 6.50 | 7.00 | 7.25 | 8.50 | 2 sprigs (W-231) no line |
| VR-382 | Sch. | 8.00 | 8.50 | 9.00 | 10.00 | 1 sprig (CO-604)      silver edge line |
| VR-383 | 3rds | 7.00 | 7.50 | 7.75 | 9.00 | 3 sprigs (VR-353) silver edge line |
| VR-384 | Sch. | 8.75 | 9.25 | 9.75 | 10.75 | 2 sprigs (J-6) gold edge line |
| VR-385 | Sch. | 8.00 | 8.50 | 9.00 | 10.00 | 2 sprigs (W-231) no line |
| VR-386 | Sch. | 8.25 | 8.75 | 9.25 | 10.25 | 3 sprigs (VR-343) no line |
| VR-387 | Sch. | Neisner Bros. | | | | 3 sprigs, A-948, silver edge line |
| VR-388 | 3rds | G. Sommers | | | | 1 sprig (CO-100) no line |

# *Official Homer Laughlin Company List, 1952*

## Virginia Rose (Light Yellow Glaze)

| Pattern | Sel | S | Unc | Mat | Description |
|---------|-----|------|------|------|-------------|
| VR-115 | R.K. | 16.75£ | 18.25£ | 19.75£ | Gold stamp and lines |
| VR-116 | Sch | 13.00 | 14.25 | 15.75 | Gold edge and verge lines |
| VR-124 | R.K. | 16.75 | 18.25 | 19.75 | Silver stamps and lines |
| VR-128 | Sch. | 14.75 | 16.00 | 17.50 | 2 sprigs (5287), silver edge line |
| VR-131 | Sch | 13.00 | 14.25 | 15.75 | Gold stamps and edge line |
| VR-135 | Sch | 13.75 | 15.00 | 16.50 | 2 sprigs (Y-137), no line |
| VR-158 | Sch | 13.75 | 15.00 | 16.50 | Red edge and band |
| VR-172 | R.K. | 16.75 | 18.25 | 19.75 | Asst'd. silver stamps and edge |
| VR-175 | Sch | 14.25 | 15.50 | 17.00 | 2 sprigs (Y-137), silver edge line |
| VR-178 | Sch | 13.75 | 15.00 | 16.50 | 1 sprig (VR-128), silver edge line |
| VR-181 | Sch | 13.75 | 15.00 | 16.50 | 1 sprig (RV-1), silver edge line |
| VR-218 | Sch | 12.75 | 13.75 | 15.25 | Silver edge line |
| VR-235 | Sch | 14.75 | 16.00 | 17.50 | 3 sprigs (4906), silver edge line |
| VR-241 | R.K. | 17.50 | 19.00 | 20.50 | 12 Silver stamps, verge band, edge line |
| VR-257 | Sch | 14.00 | 15.25 | 16.75 | 2 sprigs (VR-235) no line |
| VR-261 | Sch | 12.75 | 13.75 | 15.25 | Silver (Y-56) stamps and center |
| VR-265 | Sch | 17.50 | 19.00 | 20.50 | 7 sprigs (1439), tan edge, green verge, and con. line |
| VR-269 | Sch | 14.25 | 15.50 | 17.00 | 2 sprigs (W-7133), silver edge line |
| VR-299 | Sch | 12.75 | 13.75 | 15.25 | 1 sprig (VER-128), no line |
| VR-312 | Sch | 14.75 | 16.00 | 17.50 | 2 sprigs (VR-128), silver edge |
| VR-325 | Sch | 12.75 | 13.75 | 15.25 | 1 sprig (VR-235), no edge |
| VR-326 | Sch | 12.75 | 13.75 | 15.25 | 1 sprig (W-7133), no line |
| VR-331 | Sch | 12.75 | 13.75 | 15.25 | Gold edge line only |
| VR-332 | Sch | 12.75 | 13.75 | 15.25 | 2 sprigs (VR-128), no line |
| VR-379 | Sch | 15.50 | 16.75 | 18.25 | 6 sprigs (W-538), silver edge line |
| VR-395 | Sch | 12.75 | 13.75 | 15.25 | 1 sprig (85), red edge |
| VR-396 | Sch | 12.75 | 13.75 | 15.25 | 1 sprig (VR-395), silver edge line |
| VR-404 | Sch | 12.00£ | 13.00£ | 14.50£ | 1 sprig (Y-137), no line |

| | | | | | |
|---|---|---|---|---|---|
| VR-411 | Sch | 12.75 | 13.75 | 15.25 | 1 sprig (Y-137), silver edge line |
| VR-412 | Sch | 12.75 | 13.75 | 15.25 | 1 sprig (VR-395), gold edge line |
| VR-414 | Sch | 12.00 | 13.00 | 14.50 | 1 sprig (VR-395), no line |
| VR-422 | Sch | 18.25 | 19.75 | 21.25 | 6 sprigs, center (B-1317), asst'd. silver stamps and edge |
| VR-427 | Sch | 14.00 | 15.25 | 16.75 | 3 sprigs (Y-137), no line |
| VR-429 | Sch | 14.25 | 15.50 | 17.00 | 3 sprigs (VR-235), no line |
| VR-434 | Sch | 12.00 | 13.00 | 14.50 | 1 sprig (RV-7833), no line |
| VR-436 | 3rds | 11.50 | 12.50 | 14.00 | 6 gold stamps, center, gold edge line |
| VR-437 | Sch | 14.50 | 15.75 | 17.25 | 6 sprigs (G-3380), gold edge line |
| VR??? | Sch | 15.75 | 17.00 | 18.50 | 3 sprigs (VR-235), gold edge line |
| VR-442 | Sch | 13.25 | 14.50 | 16.00 | 1 sprig (O-79), no line |
| VR-443 | Sch | 12.75 | 13.75 | 15.25 | 1 sprig 98 (RV-7833) gold edge |
| VR-444 | 3rds | 11.50 | 12.50 | 14.00 | 1 sprig 953 (CO-100), gold edge |
| VR-445 | Sch | McLellan Stores | | | 4 sprigs 1156 (L-613), gold edge |
| VR-446 | Sch | 14.75 | 16.00 | 17.50 | 2 sprigs 3131 (L-615), gold edge |
| VR-447 | 3rds | 11.00 | 12.00 | 13.50 | 2 sprigs 6112 (W-7133), no line |
| VR-448 | 3rds | 11.50 | 12.50 | 14.00 | 1 sprig #982 (RV-7833) gold stamp rim border only |

This important official listing is dated May 1, 1952, and was submitted by Joanne Jasper

# 1952 Virginia Rose Piece List

**The Virginia Rose line is at present offered in the following items in Light Yellow Glaze only:**

| Item | Shape | Item | Shape |
|---|---|---|---|
| Tea Cup | Virginia Rose | Plate, deep 6" | Virginia Rose |
| Tea Saucer | Virginia Rose | Plate*, square 8" | Marigold (Cunningham and Pickett) |
| Dbl. Egg Cup | Cable | Coupe 7" | Virginia Rose |
| Bowl 36s | Virginia Rose | Baker 7" | Virginia Rose |
| Nappy 7" | Virginia Rose | Pickle (Dish 6") | Virginia Rose |
| Nappy 8" | Virginia Rose (Colgate Newberry) | Dish 8" | Virginia Rose |
| Oatmeal 36s | Virginia Rose (Colgate Newberry) | Dish 10" | Virginia Rose |
| Onion Soup | Nautilus lug oatmeal* (regular) | Dish 12" | Virginia Rose |
| Fruit 4" | Virginia Rose | Cream | Virginia Rose |
| Plate 4" | Virginia Rose | Covered Sugar | Virginia Rose |
| Plate 5" | Virginia Rose | Covered Dish (casserole) | Virginia Rose |
| Plate 6" | Virginia Rose | Covered Butter (oblong) | Virginia Rose |
| Plate 7" | Virginia Rose | Open Jug 24 | Virginia Rose (J.J. Newberry) |
| Plate 8" | Virginia Rose | Open Jug 42 | Virginia Rose (J.J. Newberry) |

* See p.15 for discussion

**The following items are no longer offered in the Virginia Rose line:**

| | |
|---|---|
| Cream Soup Cup | Dish 7" |
| Cream Soup Saucer | Cake Plate |
| Nappy 6" | Bread Plate |
| Fruit 5" | Salad Nappy |
| Baker 6" | Sauceboat F.S. |